003095
15

MAJOR STOCK MARKETS OF EUROPE

MAJOR STOCK MARKETS OF EUROPE

Paul Stonham

St. Martin's Press   **New York**

Printed in Great Britain
First published in the United States of America in 1982

ISBN 0-312-50482-9

Library of Congress Cataloging in Publication Data
───
Stonham, Paul.
   The major stockmarkets of Europe.

   Includes bibliographical references.
   1. Stock-exchange — Europe. 2. Finance — Europe.
   I. Title.
   HG4551.S84 1982   332.64'24   81-21279
   ISBN 0-312-50482-9   AACR2

Contents

vi

Diagrams and tables

Introduction and acknowledgements

For the past twenty years at least, the larger stock markets in Europe have all experienced similar trends. Among the most important are: a low rate of return after tax and inflation — adjustment for equity investors and borrowers; a decline of interest in equities and corporate bonds, in terms both of new issues and turnover; and relatively strong growth in the market for gilt-edged bonds, so that now they dominate most stock markets.

Since the late 1970s, European governments have paid closer attention to the internal efficiency of their stock markets in their function of allocating savings and borrowing requirements of the corporate sector. Notable among such studies have been the Committee to Review the Functioning of Financial Institutions (the 'Wilson Committee') in the United Kingdom, and the Commission to investigate stock market reforms in France under the chairmanship of M. Perouse. In other European countries, although there have not been large scale, official inquiries in recent years, there have been many *ad hoc* studies and steady improvements. The Commission of the European Communities too, has shown a sense of urgency in its issue of guidelines, directives, and continuing studies of member States' stock markets and progress in their harmonisation.

As well as wishing to bring together and document the important changes in stock market legislation and reform of practices, the author was aware of two further gaps in the literature on major European stock markets.

The first was material regarding practice, regulations, performance and control mechanisms. Although some organisations like the Fédération Internationale des Bourses de Valeurs work hard to disseminate information, as well as suggesting improvements in practice, it is frequently the case that practitioners, analysts, borrowers and lenders in one major European stock market are ignorant of conditions in others. One of the main findings of the symposium 'Towards a European Stock Exchange' organised by stock markets in Brussels in November 1980, was this widespread lack of knowledge of actual practice and conditions.

The second concerned the changes which had rapidly occurred in nearly all European stock markets. Many of these are still going on: specialised sub-markets are appearing, rules for trading are being monitored and tightened up, the position of intermediary dealers is under review, and information transfer by electronic means is swiftly taking over from slow physical methods.

This book examines the stock markets of Belgium, France, Germany, Italy, Netherlands, and the United Kingdom, being the largest six stock markets, by most measures, in the European Community. Currently, these markets lead, in annual terms, in capitalisation of listed domestic equities, average stock market capitalisation per domestic company, turnover in equities, and total equity turnover as a percentage of stock market capitalisation and of gross national product. If the Copenhagen stock market is ignored, on the grounds that it is unique in providing a large market for house mortgage bonds, then these six stock markets also lead, in annual terms, by number of companies with listed equity, number of new company listings, total listed domestic fixed interest bonds, newly-listed domestic fixed interest bonds, and domestic fixed interest bond turnover. The six countries also possess the largest GNPs in the European Community.

For these countries, the book examines savings and borrowing patterns in their public and private sectors. Special attention is given to the market for public sector bonds in each country since everywhere the weight of central and local government debt, its cost and management, closely affects the vitality of national equity markets.

For the corporate sector, there is rather more interest in equities than bonds. Although stock markets have seen growth in new listings of corporate bonds in recent years, it has been overshadowed by the large volume of new government bond issues. For the six countries, the corporate sector is examined for its position in assets, liabilities, sources and uses of funds, and indebtedness. Since everywhere (but particularly in continental Europe) companies also borrow strongly from the banking system and finance themselves with internal funds, these sources of finance are compared to stock markets. Again, nearly everywhere, most companies' financial structures are weakening, profitability is low and returns on equity unsatisfactory.

The structure and practice of each of the six stock markets is examined and it is quickly apparent that they differ in character and degree of development. The influence of national economic structure, conditions, and policies is marked. Although the computerisation of data processing and information transfer is modernising the stock markets rapidly and giving them a more uniform appearance, the free flow of capital between them still faces obstacles. Such technical aspects as types of sub-market that exist, quotation and settlement of equities, membership, and supervision, are considered.

Each stock market is evaluated from organisational and operating criteria, and the performance of equities and bonds judged by the recent behaviour of turnover, prices and yields. In addition, more academic criteria are considered in measuring the efficiency of the markets, focusing on the 'efficient market hypothesis' which relates price changes to new information. For each country, there is a sizeable academic literature on the subject.

The amount of recent legislation on stock markets varies but for the six countries considered there has generally been a quickening of interest in stock market reform. In the case of France, there exists a comprehensive plan for the improvement of the central and regional stock markets, awaiting implementation. This book makes additional prescriptions for change to improve the operational efficiency of stock markets in all six countries.

In all the countries considered there exist incentives to encourage savings and investment both through stock markets and directly by organisations and individuals. These are the subject of much controversy and evaluation, and could not be omitted in a comprehensive view of the role played by stock markets in company financing and the volume and type of saving that takes place.

The other stock markets of Europe fall well behind in size and sophistication, but not in interest. For example, the Danish stock market has a large, lively, and smoothly-operating turnover in bonds — mostly high-yielding house mortgage bonds and government stock. In Luxembourg, local companies mainly finance themselves, and the whole market is overshadowed by the new issue market in Eurobonds. The Irish stock exchange, administratively integrated with that of the UK, is small and dominated by British money. The latest country to join the European Community, Greece, can support only a rather undeveloped stock exchange. It is clear that the European savings and investment scene is dominated by the six large stock markets selected for study here.

The book was generously financed by the Anglo-German Foundation for the Study of Industrial Society. The author visited the main relevant institutions in Europe, including treasuries, central banks, departments of government, banks, stock market authorities and participants, universities and research institutes, and received much help and encouragement, for which he is very grateful. He also received much informational, translation and clerical help from his wife Joan, and Mrs Janet Connor.

1 Belgium

Company financing

Information on assets, liabilities, sources and uses of company funds, and their position of indebtedness, for example, over a long period, is rather scarce. The Banque Nationale de Belgique publishes annual data on the financial position of companies, based on its own internal sources, and on those of the Institut National de Statistique, but its definition of companies comprises joint-stock companies and partnerships, and includes public enterprises.

On the other hand, Kredietbank maintains a databank of this sort of financial information for some 109 companies (1979) which breaks down the company sector into industrial companies, public utilities and distribution companies. Table 1.1 shows the private industrial company sector, exclusive of public utilities, and from Kredietbank's databank source the breakdown of uses and sources of funds.

Kredietbank statistics include public utilities in the financing analysis of companies, and for industrial, distribution and public utility companies in 1979 the grand total of uses and sources of funds was BF180.4 billion (BF108.4 billion for industrial companies). The largest single items of use of funds by industrial companies are gross investments (61.5 per cent) and short term receivables (23.6 per cent). The largest items of sources of funds are depreciation (21.1 per cent) and transfers (17.2 per cent), out of total self-financing of 51.1 per cent and current liabilities of 40 per cent out of total external sources of funds of 39.2 per cent (one item of sources of funds is negative). Table 1.2

Table 1.1
Financing table

| | Industrial companies* | |
	in FB billion	in per cent
Uses of funds	1979	1979
Gross investments	66.7	61.5
Long term receivables	−6.3	−5.7
Inventories	16.2	14.9
Short term receivables	25.6	23.6
Portfolio	3.7	3.4
Liquidities	2.5	2.3
Total	108.4	100.0
Sources of funds		
Retained profits**	9.8	9.0
Depreciations	22.9	21.1
Transfers	18.6	17.2
= Internal sources	51.4	47.3
Capital and issue premium	4.1	3.8
= Total self-financing	55.5	51.1
Provisions (for taxes etc.)	10.4	9.6
Long term debt	−0.9	−0.7
Current liabilities	43.4	40.0
= Total external sources	42.5	39.2
Grand total	108.4	100.0

*Forty-eight companies in 1979.
**Including minority interests and evaluations.

Source: *Kredietbank Weekly Bulletin*, no.35, 26 September 1980.

Table 1.2
Combined balance sheets (in per cent of total)

	Industrial companies		Distribution companies	
	1979	1978	1979	1978
Assets				
Gross fixed assets	71.1	73.6	71.1	71.2
—Depreciations	24.3	24.9	29.7	28.9
Net fixed assets	46.8	48.7	41.4	42.3
Inventories	22.9	22.8	31.6	28.9
Debtors	24.6	23.1	13.7	13.5
Investments	2.4	2.1	10.0	8.5
Liquidities	3.3	3.3	3.0	6.8
Total assets	100.0	100.0	100.0	100.0
(in FB billion)	704.6	636.5	44.6	43.4
Liabilities				
Capital	26.2	26.7	25.8	24.2
Provisions	4.2	3.0	1.4	1.4
Long term liabilities	26.7	29.6	19.3	20.8
Bankers and advances	10.4	11.4	4.5	4.1
Suppliers	14.3	12.4	30.8	31.8
Other short term liabilities	18.2	16.9	18.2	17.7
Total liabilities	100.0	100.0	100.0	100.0
Ratios				
Solvency	26.24	26.67	25.79	24.16
Liquidity	1.24	1.26	1.10	1.08

Source: *Kredietbank Weekly Bulletin*, no.35, 26 September 1980.

3

shows the combined balance sheets for 1978 and 1979 of the two private sector groups, industrial and distribution companies.

For all companies (financial, distribution, industrial and public utilities) in the financial year 1979, compared with 1978, corporate spending increased on investment, volume of credit to customers (short term receivables) and inventory replenishment. As a result of improved (although still weak) profitability, reserves increased. There was also a shift from long term to short term borrowing. Table 1.2 shows no great change in solvency and liquidity ratios, but the solvency ratio is in fact very weak for industrial companies as a result of low profitability.

The financial year 1980 resulted in poor trading . [1] Although gross revenues of companies (including public utilities) rose 5.5 per cent (on the domestic market), prices of raw materials and inputs rose faster, by 13 per cent. The margin between gross revenues and the value of sales fell. Gross financial charges (interest paid on liabilities) which had increased by 29 per cent in 1979, rose again in 1980 by 37 per cent on the previous year. Gross company revenues reached only 8.1 per cent of national product in 1980 compared with 8.9 per cent the year before. Undistributed profits fell by 0.6 per cent of gross national product (replacement cost method). 'Fonds propres' (gross savings plus positive capital transfers) could finance 6.2 per cent of gross capital formation in 1980 (6.6 per cent in 1979). Domestic capital formation of companies reached 9.4 per cent of GNP in 1980 compared with 9.1 per cent in 1979. This, combined with the fall in 'fonds propres', increased the net financing requirements of companies from 2.5 to 3.2 per cent of national product over the year. The companies responded by trying to lower debt and financial liabilities.

Solvency and the equity debt ratio

Looking at solvency ratios of Belgian industrial companies (equity/total assets) over a long period, there is an unhealthy trend[2] — from 50 per cent in 1964 to 26 per cent in 1979. This is a position of financial weakness. The main cause over the period has been the low profitability of these companies, forcing them to borrow on fixed interest terms. Equity borrowing became very difficult for companies because of the low return to investors.[3] Loans, on the other hand, are apparently more attractive in an inflationary period, when the real burden of redemption is low. In addition, the Belgian Government encouraged loans as a means of companies financing their investments, by making interest payable on loans deductible from taxable profits — in contrast to dividends (at least until the 1978 reforms). Also Government gave an incentive to borrow on fixed terms through interest subsidies and government guarantees. Fortunately for analysis, large Belgian companies have been obliged to disclose their total indebtedness by the Royal

4

Decree of 8 October 1976.

The trend in indebtedness of Belgian companies has been analysed by Kredietbank, using information from its databank for 100 companies stored.[4] Here, the trend among private corporate sector companies is considered for two types: industrial companies and distribution companies. It is worth recalling that a company's business risk is carried mainly by its equities. Since dividends can be made variable, it is the safest source of company financing. From 1977, short term debt maturity was fixed by law at one year. Anything else is categorised as long term debt. Long term debt involves fixed periodical payments. In a period of low profitability, higher and higher debt — interest payments, redemptions and new loans — decrease the solvency ratio, and can cause severe problems, even bankruptcy.

The indebtedness of Belgian industrial companies increased from 55.8 per cent of total assets in 1966 to 69.2 per cent in 1976 and 74 per cent in 1979. The increase was partly due to inflation, as assets are valued historically. The biggest increase in indebtedness was among distribution companies — from 55.6 per cent in 1966 to 79.2 per cent in 1976, with short term debt rising especially fast. An examination in more depth for 1977, from the more detailed balance sheets required by the law of 1976, shows that equities amounted to only 31 per cent of the balance sheet totals of industrial companies, while borrowing rose to 69 per cent. Debts towards other companies, including deferred payments, drafts payable and advance payments made up 27 per cent of total indebtedness. The remainder of short term debts were to nonfinancial companies, debts towards credit institutions being 23 per cent of total indebtedness, and 62 per cent of long term liabilities. For distribution companies in 1977, 73.6 per cent of total funds was financed by borrowing. Because these have less need of fixed assets, little or no working capital is needed, and deferred payments are covered by suppliers' credits. New sales units are financed largely by real estate leasing, and short term credits finance circulating stocks.

The finance of new investments

How have companies financed new investments? In 1977 industrial companies financed 57.6 per cent of fixed assets by equities, 5 per cent by provisions, and 37.4 per cent by long term loans. Financing by means of equity fell from 85.8 per cent in 1967 to 68.7 per cent in 1976. Even when, as more recently, the level of investment has been low, equity financing has been small; again low profitability is the cause. In 1977, equity financing by capital and issue premium had fallen to 3 per cent. Depreciation grew — from 62.6 per cent in 1967 to 82.3 per cent in 1977 — and since 1974 transfers (i.e. the net book value of fixed assets sold) have also increased, pointing to a streamlining by industrial

5

companies. Among distribution companies, depreciation (as a form of equity financing) remained high in long term funding, but much new financing was undertaken by real estate leasing.

Profitabilities

Clearly, Belgian companies have greatly increased their indebtedness in the last ten to thirteen years. But more fundamentally, the share of companies' self-financing has become completely insufficient. Retained profits are very small, and depreciation cannot finance the growing cost of new investment. Therefore Belgian companies are in the very vulnerable position of high debt, and low profitability with which to redeem these debts. Even the jump in profitability in 1978 and 1979 (for forty-eight companies sampled by Kredietbank, −1.1 per cent to 4.8 per cent) was quite insufficient in comparison with risk capital deployed. In 1979, Government securities carried a net yield of 10.2 per cent, and these are riskless. Company profitability should be in the region of 16 per cent given current high business risk. In 1980 profits were brought down again.

The dangers of high gearing (leverage) are well known. The 'degree of leverage' ($\frac{P+I}{P}$) where P = net profit before tax, and $P+I$ = net profit = interest cost before tax, shows the influence of a change in the operating profit ($P+I$) on the return on equity; and should be seen together with the leverage factor (return on equity after tax/return on assets after tax). High leverage means a risk of cash deficits when income is decreasing. Companies with high leverage cannot cope well with very heavily fluctuating profits. And finally, high leverage is not attractive to investors when the company wants to make new issues of equities. For Belgian companies (Kredietbank sample of 70) profits fluctuated greatly 1966 to 1977, and the leverage factor was very high (1966 = 1.68, 1977 = 1.32) due to decreasing solvency.[5] Since 1975, company profits have been very unstable as a result of the high degree of leverage. In 1975 the ratio between net profits and net profits before financial charges was 40 per cent; which, with a solvency of 30.4 per cent, resulted in a leverage factor of 1.32. The result was a return on equity of only 0.7 per cent. There is no doubt that Belgian companies are too risky on average; the cause is deterioration in financial structure over the last ten years.

Banking loans to the corporate sector

It remains to mention the role of the banks and public credit institutions in financing private corporate enterprise in Belgium, since these play an important part in financing long term loans to industry, in particular. The increasing external financing requirements of companies in Belgium have been covered by private savings through the intermediary of private credit institutions (both savings banks and private banks) and through

6

public credit institutions. This is in spite of the fact that, as was shown earlier, domestic household disposable income has had a high consumption propensity, and the capital market has been starved of funds to some extent, so that the difference has had to be obtained by capital imports and last resort lending from the Banque Nationale de Belgique.

In the Belgian banking system, there is a high degree of specialisation. By law, commercial banks are not allowed to hold investments in industry. A large number of private and semi-State or State special institutions provides a variety of financing instruments. Freundlieb[6] distinguishes three groups of banks in Belgium. First, the private commercial banks, holding about 60 per cent of the balance sheet total of all financial institutions. The largest of these institutions are the Kredietbank, Banque Bruxelles de Lambert, the Société Générale de Banque and the Banque de Paris et des Pay Bas. About 30 per cent of the share goes to public credit institutions, of which the largest is the Société Nationale de Crédit à l'Industrie, followed by the Caisse Nationale de Crédit Professionel. The remaining 10 per cent is taken up by the private savings banks, of which there are more than thirty, dominated by the Caisse Générale d'Épargne et de Retraite. Into this group falls the Crédit Communal, a bank of long historical standing. About two-thirds of the savings banks have the legal form of a limited liability company while the remainder operate as credit co-operatives. Foreign banks are important too.

Savings increased rapidly (300 per cent) between 1970 and 1976, nearly 40 per cent of all private savings going into the commercial banks in 1976, and 33 per cent into public credit institutions. The commercial banks, in particular, offer a wide range of savings instruments. The public sector credit institutions, together with the Banque Nationale de Belgique and linked institutions, collected about half of all private savings at the end of 1977. The private sector is led by the Caisse Générale d'Épargne et de Retraite which administers the largest share of Belgium's savings deposits, including medium and long term savings from households, as well as sight deposits and certificates of deposit of one to five years.

In terms of financing investment, the Société Nationale de Crédit à l'Industrie (SNCI) provides the largest share of all investment loans. SNCI lends on long and medium term to industry via credits — borrowers' notes, customers' deposits, and 'bons de caisse' — the total of loans being determined by law. SNCI also lends to shipping and coal-mining, and guarantees industrial credits by commercial banks and other financial institutions. SNCI loans are growing fast, rising from 50 to 60 per cent of all investment loans between 1965 and end-1977. Even faster growth came from the commercial banks, increasing five times over the period.

Private savings banks continue to lend on an increasing scale to industry — the Caisse Générale d'Épargne et de Retraite (CGER) providing medium and long term loans — but mainly for housing construction. Its industrial lending is primarily indirect, via credits to SNCI through buying bonds, etc. In 1977 the institution provided some 20 per cent of all investment credit.

In the case of small and medium sized companies, the Caisse Nationale de Crédit Professionnel, a public credit institution, is a major lender. The Crédit Communal is a large lender to local authorities. Table 1.3 shows the breakdown of loans to public companies (and self-employed firms) from all credit sources.

Belgium's capital market is almost dominated by the public sector, which has contributed some 70 − 80 per cent of total investment credits and active new issues over recent years. The State is the principal capital raiser. Private placings play an important role in industrial bond issues, but the banks are forbidden to hold shares in industrial enterprises, or place new issues. They can, however, hold industrial bonds. Total growth can be seen from Table 1.3. But it should be noted that in the last two years 1979 and 1980 there has been a swing to short term financing. One jarring note: the cost of investment credit has risen markedly over recent years. The weighted average lending rate of interest of the Banque Nationale de Belgique has risen from 9.18 in 1974 to 12 per cent in August 1980; deposit rates of banks from 7 in 1976 to 9 per cent in August 1980; yield on fixed interest bonds on the Brussels bourse from 7.90 in 1974 to 11.79 per cent in September 1980; and interest rate on bons de caisse and bonds issued by public credit institutions from 7 in 1972 to 12.50 per cent in April 1980. The cost of long term credit in general, and of investment credit in particular, is high relative to other forms of credit and investment credits in other countries, which is rather a weakness. Short term credit is cheaper. There is a certain rigidity and ratchet effect about long term rates.

The role of the SNCI has certain unfavourable effects on interest rates. The Government holds half of SNCI capital; it is limited in its short term lending. SNCI is very specialised in its lending (90 per cent is by bonds of more than five years' maturity). It has no dépôts à vue or carnet de dépôts. When interest rates at short term fluctuate, it is difficult for the SNCI to place its bonds and bons de caisse. In fact, it is in a vicious circle. When short term interest rates are high, it can place its bonds easily, but registers losses on reinvestment; when short term rates fall, reinvestment is profitable, but it can place bonds only with difficulty. SNCI resources are not diversified enough, as a result the cost of its bonds is rigid and generally too high — influenced very much by the Treasury with its enormous need for financing; the State supplies 78 per cent of total public sector loans. Apart from its tap ('au robinet') current issues, SNCI is a very modest and irregular participant in the

Table 1.3
Credits for fixed capital, loans, discounted bills and
bills of acceptance by origin — Deposit Banks, CGER, SNCI, CNCP —
to public companies and self-employed firms (Belgian residents)

(credits in billions of Belgian francs)

	Open credits		Credits taken up	
	1976	1979	1976	1979
Agriculture and products	14.1	25.7	12.3	20.2
Extractive industries and products	10.6	9.1	5.1	5.1
Manufacturing industry and commerce and products	849.7	1113.1	478.2	624.5
Housing construction	74.6	117.6	42.7	74.9
Production and distribution of energy and water	31.8	47.8	20.9	30.2
Other services, e.g. transport, leasing, factoring, financial services	234.4	500.0	173.1	300.6
Total	1215.2	1813.3	732.3	1055.5

Source: *Bulletin de la Banque Nationale de Belgique*, September 1980.

Belgian stock market. The Treasury governs SNCI loans, and keeps rates up on account of its large public deficit. In turn its rates are followed by other credit institutions on the market; leaving the banks as the only institutions with relative freedom. But still the banks play a very limited role. In sum, the financing needs of the State are at the heart of the high long term cost of credit in Belgium.[7]

Central government and local authority financing

Between 1970 and 1978 taxes and social security levies by the central government and local authorities grew rapidly; faster than GNP. By 1978, the burden of taxes was the second highest in the European Community. But this growth then stabilised as a result of no new tax-increasing measures, tax exemptions in favour of companies and the index-linking of tax scales. Fortunately for Government total receipts, public financial intermediaries' non-fiscal receipts increased in 1979.

But in 1979 and 1980 the rate of growth of total public spending was very rapid; its share in GNP increased, as it had done uninterruptedly since 1970. At the same time, in 1979, the Government announced its intention of stepping up public investment. With public sector spending rising fast, the net deficit to be financed grew substantially.

The net financing requirement of the public authorities, which was 9.4 per cent of GNP in 1979, grew to 11.8 per cent in 1980. In the European Community, this was the highest percentage after Italy. This deterioration was due to higher consumption and investment costs, and lower disposable income. Other factors included an 8.1 per cent growth of the total costs of social security between 1979 and 1980, and rapid increases in wages and salaries. As a result, interest charges on the debt of public authorities increased from BF167 billions in 1979 to BF212 billions in 1980, a rise of 25 per cent. Short term interest rates shot up, and so did the total size of the public debt.

As pointed out earlier, the net effect of the movement of expenses and receipts of public authorities between 1979 and 1980 was an increase in the public authority net financing requirement from BF305 billions to BF409 billions. Table 1.4 shows how this deficit was incurred between the different sectors of public authority.

As a result of the huge rise in public debt in 1980, bank lending increased, and as Table 1.5 shows, net floating debt increased heavily and consolidated debt diminished. Since short term rates shot up during the year 1980, financial intermediaries preferred to buy Treasury certificates rather than State bonds.

The increase in public sector debt in 1980 caused a huge rise in liquidity creation; BF117 billion against BF79 billion in 1979. Issues of foreign currency debt were greatly increased, while growth in the Fond des Rentes Treasury certificates portfolio increased less. Floating debt rose hugely. By 31 December 1980, Treasury debt in foreign currencies reached BF153 billion. The other sub-sectors of public authorities also had higher net financing requirements. Borrowing from the Credit Communal was increased, and some big cities borrowed directly on the stock market.

How did these trends affect public authority deficit financing on the Belgian stock market? Short term interest rates rose steeply (three month Treasury certificates from just over 14 to 17½ per cent in early 1980, falling back to nearly 13 per cent at the end of the year). This was partly caused by fluctuations on foreign money markets. Long term domestic interest rates, on the other hand, rose steadily throughout the year. The issue rate went up from 10.5 in December 1979 to 11 per cent for the Government loan of February 1980 and to 13 per cent (for the first three years) and 11.5 per cent (for the five remaining years of the term) for the Road Fund's graduated rate loan in April 1980. These

Table 1.4
Net financing deficit of public authorities, 1972–80

	Treasury	Other central government*	Local authorities**	Social security	Statistical adjustment	Total of public authorities	Total of public authorities as percentage of GNP
			Billions of Belgian francs				
1972	–64	–22	–7	+15	–14	–92	5.8
1973	–51	–20	–16	+17	–25	–95	5.3
1974	–57	–21	–20	+18	–11	–91	4.3
1975	–110	–23	–23	+20	–22	–158	6.8
1976	–133	–21	–29	+12	–31	–202	7.6
1977	–168	–18	–19	+16	–30	–219	7.7
1978	–183	–10	–27	+3	–31	–248	8.1
1979	–212	–29	–29	–6	–29	–305	9.4
1980 (est.)	–297	–22	–45	–16	–29	–409	11.8

Source: Banque Nationale de Belgique, Rapports, 1980.

*Variations in the débudgetisée debt of the Treasury and certain other non-Treasury debt.
**Variations in debt towards the Crédit Communal and other financial intermediaries plus net loans in domestic and foreign currencies.

Table 1.5
Cover for net financing debt of the Treasury (billion BF)

	Debt variation causing creation of liquidity by the BNB				Variations in other debt in Belgian francs			General Total
	Treasury certificates held by the BNB	Treasury certificates held by the Fond des Rentes* and financed by BNB loans	Debt in foreign currencies	Total	Floating	Consolidated	Total	
	1	2	3	4 =1+2+3	5	6	7 =5+6	8 =7+4
1972	-4	+2	-14	-16	+2	+78	+80	+64
1973	-1	-2	-4	-7	-4	+62	+58	+51
1974	+5	—	-2	+3	+3	+51	+54	+57
1975	-1	+3	-1	+1	+14	+95	+109	+110
1976	+16	+1	-1	+16	+35	+82	+117	+133
1977	+16	—	-1	+15	+18	+135	+153	+168
1978	—	+13	+12	+25	+14	+144	+158	+183
1979	—	+37	+42	+79	+7	+126	+133	+212
1980	—	+25	+92	+117	+110	+70	+180	+297

Source: Banque Nationale de Belgique, Rapports, 1980.

*The Fond des Rentes is the Government organisation responsible for placing State bonds, etc., on the market.

rates were partly pulled up by money market rates, but mostly rose under the influence of the intense demand for funds by the public authorities. But despite the later fall in short term interest rates, the bond rate remained high and stood at record levels. Some city loans in September had a coupon of 12.75 per cent. In November 1980, a loan in favour of the National Housing Corporation carried an initial gross yield of 12.98 per cent. Finally, the issue calendar closed with the flotation of a Euratom 1980-87 loan offering a gross yield of 13.23 per cent. The bond rate might have gone even higher had not the public authorities borrowed heavily abroad, and had not the bond flotations met with resistance from investors looking for high yields on the money market. Only one loan was actually successful. Bond rates have shown steady increases over the years, as shown in Table 1.6.

Finally, the market for bonds, including government bonds, was influenced by high money market interest rates, and overseas borrowing in 1980. The market was tight, and bond issues placed only with difficulty.

Table 1.6
Structure of interest rates

Average yield on bond market	end 1974	end 1976	Nov. 1980
Long term bonds:			
Government funds (7–13 years)	6.94	6.79	9.88
Medium term bonds (5–10 years):			
Government funds	6.88	7.58	9.31
Issued by semi-official organisations	7.27	7.46	9.76
Issued by Gemeentekrediet (Local authorities' lending organisation) and cities	7.43	7.43	9.97
Industrial bonds	7.90	8.60	9.98

Source: *Kredietbank Weekly Bulletin*, no.48, 26 December 1980.

13

Table 1.7

Table 1.7
Public issues of bonds in Belgium (gross amounts BF million)

	1979	1980
Public sector:		
Government	196,000	154,800
RTT (telegraph and telephone)	–	–
NMBS (Belgian railways)	–	–
Road fund	60,700	40,500
Gemeentekrediet, provinces and municipalities	11,000	12,000
NMH (housing)	–	15,000
NMKN (industrial credit)	10,000	–
Private companies:	2,500	5,000
International institutions	4,000	2,000
Total	284,200	229,300

Source: *Kredietbank Weekly Bulletin*, no.48, 26 December 1980.

Structure and practice of the Belgian Stock Exchange

The structure and practice of the Belgian stock market is set out in Titre V Livre 1er du Code de Commerce, Règlement de la Bourse de Fonds Publics et de Change, Annexé à l'arrêté royal du 1er fevrier 1935 (1977), together with a number of modifications made up to 1980.

Organisation

There are four stock markets in Belgium: Brussels, Antwerp, Ghent and Liège. The first is by far the most important in terms of turnover and value of stocks. The activities of the other three are so insignificant they are not recorded separately in any centrally published official statistics. The managing committee of the Brussels stock market is the Commission de la Bourse. Its fifteen members are all stockbrokers; it represents the association of stockbrokers, and establishes their yearly list. It directs the daily operations of the stock exchange, and publishes the official quotation of public funds. It ensures that stockbrokers fulfil their duties to each other and to third parties and, finally, can penalise indiscipline in the market by any of the following means: warning, reprimand, suspension and expulsion. Ultimately, it makes proposals to the Minister for Finance.

Responsible to the Commission de la Bourse is the Comité de Cotation (Quotations Committee). Its three members are appointed from among the Commission's members. They take note of daily price fluctuations, and act if these are abnormal; assure the regularity of quotations and execution of orders; and keep the Commission de la Bourse informed about abnormal movements of écarts (margins) between equities and bonds.

Directly responsible to the Minister for Finance is the Comité de la Cote (listings Committee) made up of six to twelve active members and one or more deputies, themselves either stockbrokers or bankers. This committe makes decisions on the admission of equities and their removal from the list if necessary. All companies must notify the Comité de la Cote of all changes in their structure, detachment of coupons, etc.

Also directly responsible to the Minister for Finance is the Commission d'Appel (Appeals Commission). This body has seven active members and five deputies. Its function is to rule on appeals: against refusal for membership of the stock exchange, against a disciplinary decision of suspension or expulsion, against refusal of a request to enter the market, by the Commissaire du Gouvernement (Government Commissioner), against all decisions taken by the Commission de la Bourse or the Comité de la Cote.

The Commissaire du Gouvernement, mentioned earlier, through all committees and other commissions, supervises the application of the laws and regulations of the stock market, and can arrange relevant meetings.

Finally, any application for listing must be made not only to the Comité de la Cote, but also to the Commission Bancaire (Banking Commission) whose members are nominated by the King. In addition to legal powers entrusted to it to control all banking functions in Belgium — commercial banks, savings banks, holding companies, etc. — the Commission has a primary legal responsibility to supervise all matters relating to the introduction of equities and bonds to public dealings on the stock market. Its total powers are wide and may be compared in some respects to the Belgian equivalent of the American Securities and Exchange Control. The Commission is limited by its charter, which specifies the protection of the saving public, but for some years it has tended to assume a wider brief, to include, for example, the question of private transfers of controlling shares. This problem extends to local authority enterprises as well. The laws of 1970 and 1973 require local authorities to inform the Minister for Economic Affairs, the Minister for Finance and the Secretary of State for the region concerned of such transfers over BF100 million. In the case of transfers of private sector controlling shares, the Commission has recommended: (i) such transfers should be notified to the Commission before the event takes place; (ii) all stockholders should be treated (informed) equally: this accords with the EC Code of Conduct; (iii) if a premium ('prime de contrôle') is paid, the proceeds should go to the stockholders, not the company; (iv) following a controlling takeover, the general public should be rapidly and clearly informed; (v) generally, the 'offre publique d'achet ou d'échange' best assure equal treatment between stockholders. There are well known rules and regulations attached to these. The Commission does not favour 'partial' public take-overs; they discriminate between stockholders. Neither does the Commission object to convertible bonds, as long as they are provided for in the company's articles. The Commission has similar surveillance over the Sociétés de Gestion de Fonds Commons de Placement (investment trusts), Belgian and foreign.

The markets

The marché du comptant (cash market) which deals with local shares, is divided into three distinct sub-markets: le marché des Rentes (Government broker market), le marché des Corbeilles (continuous price market for large transactions) and le marché du Parquet (for smaller transactions, where only one price is established). The Commission de la Bourse can, as it requires, organise a marché des droits de souscription (rights market) on the Corbeilles or Parquet.

There is also a marché à terme (account settlement market). Here, trading is settled only at the end of each fortnightly account; it is not strictly a forward market as normally understood. Foreign shares are mainly dealt in this market. There is, of course, a large market for Government bonds, reflecting the size of the State deficit. The Government issues the following types of loans:

(a) Budget loans: dette directe de l'État (three issues per annum); dette indirecte de l'État (issued by the Fonds des Rentes); emprunts dont l'État garantir l'intérêt et l'amortissement, e.g. for parastatal institutions like SNCB, RTT; emprunts des associations intercommunales (e.g. autoroutes); emprunts des villes (no guarantee).

(b) Fixed price loans − taken up by the banks.

(c) Fixed price loans taken up by consortia of banks, including, since 1973, consortia of the savings banks.

Finally, there is the market for Eurobonds. These are taken up by self-employed firms, investment clubs and private institutional investments, and the central bank. Issuers of Eurobonds are local authorities and large companies. Banks are the intermediaries in Eurobonds. Most Eurobond issues are quoted on the bourse, but the secondary market is principally a 'network market' undertaken between banks. Eurobond issues are not public issues in Belgium, and therefore issuers are not subject to authorisation by the Commission Bancaire, nor obliged to publish prospectuses, but information is given to the Commission. Relatively little trading takes place on the bourse. The main purposes of listing are to provide information, to give investors confidence and to allow exchanges to provide some barometer of approximate quotations and to make Eurobonds eligible for the portfolios of many institutions which are restricted to investment in quoted stocks. In practice most Eurobonds are traded 'over the counter' by secondary market makers recognised by the Association of International Bond Dealers.[9]   But issues in Euro-Belgian francs are prohibited.

Orders

In the marché à terme, brokers deal through the Quotations Department which ascertains a situation with the EDP centre, and communicates the results to the Commissaire. The system of quotations is then by auction, either directly with brokers or through the Commissaire aux criées. In the marchés des Corbeilles and du Parquet, brokers deal through a 'specialist', a stockbroker centralising orders, and an action system is conducted by the Commissaire. The maximum spread of price is established in the rules and ranges from 2 per cent in the marche des Rentes to 10 per cent in the Corbeilles.

Orders can be placed in various ways in both the terme and au courant markets. The most simple is 'au Cours' (opening price), opening on the Corbeilles being 1250 hours, 1230 hours for the Terme, 1310 for the Parquet and 1330 hours for the Ventes Publiques Supplémentaires (monthly public sales market, unlisted stock admitted through the Commission de la Bourse). Orders are therefore executed at the opening price by the Commissaire aux criées; 'à court limité' = orders are fixed at maximum and minimum prices by the person placing the order; 'au mieux' = price fixed at the discretion of the broker. Other orders are 'stop' as in other major bourses like Paris, to stop excessive loss or gain. On the marché à terme, there are special orders — definite 'ferme' or conditional 'terme conditionel'. Definite means predetermined price. Conditional prices are 'à prime' (optional): one party reserves a right, by paying à prime (premium), either not to 'call' or 'put' before the option day, or to annul the purchase. Call options are called 'prime dont' and put options 'prime ou'. Between the two options markets (put and call) there are also operations called 'le stellage' (double option or put and call) where one of the two parties (le 'preneur', giver) reserves the right, on paying a prime, not to call or put a fixed quantity of stocks at a fixed price until the term. As far as orders 'dont' and 'ou' are concerned, the more distant the payment date, the greater the margin between le ferme and la prime, since the time in which to choose is long and favours the buyer of a 'dont' and the seller of an 'ou'. The other party, in each case, pays the highest prime.

There are more complicated orders, e.g. 'achet ferme contre vente à prime 'ou', i.e. an optimist will buy at a definite price and sell 'ou', on the expectation of a rising price. If the rise occurs, the buyer can sell before the put date, and lose his 'prime', and still profit. There are other combinations. To cover intense speculation, Belgian law limits the size of the margin. Investment clubs use even more sophisticated techniques of ordering.

Finally, orders are actually executed 'par criées' (auction) used to determine the opening price, par opposition (on the Corbeille — several prices proposed) and par casier (on the marché à terme) in which brokers leave their buy and sell orders in a pigeon-hole, and the Commissaire bases his quotation à la criée on these. Settlements of spot transactions are carried out by a designated Caisse under the supervision of the Commission de la Bourse, and à terme operations by the Coopérative de Liquidation des opérations à Terme.

Listing and transactions costs

Listing fee is BF50,000 plus (a) an annual fee of BF5,000 for companies whose market value is less than BF50 million or (b) an annual fee of BF10,000 for companies whose market value is more than BF50 million.

Transaction fees are complex. The investor in securities has to bear the following costs on security transactions: [10]

A brokerage fee charged by the Minister for Finance:

BF4.50 per 1,000 on the actual value increased by interest for spot transactions in Government bonds with a degressive rate over BF2 million. Short dated bonds, with less than one year's maturity, carry a fee of 3 per cent up to BF250,000 and 2 per cent over BF250,000.

BF8 per 1,000 for forward transactions with a degressive rate over BF5 million.

BF10 per 1,000 for spot transactions, with a degressive rate over BF2 million.

For equities traded on the spot market, the following scale is applied on the first portion of BF2 million of the amount of a transaction or on an operation of at least BF2 million; for the part above this amount, the degressive normal fee is applied. The total of the fees including the fixed duty may not exceed 10 per cent of the amount of the operation. The loans whose redemption is before one year are not subject to the scale (for low value securities).

Scale		
from BF1 to BF15:	10 per cent of value of equity
from BF16 to BF100:	BF1.50 per share
from BF101 to BF200:	BF2.00 per share
from BF201 to BF400:	BF4.00 per share
from BF401 to BF600:	BF6.00 per share

This brokerage is increased by a fixed duty of BF100 for each transaction mentioned on the contract note with the exception of the transactions carried forward to the next account and the transactions in subscription rights.

A Government tax on equity transactions amounting to:

BF0.70 per 1,000 for Government stock

BF1.40 per 1,000 for other Belgian and foreign Government bonds

BF1.70 per 1,000 for forward transactions

BF1.40 per 1,000 for forward transactions in certificates issued in Belgium for foreign shares

BF3.50 per 1,000 in the spot market for Belgian and foreign company shares

Costs relating to the functioning of the market: a complementary quotation charge of:

BF0.25 per 1,000 is made on the total of transactions on the cash and forward markets

BF0.10 per 1,000 on the total transactions for Government bonds

For contangoes there are 3 charges:

up to BF5m	4 per cent
from BF5m and BF1—10m	3 per cent
over BF10m	2.5 per cent
(minimum commission per share: BF.075)	

For options (put, call and straddle):

Options for the next market day

if not exercised — 3 per cent of value of premium plus ordinary commission rates

if exercised — ordinary commission rates apply

For long-term options:

not exercised — 6 per cent of value of premium

exercised — normal commission rates

Commission sharing:

to foreign stockbrokers — 15 per cent

to banks included in the list of the Belgian Commission Bancaire — 40 per cent

N.B. The above commission rates are increased by small complementary charges. The same commission fees are charged for unlisted securities.

The Stamp Duty on market transactions in Belgium is:

Government stock	0.07 per cent
Bonds, including certificates issued by Belgian nominee companies	0.14 per cent
Shares	0.35 and 0.17 per cent respectively on cash and account transactions
Options	nil
Carry-overs	0.085 and 0.170 per cent are respectively charged if such deals lapse within or after 20 days.

Types of shares

The Belgian Stock Exchange displays a variety of instruments in which to deal:

1   *Actions* (equities) — the following are registered in form:

(a) actions de capital sans désignation de valeur nominale — fluctuating value, part-social equities

(b) actions de priorité ou préférence (preference equities, fixed dividend, paid first). These are also called parts privilegiées

(c) parts bénéficiaires — not related to capital, simply carry a right to annual pay-out or put in reserve, no nominal value or voting rights
(i) le part de fondateur (company promoter)
(ii) actions de dividende — right to a part of dividends, but no share of capital or reserves on liquidation

(d) actions de jouissance — replace equities drawn out by amortisation of capital. Represent only a right to dividend of second rung, after actions de capital prioritaires

(e) part de réserve — right to part of reserves in case of liquidation.

Equities may be 'nominatif' in title (registered) or 'au porteur' (bearer) (anonymous) — or mixed 'nominatif' and 'au porteur' (coupon).

2 *Obligations* (bonds) — these may be:

(a) en deviser (foreign currencies) — including emprunts (loans); à option de change (several foreign currencies). Rates of interest may be floating or progressive.
Payment (i) anticipé, (ii) au pair, (iii) à prime, (iv) par tirage ou rachat en bourse

(b) Garanties: paid out before equities, but after other bonds; some may be privilégié (e.g. emprunt hypothécaire)

(c) Emprunts indexés

(d) Bons de caisses (medium term loans), and bons de caisses de capitalisation: no longer used (reinvestment of interest)

(e) Obligations participantes: fixed interest plus fraction of dividend as per equities.

3 *State bonds*

(a) bons du trésor or certificates de trésorerie: State loans reserved for financial institutions

(b) rentes perpétuelles: no repayment date

(c) emprunts forcés: necessity to convert or unify past debt

(d) bonds convertible into equities

(e) obligation avec warrant: right to convert to subscription at fixed price.

4 *Fonds commun de placement* — placed by investment clubs in diversified safe investments. Investors are collectively treated.

(a) fonds communs immobilières: flexible bonds in a flexible portfolio

(b) certificats fonciers: collective ownership in a fixed portfolio. Yield is indexed or blocked.

Intermediaries

Only 'agents de change' (brokers), 'agents de change correspondants' and authorised banks are allowed to receive Stock Exchange orders. Only agents de change have the monopoly to execute orders. The latter two intermediaries must go through an agent de change to execute their clients' orders. There were 302 agents de change at 31 December 1979. But there are two exceptions under the system 'cession à titre onéreux', when direct sales and purchases in the market can take place without an agent de change:

(a) rare transfers between sellers and buyers
(b) for large orders (greater than BF10m).

Agents de change *may* act as contrapartistes (jobbers) in cases of incompatible bargains, listed or unlisted. Normally, this role is forbidden. Agents de change correspondants are subject to the same rules as agents de change. By a law of 1955, agents de change may undertake arbitrage, but only a small number of agents in fact do so. Limited to the role of intermediary, agents de change cannot undertake new public issues of securities. Agents de change may not accept deposits of capital, other than those directly concerned with their business as brokers, i.e. accepting clients' orders, nor turn such payments into savings deposits. Neither may they make any discount transactions for their own account. They must not make settlements outside the Stock Exchange.

International aspects of the Stock Exchange

The Belgian Stock Exchange is considered restricted with respect to dealings in foreign bonds. Although Belgian law does not forbid bond issues by foreign borrowers on the Belgian stock market, issues of public bonds by foreigners are not encouraged by the Treasury. By virtue of membership of the IBRD and EIU, Belgium is obliged to give access to its stock market to bond issues from these institutions. But the Ministry of Finance makes it costly and slow for them. In total, for the period 1972—76, less than 1 per cent of public issues in Belgium were by these organisations.[11] The same applies to private issues of foreign bonds on the Belgian Stock Exchange; although no formalities are required, the total of issues was insignificant in 1972—76. The right to subscribe to these bonds by the main borrowers (insurance companies) is strictly controlled.

Private issues of Belgian bonds on foreign stock markets are rare, due to the Belgian tax system. The 'précompte mobilier' applies with very few exceptions to Belgian borrowers; this interest rate is 20 per cent. The same applies to Belgian State loans overseas.

Clearing

Partly to promote the introduction of foreign stocks on the Brussels Stock Exchange, a computer-based 'clearing house' was set up in 1967 for transactions in bonds and equities. The Caisse Interprofessionelle de Dépôts et de Virement de Titres provides physical safekeeping for certificates, and enables securities to pass from one holder to another automatically, without their exchange. It services bearer or registered securities, Belgian or foreign. Originally, it was set up by a group of 200 Belgian banks and stockbrokers. In the first stage, CIK limited its activities to Belgian securities and members, but since 1980 it is open to foreign securities and members. Foreign financial institutions (banks, brokers or other similar clearing systems) can become shareholders and affiliates of CIK. The system of appointing nominees makes clearing easier, e.g. CIK can appoint foreign nominees who keep certificates abroad for CIK, so there is no need for a foreign company either to print certificates in a foreign language, or send certificates out of the country. Similarly, CIK can be appointed nominee by foreign banks and brokers for Belgian securities bought by foreign investors or listed abroad. A large percentage of all institutional dealings take place wholly with the CIK. The advantages claimed are as for other EDP clearing systems: reduced paperwork, postage and administration, and a faster clearing service. As CIK gets tied into other automated clearing systems in national stock markets abroad, the ease with which international dealings are cleared will improve. Already, CIK has access to French securities through SICOVAM.

The after-hours market

The after-hours market is not very respectable in Belgium. Its statistics do not show up in the official publications, so it is difficult to gauge its size and importance.

23

Evaluation of the Belgian stock market structure and practice

The overwhelming role of the Brussels Stock Exchange compared with the provincial exchanges is understandable. But the provincial exchanges do not seem to have the integrative, complementary, or supportive role that, for example, those in France have. They give the impression of being neglected, and contributing little to the role of bringing borrowers and lenders together, even in a modest and regional way.

The Commission de la Bourse operates in a normal fashion as 'watchdog', in much the same way as the Council of the Stock Exchange in the UK. The Commission is composed of stockbrokers who act as a managing committee in much the same way as the British Stock Exchange Council, but the difference is that its functions and responsibilities are set out in Titre V, Livre 1er du Code de Commerce, Règlement de la Bourse de Fonds Public et de Change, annexé à l'arrêté royal du 1er février 1935 (with subsequent amendments). It is the continental system, and generally more rigid than the British, although within its own framework it has some discretion on decision-making.

The weakness of the system is the subordination of the Commission de la Bourse to the Minister for Finance. The Ministry is very powerful, and since it also acts in accordance with Belgian monetary policy, tends to subordinate its stock market decision to that. The Ministry directs unequivocally the Commissaire du Gouvernement, who supervises the application of the laws and regulations of the stock market according to the arrêté royal and subsequent amendments. It also controls directly the Comité d'Appel. The Commissaire du Gouvernement can be called or heard in the Comité d'Appel, and he also has the right to attend, in a consultative capacity, the Commission de la Bourse, as well as attending the Comité de la Cote, also in a consultative capacity. The Comité de Cotation surveys abnormal price movements under the control of the Commission de la Bourse, but can only discipline by calling for agents' books and making proposals to the Commission, which, in turn, makes proposals to the Ministry. It is not clear what are to be considered abnormal price movements, or how criteria are drawn up to judge what may be considered justified or unjustified movements. The Commission de la Bourse has disciplinary powers of its own, but by and large these relate to unprofessional practices by agents de change, and to their professional standing (e.g. bankruptcy, undertaking other work) rather than practices which breach the accepted standards of behaviour and techniques available in the market itself.

Thus, although the Commission de la Bourse is, to some extent, a self-regulating management committee, it and all the associated bodies connected with the stock exchange exercise their powers by right of statute, not time-honoured practice. In order for their powers to be changed, the statutes must be amended. It turns out in the end that, even discretionary decisions, by the Commission de la Bourse for example, must be reported to the Minister for Finance.

Superimposed on this system of control is the Commission Bancaire, a powerful body, whose members are nominated by the King, and which has powers to regulate all banking functions, as well as a legal responsibility to supervise listings and dealings of stocks on the market. This is the nearest Belgium comes to an SEC. But, although it can call for information on transfers of controlling shares (take-overs and mergers), it has no powers to prevent them if they are thought undesirable. There is no body comparable to Britain's Panel on Take-overs and Mergers, which has the right to hear appeals by parties to take-over transactions against rulings by the executive. In the UK statutory arrangements for supervision of the UK securities industry are administered primarily by the Department of Trade, which provides a legal framework rather than a system of regulating markets. The relevant Acts in the UK are the Companies Act and the Prevention of Fraud (Investments) Act 1958. The Director of Public Prosecutions can intervene in matters of suspected fraud. Within the realm of non-statutory regulation in the UK Stock Exchange comes not only the Stock Exchange Council, but also several other bodies like the Council for Securities Industries, the Bank of England, the Panel on Take-overs and Mergers, the Issuing Houses Association, and others.

The Belgian system of stock market supervision can therefore be criticised in that it is overly statutory, and powers overlap between different supervisory bodies, e.g. the Commission Bancaire and Commission de Cotation. There is no real forum for looking at 'insider trading' for example, although the Commission Bancaire is exploring this, as well as take-overs and mergers. No definite rules or penalties have been produced yet. Belgian company law is outdated in such areas as the protection of small savers, but a new law before Parliament in 1980 may increase supervision of companies in this respect.

The organisation of cash markets appears overly complicated: the Corbeilles, Parquet and Rentes. The recommendations of the Commission Perouse, in Paris, point to savings and greater efficiency through integrating such markets, and especially through attempting to set up continuous pricing in a trading period of longer opening hours. Similarly, the spot settlements market and the fortnightly account market might be brought closer together. The system of orders à la criée has been criticised elsewhere as disruptive, and the par opposition and par casier seem outdated. On the other hand, the complicated system of ordering in options trading seems an advance, except that the market is thin, and therefore would tend to be speculative.

Listing and transacting costs seem high on the Brussels Stock

Exchange, although they are not necessarily a bar to admission to the Exchange or to transactions on the secondary market. But transaction fees seem complex, and fiscal measures certainly operate against equities in favour of bonds.

The borrowing instruments or notes in the market seem unusually complex; this may reflect the opportunities for speculative activity in a thin equity market, and the need to increase returns by sophisticated practices of investment.

Agents de change on the Brussels Stock Exchange do not have a great deal of official freedom, and, as far as one can tell, profits are not high; it is surprising that over 300 stockbrokers continue to deal. Some of them are large by any European standards. They gain by certain unofficial activities, e.g. they unofficially act as specialist 'market holders': i.e. although there is no formal jobbing function, brokers may offer themselves to companies. They may unofficially act as contrapartistes, and need not be on the Stock Exchange's books or the Commissaire's List. Certainly, a fair amount of block trading in equities takes place outside the stock market. Buying and selling institutions must pass their order through an agent de change, but this may not take place on the Stock Exchange. On the other hand, it must be recorded on the Stock Exchange. The weak point is that the price can never really be trusted. There is now a draft bill for the reform of company law before Parliament, which includes measures to improve the capital market, and also fiscal incentives are being explored. As yet, it is not a criminal offence in Belgium (as it is in France) not to apply EEC codes e.g. on admission, listing and disclosure of information. There is, for instance, no law on 'insider trading' in Belgium. The agents de change are in a delicate position, which should really be cleared up by amendments to the arrêté royal.

The rules and practice regarding the ease with which Belgian and foreign borrowers may issue bonds on each other's markets has already been explored, and quite clearly, Brussels is being held back by unnecessary rules and practices of the Treasury, as well as some aspects of Belgian law.

The after-hours market, which is a strength in other national financial centres, is held in low esteem in Belgium. But unofficial markets are growing everywhere, and it would probably be a mistake to cast this in a Cinderella role.

Performance and efficiency of the Brussels Stock Exchange

We have already seen in earlier analysis and tables, that by 1979 and 1980 there appeared a shortage of funds on the Belgian Stock Exchange to cover net financing requirements of Belgian companies and public sector net borrowing requirements, causing interest rates to rise. This is reflected in the various statistical indicators of the stock market over a longer period than just those two years.

The performance of Belgian equities

1   *Volume of transactions*   Both 1979 and 1980 were years of increased activity for Belgian equities; only 1973 surpassed 1980. Table 1.8 shows the pattern since 1971.

Table 1.8
Volume of equity transactions, Brussels Stock Exchange

	Total BF billions	Per cent	Belgian equities* BF mill.	Per cent	Foreign equities BF mill.	Per cent
1971	40.9	100	29.5	72	11.4	28
1972	47.9	100	28.8	60	19.1	40
1973	66.0	100	40.9	62	25.1	38
1974	44.6	100	25.1	56	19.5	44
1975	48.8	100	23.1	47	25.7	53
1976	50.3	100	18.7	37	31.6	63
1977	36.9	100	17.9	49	19.0	51
1978	38.5	100	20.5	53	18.0	47
1979	52.8	100	29.7	56	23.1	44
1980 (prov.)	62.5	100	24.9	40	37.6	60

Source: Banque Bruxelles Lambert: *Bulletin Financier* no.1, 9 January 1981.

*Excluding industrial bonds, communal funds, sales of public supplementaries.

An even higher turnover in equities took place in 1980 than in 1979, almost exclusively due to foreign equity turnover. Investment in Belgian equities fell by 16 per cent between 1979 and 1980, reversing the trend of previous years. The volume of turnover on the terme market continued to increase. Terme market equity turnover represented three-quarters of turnover in 1980. Terme market turnover has been increasing as a proportion of total stock market turnover in equities since 1973.

But it is important to note, in the context of the structure of purchases and sales of equities on the stock market, that in 1980 only ten active equities accounted for the majority of turnover of Belgian equities (64.8 per cent); the 220 other equities contributing only 35.2 per cent of the total value. Closer examination is even more revealing: the company, Pétrofina, with 21 per cent of market capitalisation, alone contributed 35.7 per cent (BF8,135 million) of the total of transactions in Belgian equities between January and November 1980. Turnover in other Belgian equities in the year was quite small, e.g. Intercom 7.5 per cent (BF1,716 million), and Gevaert 2.4 per cent (BF537 million). Among foreign equities quoted on the Belgian Stock Exchange, although the total value of turnover was much higher per company, for the ten most active equities the value per company was not greatly different, e.g. the highest was Royal Dutch 7.3 per cent (BF2,508 million), lowest Minorco 3.4 per cent (BF1,157 million). Between 1980 and 1979, the average daily turnover of Belgian equities dropped 21 per cent, while that of foreign shares rose by 56 per cent.

2   *Equity issues*   Issue activity in 1980 was very weak. No convertible bonds were issued during the year. The only companies which issued stock in 1980 were Delhaize Gedbroeders en Cie, 'De Leeuw', FN, Wagon-Lits et due Tourisme and Crédit Général SA de Banque.

Table 1.9
Issues (in BF billion)

	1975	1976	1977	1978	1979	1980 (Jan–Oct.)
Equities	3.4	0.4	10.2	9.3	5.4	1.7
Convertible bonds	4.9	2.0	0.6	0	2.5	0
Total	8.3	2.4	10.8	9.3	7.9	1.7

Source: *Kredietbank Weekly Bulletin* no.48, 28 December 1980.

There has been a steady decline in issues of company equity shares since 1977, for reasons already explained, a major one being the relative attractiveness of Government bonds.

3   *Market capitalisation*   At the end of November 1980 market capitalisation of Belgian companies quoted on the cash market attained BF325.6 million against BF378.5 million in 1979, a reduction of BF52.9 million (in 1970 the figure was BF302.0 million). If the breakdown of companies is examined, according to statistics of the Banque Bruxelles Lambert, only the petroleum sector, led by Pétrofina, increased its share, to 22.58 per cent. Since 1974, most industrial sectors

fell, e.g. electricity and gas to 18.08 per cent in 1979—80. Steel and textiles accounted for only 1 per cent of total market capitalisation in 1980. All the financial service industries were down in those two years, all non-ferrous industries up.

4   *Equity yields*   For Belgian equities the relatively low yields on shares up to 1980 are shown in Table 1.10.

Table 1.10
Percentage yields on Belgian equities 1972—80

	Total of companies	Industrial companies
1972	4.1	3.9
1973	3.8	3.7
1974	5.3	5.4
		(new series)
1975	5.8	5.8
1976	5.5	4.9
1977	5.9	5.4
1978	6.0	5.8
1979	5.9	5.4
1980	7.3	6.2

Source: Bulletin de la Banque Nationale de Belgique, Rapports, 1980.

5   *Equity price movements*   The Bulletin de la Banque Nationale de Belgique has constructed an index (base 1970) for equity prices on the Belgian Stock Exchange as shown in Table 1.11. The weakness of prices is apparent, except for the exceptional year 1979.

Table 1.11
Index of prices of Belgian and foreign equities 1972—79

	Belgian equities			Foreign equities	
	Au comptant market	Terme market		Au comptant market	Terme market
	Total industrial companies				
	(indices 1970=100)			(indices 1970=100)	
1972	121	125	118	113	110
1973	143	148	142	117	111
1974	118	119	122	98	96
1975	114	114	115	100	96
1976	109	105	107	102	97
1977	101	97	92	92	89
1978	105	99	91	96	89
1979	113	108	n.a.	112	n.a.

Source: Bulletin de la Banque Nationale de Belgique, September 1980.

The performance of Belgian bonds

1   *Volume of transactions*   The rapidly increasing turnover of Government bonds (in BF billion) since 1979 is shown in Table 1.12.

Table 1.12
Turnover of public sector bonds (period Jan.—Oct.) (BF billion)

	1976	1977	1978	1979	1980
Public sector bonds	51.3	56.8	57.8	74.5	91.6
Belgo-Congolese Fund	0.3	0.3	0.3	0.2	0.3
Total	51.6	57.1	58.1	74.7	91.9
Per cent shares/private and public bonds in total turnover of securities	84.8	54.9	53.2	57.3	54.1

Source: *Kredietbank Weekly Bulletin*, no.48, 26 December 1980.

2   *Bond issues*   Government bond issues have tended to crowd out equities. Using statistics from the Banque Bruxelles Lambert, Table 1.13 compares bond issues with equity issues (already shown in Table 1.9) to give some indication of the extreme imbalance.

Table 1.13
Issues of company equities, convertible bonds and certificats immobiliers in comparison with private loans, state loans and other public sector loans (BF billions)

	1976	1977	1978	1979	1980
Equities	0.69	10.23	9.54	5.59	1.70
Convertible bonds	0.28	0.63	–	2.50	–
Certificats immobiliers	0.89	0.33	0.90	2.45	0.38
Loans (bonds):					
private sector	7.50	3.63	–	–	5.00
Belgian Government loans	129.00	167.80	185.00	196.00	154.00
other public sector loans	67.00	102.50	95.00	81.70	67.50
loans by public institu- tions	–	1.50	4.50	4.00	2.00
Total	205.36	286.62	294.94	292.94	231.38

Source: Banque Bruxelles Lambert, *Bulletin Financier,* no.1, 9 January 1981.

In 1980, the total of effective issues on the Belgian Stock Exchange was only BF231.38 billions compared with BF294.94 billions in 1979. This tight situation in the market plus high short term interest rates led Governmental and public sector borrowing to seek funds overseas. Even so, the public sector is by far the largest domestic borrower, with 96.1 per cent of capital raised on the Belgian market. This still does not count bons de caisse issued by banks, savings banks and parastatal credit institutions. A poor market climate has inhibited equity issues in Belgium: the low level of quotations, discriminatory treatment against dividends in favour of debt, and the absence of capital increases in the electricity sector. Table 1.14 shows the size and trend of public debt issues in billions of BF from 1972–79 (provisional) in detail.

Table 1.14
Issues of public sector debt in Belgian francs of more than one year (net total issues*)
(BF billions)

	State direct debt	Parastatal institution	Autonomous funds+social securities	Public financial institutions	Local authorities inter-communale	Totals
1972	68.6	7.8	7.1	10.5	25.1	119.1
1973	65.6	5.5	– 3.8	15.7	37.2	120.2
1974	55.4	7.0	– 5.0	29.7	22.7	109.8
1975	69.4	0.4	24.5	19.4	26.3	140.0
1976	71.7	15.9	10.8	31.1	40.5	170.0
1977	113.3	–1.6	21.1	98.3	56.0	287.1
1978	113.1	16.2	30.6	18.2	38.7	216.8
1979 (prov.)	89.4	–6.3	36.8	27.1	52.3	199.3

Source: Bulletin de la Banque Nationale de Belgique, September 1980.

*All notes accessible to placements by public subscription – on the bourse (on the official list) or hors-bourse – as well as bons de caisse issued au robinet by the Crédit Communal de Belgique, SNCI, INCA, OCCH, CNCP, and savings bonds issued by the CGER.

3   *Yields on bonds*   Table 1.15 shows the steadily increasing structure of interest rates (average yields after deduction where applicable of 20 per cent advance levy)(précompte immobilier) in each case at the end of the year.

Table 1.15
Average yields on Belgian bond market*

	1972	1973	1974	1975	1976	1977	1978	1979
Long term bonds								
Government funds (7–13 years)	5.72	6.22	6.94	6.65	6.79	6.59	6.64	8.18
Medium term bonds (5–10 years)								
Government funds	5.91	6.37	6.88	7.03	7.58	6.96	6.75	8.30
Issued by semi-official organisations	5.64	6.24	7.27	6.78	7.46	7.16	7.06	8.71
Issued by Gemeenkrediet (local government authorities) and cities	5.72	6.31	7.43	6.98	7.43	7.01	6.91	8.78
Industrial bonds	5.95	6.68	7.90	7.37	8.60	7.71	7.34	8.85

Source: *Kredietbank Weekly Bulletin*, no.48, 26 December 1980.

*Taking account of purchase costs and the premium or loss on redemption.

It is worth noting later figures from the Bulletin of the BNB, which show large rises in bond yields (Table 1.16).

Table 1.16
Yields on fixed-interest bonds quoted on the Brussels Stock Exchange

	Maturity 2–5 years		Maturity > 5 years			Average weighted yield
	State	Parastatal and cities	State	Parastatal and cities	Private companies	
September 1980	11.24	11.58	12.08	11.81	7.3	11.79

Source: Bulletin de la Banque Nationale de Belgique, September 1980.

The difference between State and parastatal yields and company yields is startling, and a major reason for disinterest by Belgian investors in equities.

An instructive way of comparing stock market performance is to consider returns to equities in the Belgian Stock Exchange. The method has been developed in relation to bond rates by the Banque de Paris et des Pays-Bas using the concept of 'return actualisé'. For several years PARIBAS has calculated an 'up-dated' or 'real' return on Belgian 'growth equities' (valeurs de croissance) in relation to face-value of the yield of fonds d'État (State bonds). The equities in question are those whose dividend has increased every year for at least the preceding five years. The relationship between the two rates indicates by how much a purchase for twelve months of a growth share is superior or inferior to a similar purchase in a State bond. 'Return' of a growth equity in this case can be illustrated by the following example: an equity is bought for BF1,000, having given a dividend of BF50, and sells for BF1,030 a year later, giving a return of BF80 or 8 per cent.

The general deterioration of the 'return actualisé au rendement facial des fonds d'État' since 1978 is shown in Figure 1.1. In fact the 'return actualisé' was below the equivalent State bond investment from 1973 to 1975 and again from 1976 to 1977.

The 'return actualisé' in the stock market is a variable which precedes price movements in the market. In February 1980 the 'return actualisé' at the last statistic was –9.1 per cent; the yield on State bonds of more than five years was +11 per cent. All Belgian banks, insurance companies, holding companies, energy concerns, trust and construction

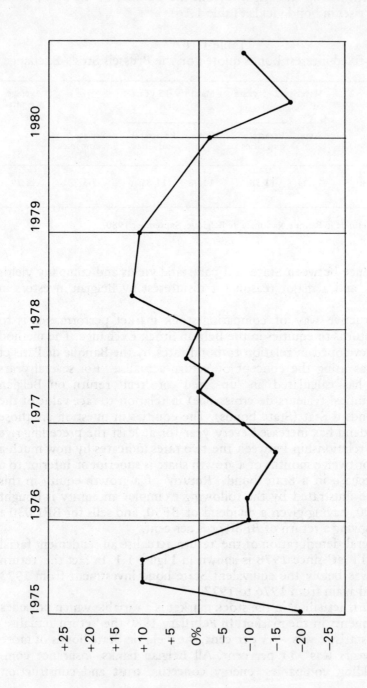

Figure 1.1 Real return* on Belgian growth equities

*Return = total yield (dividend + difference in prices) in relation to the yield on State bonds. The horizontal line (0%) represents a 'nil match' with the State bonds.

companies were sectors showing negative returns.

A more analytical study of real returns to Belgian companies quoted on the Stock Exchange has been undertaken by Friesewinkel, Kirschen and Morelle.[13] The authors note first that the number of Belgian companies quoted on the Exchange fell between 1953 and 1969 by 162, an annual average fall of 2.3 per cent, and from 1969 to 1977, by a rate twice as fast -- 148 firms at an annual average rate of 4.8 per cent. The authors give small Exchange turnover as one reason, the attraction of dealing in foreign equities as another, but most important of all inadequate real returns to companies.

For example, at the end of 1976, the total value of quoted Belgian equities was BF333.2 billion. In 1977, these equities distributed dividends of BF19.6 million at end-1976 prices; nominally yielding 5.9 per cent. But the value of the equities, at end-1976 prices, fell by 12.4 per cent, giving a real annual rate of return of -6.5 per cent (even before taxes on dividends). For the period 1969 to 1977, the annual real rate of return was on average -2.4 per cent (before taxes on dividends). Between 1969 and 1976 all annual real rates of return were negative, except one. A more sophisticated study by Gheysens, Regidor and Vanthienen also considered the problem from the viewpoint of the cost of equity capital.[14]

The efficiency of the Brussels Stock Exchange

The term 'efficient market' is applied in at least three senses.[15] 'Allocational efficiency' allocates capital to uses in an optimum way, and ensures savings are channelled into the most productive uses. National welfare is maximised. 'Operational or internal efficiency' is concerned with the monetary and real costs and speed of stock market operations and mechanisms, and is a major focus of this book. In addition, there are a number of tests of what might be called 'external efficiency', concerned with information and prices. An efficient market in the last sense is one in which equity and bond prices reflect *all available* information and in which stock prices sensitively react to changes in information relating to the real value of equities.

In the case of the Belgian Stock Exchange, some mention has been made already to weaknesses of structure and practice. No attempt has been made, except in passing, to evaluate the allocative efficiency of the stock market. (For example, it was noted earlier that the capacity of the stock market to absorb capital requests is limited.) But there have been a number of sophisticated statistical tests of the 'efficient market' hypothesis in various forms in Belgium and the evidence is at least interesting. Three major centres of learning in Belgium which have been responsible for testing 'efficiency' in various forms are the Katholieke Universiteit de Leuven (Department of Applied Economics), the Université de Liège, and the University of Antwerp. Without going into the debate here, it is important to realise that the Capital Asset Pricing Model, developed originally by Sharpe[16] is a theory about an optional portfolio of risky shares. It supports or uses the 'efficient markets hypothesis' when it assumes all investors' expectations are identical.[17] It is plausible in an 'efficient' market, but not a *sine qua non*. As Pogue, Modigliani and Solnik[18] point out, although 'systematic risk is an important factor in the pricing of (European) securities . . . it is not the only dimension of market efficiency. Even if the pricing of risk is rational, institutional factors or thin markets might create market inefficiencies which are not revealed by these (CAPM) tests'.

In an unpublished paper by Hawanini and Michel[19] the authors seek to answer the broad question, 'Is the Brussels Stock Exchange an efficient market?' by use of the 'random walk model' and the 'efficient market hypothesis' (EMH). The two tests of efficiency used were (i) a statistical study of first order serial correlation of historical price changes (closely related to the random walk model of price behaviour), (ii) a statistical study of the structure of leads and lags which exist between certain stocks and the rest of the market (closely related to the EMH). The authors found that there was not sufficient statistical dependence, on a sample of twenty-six stocks tested weekly, to permit the predictions of price movements by using the history of price changes themselves, i.e. in the short run, price changes were not predictable using linear combinations of previous price changes. The result provides some evidence of efficiency. The second test analysed stock price behaviour to determine if certain stock price movements preceded, occurred simultaneously with, or followed, movements in the market index. An efficient market would show no such evidence. Arbitrage would bring leading or lagging in prices in line with the market movement. The tests showed that no one stock out of the twenty-six had significant lead or lag statistics with the market which were better than those of the market model with zero lag regression: again some indication of efficiency, but no measure of it.

In an interesting paper by Fabry,[20] EMH was investigated for the Belgian Stock Exchange with respect to financial ratio information. For all practical purposes, the BSE could be considered efficient in this respect. Some adjustment of stock prices took place after the announcement date (e.g. dividends), but these inefficiencies were rare enough not to permit profitable trading. One of the assumptions of the study was restrictive, and could be relaxed with loss of validity, i.e. that all stocks reacted at the same time relative to the announcement month.

Daems[21] points out that large holding companies are a characteristic controlling participant in the Belgian savings—investment process. These companies issue equities in the stock market in order to finance their controlling interests in large industrial and financial companies, and some of the equities trade on the secondary market. But in a perfect market, there is no reason why small investors should benefit from buying into diversified portfolios of holding companies. Small investors may benefit when transactions and portfolio-management costs are high, as they can economise on the number of shares they hold, and still diversify. Otherwise, they will be indifferent between private and institutional diversification. Daems found that the Belgian Stock Exchange was efficient to the extent that no performance difference could be found between the stocks of holding companies and non-holding companies; small investors do not need holding companies to enable them to possess diversified portfolios returning at least the same level of remuneration. The one advantage for small investors was the smaller number of stocks they could carry in a holding company without increasing the total risk.

Regidor and Sercu[22] considered whether quoted Belgian equity prices demonstrated randomness. Testing for independence by serial correlation and runs analysis, the authors showed that Brussels equity prices did not exhibit a consistent pattern of non-randomness. Although for some stocks, a significant statistical dependence was observed for the entire period considered, further tests on sub-periods showed that the statistical dependence behaved erratically. It was considered doubtful whether these dependencies could be exploited for successful forecasting, given security analysis and transactions costs.

In an article by Pogue and Solnik,[23] the authors draw inferences from the application of the market model (which says that the risk premium on a security is a linear function of the market risk premium) for the 'efficiency' of European stock markets, including Belgium. Belgium had the longest adjustment lags to movements in equity prices among eight countries examined. It also had the largest percentage variation in equity returns explained by market movements (mainly because of price adjustment lags). In an efficient market (all else equal) the beta (β) value would not be sensitive to the length of return interval, i.e. β (a stock's risk derived from the systematic risk of the market, not its individual risk) should not vary with data (price changes) taken over daily, weekly, or monthly intervals. It was highest (least efficient) for Belgium. On the positive side, for Belgium, measures of total and systematic risk were as predictable as for any other country, i.e. equities were properly priced. Belgium, by these measures, is one of the least 'efficient' stock markets, but as Pogue, Modigliani and Solnik[24] point out, rational pricing of equities does not mean a stock market is wholly or even partially efficient by other criteria.

New legislation and stock market reform

Despite the imperfect performance of the Brussels Stock Exchange out-lined above (falling numbers of agents de change, low returns on equities, high Government bond interest rates drawing liquidity from potential equity investors, declining rates of return on capital invested and on returns to investors, thin trading in the secondary market, weak activity in new issues, few active companies on the Exchange, falling equity prices, inability of the Exchange to absorb all capital required) and despite several studies of the Brussels Stock Exchange showing it to be at best 'weak efficient', there has been, and is proposed, very little in the way of the reform or amelioration of Stock Exchange practice to encourage borrowers and investors to make more use of the market. Most recent reform measures have taken place in the 'environment' of the Exchange, e.g. taxes, more than in the internal organisation and practice of the Exchange itself.

To be fair, there is no lack of concern within the Stock Exchange itself, to improve the market-place for savings and investment and, particularly, to encourage companies to raise more equity. In the words of the President of the Stock Exchange, M. Jean Reyers, 'Let us hope . . . that there may be an end to demogogical behaviour which has led our country to budgetary deficits reaching, with respect to the gross (national) product, twice the average of other countries of the Common Market, despite a (demented) fiscal regime, giving the lie to all electoral promises, which should be remembered when the next occasion arises'. Writing briefly on statistics of the Exchange's performance, M. Reyer stated '(the volume of national stocks is inadequate) due to the lack of concern by our ruling party for national companies and shares, to the absence of an adequate fiscal regime, and to the lack of encouraging initiatives. Is it the (Government's) intention to do away with companies and people willing to take the risk of investing?'.[25]

Among current changes and improvements is the more scientific drawing up of the official list, which will become a good deal clearer to use. Settlement between the Stock Exchange and the banks, based on settlement in the à terme market, is being rationalised. Also, the EDP centre is gradually taking on more functions in the administration and accounting of securities, and generally increasing the speed of trans-actions and settlement in the Exchange.

The EDP centre of the Commission de la Bourse (Parquet and

Corbeille cash markets) is involved in the following functions. It:

- (a) transmits buying and selling orders received from customers,
- (b) proposes a price at the auction,
- (c) introduces the possibility of direct intervention at the auction,
- (d) ascertains the quotation,
- (e) records (by the specialist [stockbroker centralising orders]) of contra,
- (f) communicates the volume of the market,
- (g) confirms transactions effected.

In the account settlement market, it:

- (a) from 11.30 a.m. to 12.15 p.m. transmits buying and selling orders,
- (b) ascertains a situation,
- (c) communicates situation to Auction Commissaire,
- (d) introduces possibility of direct intervention at the auction,
- (e) ascertains the opening price (based on the situation and interventions),
- (f) deals with interventions which will create successive prices,
- (g) transmits prices,
- (h) confirms transactions effected.

The Exchange continues to work on the question of opening an options market; it is not an easy task, since already the turnover of equities on the market is thin, and there is a minimum volume of options trading necessary to make the market viable. The options market in Amsterdam, although developing well, is still not considered to be profitable for intermediaries in the same way that the much larger Chicago market is. However, there is no doubt that the official establishment and encouragement of such a market in Brussels would be an imaginative move, and add greater variety to trading there, especially in a period of volatile prices.

Amongst work in progress in 1979 was solving the difficult fiscal problem raised by the contango business, and the successful stabilisation of the CIK situation. During that year there were lengthy negotiations with the European Commission on establishment freedom; the outcome being abandonment of the plan, which did not displease the authorities of the Brussels Stock Exchange.

A major new development during the year was the consolidation of the guarantee fund, whose draft by-laws were unanimously approved by the four Stock Exchange Committees and the professional associations. This draft will be submitted shortly to the Minister for Finance for approval. Finally, the reform of accounting disclosure. The Brussels

Stock Exchange is not happy with the European Commission's recommendations, since the actual cost of the markets' transactions is such that the cost of such sophisticated accounting information requirement is out of proportion.

Praise must be given to the continuing development of statistics and information by the Brussels Stock Exchange, which has no institutional implications, but can only add to the efficiency of the market in terms of the quantity and quality of information available to investment analysts and their clients, and to the Government.

Other prescriptions for stock market reform

Some of the apparent weaknesses of Stock Exchange organisation and practice were pointed out earlier in this chapter. Here, some prescriptions will be made which would contribute to their amelioration.

Although the Commission de la Bourse, together with its subordinate and complementary committees, has a range of disciplinary powers, these largely relate to the professional conduct of agents de change, correspondents and banks. For example, although the Comité de Cotation has a brief to survey and note abnormal price movements in the market, and report them to the Minister for Finance, there do not appear to be any criteria to judge insider trading which can give rise to such price movements, and cause a transfer of control within companies. Other operations, known as 'dawn raids' in the UK, do not appear to have been recognised in Brussels, although there is no official evidence that these have ever taken place. Although the Commission de la Bourse is a self-regulating management committee, to a large extent, the rigidity introduced by its need to report infringements of rules to the Minister for Finance, established by the arrêté royale, has already been mentioned. Rules and criteria should certainly be established on 'insider trading' if investor confidence is to be maintained.

The overlap of surveillance functions with the Commission Bancaire has also already been mentioned. Whilst the Commission Bancaire's role is largely confined to supervision of banks in Belgium, it has important powers to regulate listings and dealings of stocks on the Exchange. It is appointed independently by the King, and can be compared to the USA's Securities and Exchange Control in some respects. In its role of supervisor of issues of securities, derived from the 1935 arrêté royale, it has also met many cases of private transfers of shares in companies giving controlling interest to parties involved. The Commission, with this experience, has made a number of recommendations, and drawn up some reports dealing with the problem. In spite of several refusals by the Commission to approve them, most 'offres publiques d'acquisition' (take-overs) in the last ten years have resulted in a private transfer of controlling shares. The Commission's brief is limited to the protection of the saving public; but the problem of take-overs is very large, and also concerns local authorities. Since the law of 30 December 1970, such take-overs involving funds of at least BF100 million must be notified to the Ministry of Economic Affairs, the Ministry of Finance, and the Secretary of State for the Economy. The Commission has noted the complexity of rules governing take-overs and mergers in other countries possessing developed financial markets, and the general agreement with which these countries treat the problem, although several formulae exist to cope with them.

In Belgium, the law regulating companies does not concern itself with matters of internal control, but the Commission has a brief to protect the interests of security holders, and ensure their equal treatment. So the Commission calls for full prior information but, regrettably, does not always receive it. Also, the Commission has no unequivocal criteria to guide it. The powers and criteria to be used by the Commission in matters of mergers and take-overs could certainly be clarified and strengthened.

On stock market costs, Belgian charges on cash transactions seem relatively high, e.g. basic charge BF100+

up to BF2m	10 per cent of market value
from BF2m + 1 – BF5m	9 per cent of market value
from BF5m + 1 – BF10m	8 per cent of market value
over BF10m	6 per cent of market value

This compares with (say) Italy, flat rate 0.50 per cent, plus discounts at high value transactions; UK, 1.5 to 0.125 per cent on sums from £7,000 to £1m; and Germany, 1.0 per cent flat rate.

Even for lower value securities in Belgium, there is not much financial incentive to deal in equities. Charges on public sector bonds are lower, often less than half *pro rata* with value of transaction. The variety of cash markets and marchés à terme as well as the complex system of types of equities may be seen as an advantage or disadvantage. However, it is worth noting that the Commission Perouse in Paris, after careful deliberation on the French Stock Exchange's variety of markets and notes, decided that many investors were put off by the complexity, and has recommended an integration – particularly of markets. In a thin market, this may have relevance to Brussels.

A more controversial area is the role of financial intermediaries on the bourse. Agents de change have a monopoly of the execution of orders, they do not usually deal on their own accounts. Banks may not undertake executions of orders except through the medium of agents.

The arguments for and against brokers acting also as jobbers (dealers) are complex, but it must be said that a broker-only market has disadvantages. It suits the investor who is willing to buy or sell at a specific price a small number of shares, and who is in no hurry to complete a transaction. For the investor (perhaps institution) who is in a hurry, needing to receive or dispose of cash, and for whom delay is costly, a dealer market may be more satisfactory. A dealer stands ready to buy or sell and to quote bids and offers separated by a narrow spread. It is probably true that, although there are some large brokerage firms in Brussels, they may nearly all be too under-capitalised to deal. However, banks do not suffer in this respect, and could easily take positions as jobbers or dealers. It is worth considering whether banks, with their massive liquidity bases, could be licensed as brokers and dealers, with suitable safeguards. At the present time, the picture is not entirely clear, there is no official position or role of jobber on the Brussels Stock Exchange, but agents can be specialist 'market holders', and may offer themselves officially or unofficially to clients. They are known to act as contrapartistes, and need not be on the Commissaire's list. To some extent, the process is speeded up by brokers trading in blocks of shares outside the official market.

In fact, institutions (like banks) may trade on the after hours market, but they must still pass through an agent, and the transaction must be recorded on the Stock Exchange. As pointed out earlier, the weak point about the after hours market is that participants can never be sure of prices. The general conclusion is that there is room for further enquiry into the role and activity of agents de change as they presently operate on the Brussels Stock Exchange. It may be, as the Perouse Commission concluded in France that a thin market could be improved by the increase in liquidity and flexibility that official dealing or contrapartiste operations could bring to the market.

Much could be done to internationalise savings and investment on the Belgian Stock Exchange. The domestic bond market is available for the flotation of foreign bonds to only a very limited extent. Belgian banks are officially encouraged to deal only in non-Belgian franc bonds to Belgian investors, in order to preserve the domestic bond market for Belgian Government borrowing. Neither does the Belgian Government wish to abolish withholding tax or see wider use of the Belgian franc internationally. Withholding tax is deducted at source by Belgian issuers, whether State or private sector, effectively killing foreign interest in buying domestic Belgian bonds. Finance companies can issue bonds to foreign investors only on registered forms; these are less marketable and therefore less popular. Also Belgian banks cannot bring foreign issues to the Belgian issue bond market, and the withholding tax keeps Belgian issues out of foreign bond markets. Effectively, there is no Euro-Belgian franc market. Clearly, if withholding tax were dropped, the flow of international funds into and out of the Belgian Stock Exchange would be greatly encouraged — although it would not make Belgian Government borrowing on the domestic market easier.

On other reforms which might be explored for the Brussels Stock Exchange, there is little that can be said in the absence of concrete evidence. For example, are new issue premia and underwriting costs reasonable, are the amount and costs of research by agents de change such that they contribute to efficiency in the Exchange? Although the study of external efficiency of the Brussels Stock Exchange is quite impressive in volume and of high standard, there seems to be little continuous work on the operational aspects of improvement, which could do much for the market's efficiency.

Fiscal, company and savings/investment incentives

In 1978, the Belgian Government, faced with mounting economic crises, introduced the so-called 'Loi Anticrise'. In fact, this was the Loi de Réorientation Économique of 4 August 1978.[26] One of the anticrisis laws contained a number of important fiscal measures designed to assist company investment and risk capital.

All companies which increased their capital in 1979 were exempt from taxes on their dividends. This exemption continues for five dividend declarations and applies to dividends not in excess of 5 per cent of paid-up capital. For 'associated' or 'complementary' investment by 'development' companies (mining, etc.) 15 per cent of profits were considered tax free for 1979 and 1980. However, the total of the tax exemption was limited to 6 per cent of total investment for 1979 and 1980. And there is the possibility of exemption from tax on appreciations. For financial companies there was no such exemption. The tax immunity on betterment for companies, established in 1977, was continued for two years.

For small and medium sized companies (petits et moyens entreprises — PME) defined as those employing less than seventy persons, depreciation allowances were doubled for a three-consecutive-year period from 1978. Similarly, such companies were exempt from the précompte immobilier (advance levy) for five years. Also, they were exempt from the 1 per cent registration charge on contributions to capital. Interest subsidies on loans by PMEs for direct investment in fixed capital was continued. This subsidy, granted on a maximum of 75 per cent of the investment, can amount to 5 per cent over a period of five years. Provided that at least half the investment is financed with stockholders' equity, outright capital grants may be made. It is thought, however,[27] that it might have been better to reduce the tax burden on PMEs further, rather than bringing in a complicated system of subsidies.

For individuals, the index-linking of tax scales introduced early in the 1970s was continued in favour of those whose incomes did not exceed a certain ceiling.

But it is very difficult to judge the effect of these measures on public equity issues. True, their movements increased to eight in 1978, but still companies were unable to compete effectively for funds against high interest rate, tax-exempt Government bonds in that year.

More recently, under the Projet de Loi de Redressement (relative aux dispositions fiscales et financières) (Law of Rectification regarding fiscal and monetary arrangements) approved by the Chambre des Représentants, session 1980-81, 12 January 1981, further fiscal relief was brought in to encourage investment, energy conservation, scientific research and the formation of risk capital. The 5 per cent exemption for company dividends was continued. For research and development, tax exemption equal to BF100,000 on personnel employed in scientific research, and depreciation equal to 110 per cent of the value of investment in scientific research were allowed.

The law of 8 August 1980 prolonged until 31 December 1983 tax exemptions on distributed company profits (dividends) relating to new equity issues. Simultaneously, for the same period, tax exemption was granted to individuals for the first BF30,000 tranche of income received as dividends. To encourage the small saver, the limit of tax exemption was raised to BF75,000 starting in 1982. This benefit was reserved to holders of registered equities. The fiscal advantages mentioned earlier were prolonged for specified years depending on recruitment patterns; e.g. a company of forty employees recruiting one extra employee in 1981, and maintaining a workforce of forty-one until the end of 1984, would benefit from tax exemption of BF400,000.

Persons earning more than BF5 million after tax in 1981 and 1982 (1980 and 1981 tax years) were obliged to invest a sum equal to one-tenth of their tax payments in State bonds, or industrial bonds or equities, to be held for a period of at least two years. They were deposited in the central bank or CDC.

In 1981, a major new draft bill on company law was placed before Parliament, reforming many aspects of commercial companies. The draft bill is the result of long discussions by a committee of specialists set up in 1951, called the Commission Struye, after its first president. The final code contains sixteen chapters and 423 pages. It has especially important clauses relating to equity holders. Its general trend is to follow the guidelines set out by the EEC directives.

The main changes are as follows: recognition of a new type of company — la société à capital variable, instead of one of the old forms — la société en commandite des actions; radical changes in the management and control of limited liability companies; simplification of rules regarding the transfer of shares in the renamed Sociétés Privées à Responsabilités Limitées, and in a more general way, a strengthening of this form of company among the capitalised companies; a reorganisation of the co-operative companies into a form more appropriate to their aims; a total overhaul of the procedures and standing of annual general meetings; modifications to company statutes; submission of annual accounts — all reforms which allow much closer integration of rules for all the main types of companies.

But there are several gaps and omissions, even after the lengthy negotiations and consultations which preceded the draft bill. The protection of minority shareholders is inadequate. Minority shareholders are given responsible status towards directors of companies, and the bill foresees the grouping of bondholders into an organisation having a clear identity. A notable gap in the bill is any provision for cases of mergers.

Particular attention has been paid to the small saver. Security holders have much better access to information, which company administrators will be obliged to produce periodically or occasionally, to inform them of all company decisions which could influence prices on the Stock Exchange. The security holder is also given a stronger voice in the company's affairs by the facility of a vote by correspondence, and by public request to exercise his vote at annual general meetings. His control is strengthened also by the establishment of a 'social minority security', and by extending the investigatory powers of directors.

Several penal measures are introduced, and applied to the abuse of company assets, and abuse of privileged information which could assist in Stock Exchange transactions. These preventive measures are not yet complete, neither are questions of participation. But the law does define 'mother companies' (sociétés dominantes) and their relation to 'daughter companies' (filiales). This matter and its implications for minorities will come under the jurisdiction of the Commission Bancaire, guided by the directives of the European Commission.

On the structure of corporation tax, Belgium applies a 'modified classical system', with some relief on the tax paid by the receiver of the dividend. (A 'complete classical system' would entail company profits fully subject to corporation tax, and dividends completely taxed at personal income tax rates.) In addition, there is another concession. Yields from capital contributed to newly formed companies, or to companies which have increased their capital, are exempted from corporation tax for a period of five business years.

Like some other countries in the Community, Belgium has special exemptions for income received on some fixed interest instruments — bonds and deposit certificates, and savings deposits. There are also exemptions relating to equity dividends. In Belgium, this last exemption is BF30,000 *per annum* and limited to distribution by newly created companies or companies which increase their capital between March 1977 and December 1983, under the same conditions as the exemption from corporation tax.

A withholding tax on dividends is levied in Belgium at the rate of 20 per cent, and this treatment leaves equities and bonds in an equally favourable position regarding tax.

There is no tax incentive as yet for investment in equities, like the Loi Monory in France, which allows deduction of a certain sum of capital invested in equities from taxable income. Neither are there any Government premiums for saving in equities, such as exist in Germany.

But, on the other hand, capital gains, which are incorporated into profits (in the normal way) are exempt from taxation in Belgium under the argument that such gains are a part of the 'normal management of portfolios'. Where it has been decided that capital gains do not meet this requirement, then they are included in the income tax base, on an optional basis.

There are detailed rules on the extent to which institutional investors can invest in equities in Belgium. First, the proportion of their equities permitted in investors' assets is as follows: insurance companies, not more than 25 per cent of reserves in equities of Belgian companies; old age and life assurance institutions, not more than 20 per cent of reserves in equities of Belgian companies; mortgage loan companies, not more than 15 per cent of capital in equities of Belgian companies; saving fund, authorisation required by Minister of Finance; pension fund, not more than 10 per cent of actuarial reserves in Belgian listed equities. Second, as far as participation in a single company is concerned, insurance companies must not invest more than 5 per cent of their capital and reserves in a single company. There are no restrictions of this kind on the other financial institutions. Third, regarding limitations on investment in equities in foreign companies, insurance companies must not hold more than 25 per cent of their reserves in foreign securities listed on the Brussels Stock Exchange, and mortgage loan companies must not hold more than 10 per cent of their capital in bonds or equities of foreign companies. There are no restrictions of this third kind on the other financial institutions.

Summary

Belgium has serious economic problems, reflected in the performance of the Brussels Stock Exchange and the participants in it. The Stock Exchange is unable to supply the massive and growing financing needs of Government, even at high bond yields. This 'crowding out' effect is compounded by consistently low real returns to Belgian companies which now find themselves high geared. Their ability to self-finance is much reduced through low profitability. All measures of performance of the Stock Exchange: turnover, new issues, equity yields are poor. Even high yielding State bonds are difficult to place in a market which has low absorption capacity.

The Stock Exchange itself is organised on statutory lines, and has a complex of markets, and types of notes. The scope for foreign bonds or foreign investment by Belgium is strictly limited. Control of the Stock Exchange seems weak, and abusive practices, such as insider trading not properly curbed. The Commission Bancaire's slightly ambiguous role gives it no clear-cut powers. Costs on the market are relatively high, and trading thin, not helped by restrictions on brokers going outside their traditional role. The many large banks cannot play a useful role in the Exchange. Whilst the clearing system is improving, the position of the after hours market remains under-utilised and poorly controlled. Tests of external efficiency of the Exchange show weak values, but contribute no insight into the operational weakness of the market. Whilst the Stock Exchange itself is well aware of needed improvements, those actually undertaken recently have not been radical, but more of a modest technical kind. Prescriptions to improve include strengthening the role of brokers and banks, liberalising international dealings, rationalising the complex of markets and instruments and strengthening surveillance of abusive practices.

The Government has recently introduced modest fiscal measures to encourage company investment, especially by PMEs, and the new draft bill on company law before Parliament could prove the beginning of a good deal more encouragement to invest in company equities.

Notes and references

1   Banque Nationale de Belgique, Rapports 1980.
2   *Kredietbank Weekly Bulletin*, no.11, March 1979.
3   L. Gheysens, B. Regidor, L. Vanthienen, 'Cost of Equity Capital of 185 Belgian Companies', *Tijdschrift voor Economie en Management*, vol.XXIV, nr.1, Katholicka Universiteit, Leuvan 1979.
4   *Kredietbank Weekly Bulletin*, no.11, March 1979.

5   *Krediethank Weekly Bulletin*, no.27, 6 July 1979, pp.1-5 'Financial Leverage'.

6   Konrad Freundlieb, 'The Role of the Banks in Financing Investment in Belgium', *Euro-cooperation*, no.21.

7   De Suret and G. Martin, 'le Coût du Crédit d'Investissement en Belgique — Un Exemple de la Rigidité de Nôtre Système Financier', Revue de la Banque, no.6, Bruxelles, 1978, pp. 391-407.

8   Commission Bancaire, Rapport Annuel, 1978–79.

9   Bourse de Bruxelles, 1979.

10   M.S. Mendelsohn, *Money on the Move: the Modern International Capital Market*, McGraw-Hill, London 1980.

11   G. Ugeux, 'L'Internationalisation du Marché Belge des Capitaux', Revue de la Banque, no.2, Bruxelles, 1978.

12   Banque de Paris et des Pay-Bas, Notes Économiques, no.30, March 1980.

13   M. Friesewinkel, E.S. Kirschen, B. Morelle, 'Les Returns sur les actions Belges Cotées en Bourse de Bruxelles (1969–1977)', *Cahiers Économique de Bruxelles*, no.80, 1978.

14   L. Gheysens, B. Regidor, L. Vanthienen, 'Cost of Equity Capital of 185 Belgian Companies', *Tijdschrift voor Economie en Management*, vol.XXIV, nr.1, 1979. The authors found that '(during the seventies) the cost of equity funds for the "average" Belgian company quoted on the Brussels Stock Exchange is approximately 11.5 per cent assuming a risk-free rate of interest equal to 6.8 per cent. During the period investigated, most of the individual companies included in the sample realised a rate of return on equity (based on stock market data) that was below their minimum required rate of return on equity funds. This conclusion appears to hold also at the industry level'.

15   *Proposals for a Securities Market Law for Canada*, vol.3, chapter 2, Consumer and Corporate Affairs, Canada, 1979.

16   W.F. Sharpe, 'Capital Asset Prices: a Theory of Market Equilibrium under Conditions of Risk', *Journal of Finance*, vol.19, no.3, September 1964.

17   M. Firth, *Investment Analysis — Techniques of Appraising the British Stock Market*, Harper and Row, 1975.

18   G.H. Pogue, F. Modigliani, B.H. Solnik, 'A test of the Capital Asset Pricing Model on European Stock Markets', paper presented to the First International Congress on Stock Exchanges, Milan, March 1972.

19   G.A. Hawanini, P. Michel, 'Market Efficiency of the Brussels Stock Exchange', unpublished paper, February 1975.

20   J. Fabry, 'Annual Reports in Belgium: the Information Content and Reaction Time', University of Antwerp, UFSIA (photocopied).

21   H. Daems, 'An Empirical Study of the Efficiency of Security Sub-stitution by Holding Companies. The Brussels Stock Exchange, 1964–1973', *Tijdschrift voor Economie en Management*, vol.XXI, nr.3, 1976.
22   B.V. Regidor, P. Sercu, 'Behaviour of Share Prices of the Brussels Stock Exchange', *Tijdschrift voor Economie en Management*, vol.XXI, nr.3, 1976.
23   G.A. Pogue, B. Solnik, 'The Market Model applied to European Common Stocks: Some Empirical Results', *Journal of Financial and Quantitative Analysis*, December 1974.
24   Pogue, Modigliani and Solnik, op.cit. (note 18).
25   M. Jean Reyers, Président de la Bourse de Bruxelles, Bourse de Bruxelles, 1979 (President's message).
26   *Moniteur Belge*, 17 August 1978.
27   *Kredietbank Weekly Bulletin*, no.3, 19 January 1979, 'New Support Measures for Small and Medium-Sized Firms'.

2 France

Company financing

Whilst the current structure of company financing in France is of primary relevance to the state of the present Stock Exchange, this structure has undergone changes in the last few years which are in themselves instructive.

During the period 1967 to 1976, sociétés anonymes (excluding the nationalised enterprises and self-employed firms) suffered from a big fall in the rate of self-financing, due to a similar fall in returns on added value, and at the same time they borrowed on fixed interest on a larger scale. However, continuing inflation lightened the real burden of fixed interest debt. It has been estimated that rising prices of 10 per cent on average a year diminished the real burden of the sociétés' debt by some FF100 billion over the period, more than their annual gross self-financing.[1]

The rate of self-financing can be traced with the aid of two ratios: gross company savings/gross fixed capital formation (excluding VAT deductible); gross company savings/total gross capital formation + fixed capital + growth in stocks. From 1968 to 1976, the two ratios, although fluctuating, generally showed steady decline. The first ratio moved from 86 to 58, the second fron 78 to 50.

The deterioration in companies' self-financing can also be analysed from the viewpoint of their investment. The rate of self-financing can be analysed by the use of the ratio: proportion of profits not distributed (savings/value added) — rate of investment (capital formation/value added). The deterioration in the rate of self-financing over the period came about because the proportion of profits not distributed fell between 1968 and 1976, from 16 to 10 per cent. It was also affected by a long decline in the rate of investment, but not so markedly until 1974. Furthermore, over the whole period, the share of salaries in value added increased from 59 to 68 per cent. This, plus a fairly steep rise in interest charges, explains why gross savings of companies fell steadily from 1967 to 1976.

In sum, for French companies between 1967 and 1976, value added increased by a multiple of 3.1, gross fixed capital formation by 2.6, salaries and taxes by 3.5, and interest charges by 5.9. The counterpart to the fall in self-financing by companies was greater recourse to external finance, particularly to bank borrowing. Table 2.1 shows this by value and percentage. The most striking changes are the growth in medium and long term borrowing, fall in gross savings, and rise in net capital transfers.

The changes are reflected in movements within the balance sheets of French companies (table not shown). Between 1967 and 1976, Fonds Propres (equity capital) fell from 36 to 25 per cent of liabilities. By contrast, short and medium term debt rose from 62.4 to 73.9 per cent of liabilities. Over the whole period, short term debt was usually about three times the size of medium and long term debt. This increase in debt was less punishing than would be thought at first, because of accompanying high rates of inflation.

In 1969 total debt of all companies (including nationalised enterprises) was FF366 billion; in 1975, FF859 billion. Yet this massive rise in total debt was compensated for so totally by inflation that the ratio of debt/gross capital at replacement cost (in percentages) was almost unchanged; 81 in 1970, 80 in 1975. Similarly the ratio interest/total debt moved from 8 per cent in 1970 to 9 per cent in 1975. Recourse to the Stock Exchange was modest over the whole period. Table 2.1 shows that companies were able to finance their fast growth in capital accumulation more readily than their gross profits increased, by recourse to borrowing. The table also shows the general disruption (particularly to stocks) caused by the oil price rise in 1974.

The recession of 1974-75 marked the beginning of a slowdown in production, from an average increase of 5.4 per cent between 1963 and 1973, to 1.2 per cent between 1974 and 1978.[2] In 1974 and 1975 themselves, the proportion of self-financing fell dramatically, but 1976 soon saw recovery. Companies reporting themselves in the quarterly inquiry by INSEE as being in financial difficulties were at their maximum in 1974, but from the end of that year to the end of 1979 companies reported a continuous, if irregular, improvement

51

Table 2.1

Capital and consolidated finance accounts for companies (excluding nationalised enterprises) 1970–76
(in billion francs and percentages)

	1970	1971	1972	1973	1974	1975	1976
Uses	130.7	136.1	167.5	177.2	215.7	176.9	240.6
Gross fixed capital	69.1(53)	78.2(57)	87.8(53)	97.7(55)	111.3(52)	112.1(64)	133.8(56)
Variations in stocks	16.0(12)	9.4(7)	10.4(6)	20.5(12)	28.3(13)	-8.1(-5)	19.7(8)
Growth in credits	24.9(19)	19.8(15)	35.8(21)	25.6(15)	45.6(21)	38.9(22)	47.2(20)
Redemption of medium and long term credits and bonds	17.8(14)	19.6(14)	25.1(15)	23.7(13)	21.9(10)	23.7(13)	32.2(13)
Adjustment	2.9(2)	9.1(7)	8.4(5)	9.7(5)	8.6(4)	10.3(6)	7.7(3)
Resources	130.7	136.1	167.5	177.2	215.7	176.9(38)	240.6
Gross saving	50.9(39)	55.9(41)	64.6(39)	66.4(38)	62.6(29)	67.5(38)	76.8(32)
Net capital transfers	0.8(-)	0.3(-)	0.8(-)	1.1(-)	1.6(1)	2.7(1)	8.6(4)
Securities	10.3(8)	12.8(9)	14.1(8)	16.3(9)	15.7(7)	20.5(12)	22.7(9)
Bonds	3.1(2)	5.9(4)	4.9(3)	4.5(3)	3.5(2)	8.1(5)	6.0(2)
Equities	7.2(6)	6.9(5)	9.2(5)	11.8(6)	12.2(5)	12.4(7)	16.7(7)
Medium and long term credits	40.2(31)	44.1(33)	54.5(33)	57.8(33)	58.2(27)	77.1(44)	89.8(37)
Short term credits	28.5(32)	23.0(17)	33.5(20)	35.6(20)	77.6(36)	9.1(5)	42.7(18)
Loan redemptions	25.5	30.4	34.3	38.5	39.8	61.5	63.6

Source: Paul Dubois, op.cit., note 1.

in their positions. But increasing salaries, the continuing total cost of debt, and high interest rates since 1974 have caused a steady fall in the rate of return on invested capital during the period.

French companies responded by investing in more modern equipment rather than extending the capacity of existing plant. They also looked for new outlets, particularly in overseas markets. By 1978 and 1979 these policies appeared to have paid off and companies had improved their financial position; even the rate of growth of debt had slowed down. They were helped in 1979 by the lifting of restrictions from industrial prices and a fall in the proportion of salaries in value added. With companies restraining current expenses, gross savings grew strongly in 1978 and 1979, although never reaching the high levels of the years before the 1974 oil price rise. Recent investment has grown modestly, around 2 per cent per annum.

Table 2.2 shows changes in the major components of sources and uses of funds in the second half of the 1970s. Some movements are immediately apparent. The steady increase in the value of new investments and the growth of stocks between 1976 and 1979 has been financed by continuing high, though reducing, bank and non-bank borrowing, a noticeable increase in the issue of bonds and equities on the stock market, and less reliance on foreign loans. A large jump in the liquidity position of companies became apparent in 1979. Applying some financial ratios to the companies' data reveals generally favourable trends (Table 2.3).

These financial improvements had much to do with the modernisation of French industry, and investment which had this objective rather than the increase of current capacity. But this restructuring has not applied across the board to French industry. From the INSEE inquiry of June 1980 it appeared that some sectors of industry would see a slowing down of the rate of investment, and others the reverse, namely the car, steel and oil industries which were making great efforts to modernise.[3]

Banking loans to the corporate sector

There are three types of registered banks in France, grouped according to their major activity:[4] (a) the 'banques de dépôts', which are deposit banks and carry out credit operations, (b) the 'banques d'affaires', basically investment banks, which grant loans and take equity participations, and (c) the 'banques de crédit à long et moyen terme', which are long and medium term credit banks (minimum maturity two years). But in 1966-67 new banking laws were introduced which blurred the divisions between these groups (the Debré reforms). Banques de dépôts

Table 2.2
Uses and sources of company finance (FF billion)

Uses	1976	1977	1978	1979
Net current spending:	770.5	874.2	978.8	1112.6
of which salaries	(607.8)	(686.5)	(773.0)	(876.9)
investment	171.5	187.0	206.5	231.8
stock variations	+21.0	+20.4	+12.3	+32.4
variations in M3	8.9	28.6	20.1	33.0
Net changes in Security Portfolio	9.1	7.4	7.3	5.6
bonds	(0.6)	(0.6)	(0.8)	(0.9)
equities	(8.4)	(6.8)	(6.5)	(4.7)
Total uses	981.0	1117.6	1225.0	1415.4

Sources	1976	1977	1978	1979
Gross value added	869.9	985.2	1114.8	1217.5
Investment aid	11.5	6.3	6.8	7.4
Variations in banking and non-banking credit	61.2	64.9	60.0	59.6
of which: banking credits	(32.4)	(33.8)	(30.9)	(31.7)
Security issues (net)	32.3	31.4	36.3	35.6
bonds	(12.4)	(12.3)	(10.1)	(12.6)
equities	(19.9)	(19.1)	(26.2)	(23.0)
Net direct foreign borrowing at medium and long term	5.9	7.8	3.3	4.1
Various	0.2	22.0	3.8	37.2
Total sources	981.0	1117.6	1225.0	1415.4

Source: Conseil National du Crédit, op.cit., note 2.

Table 2.3
Principal financial ratios (in percentages)

	1976	1977	1978	1979
Rate of return on assets:				
$\dfrac{\text{Variation in financial assets}}{\text{Gross value added}}$	2.1	3.7	2.5	3.0
$\dfrac{\text{Variation in liquidity}}{\text{Gross value added}}$	1.0	2.9	1.8	2.6
Rate of debt:				
$\dfrac{\text{Variation in debt}}{\text{Gross value added}}$	11.4	10.6	8.9	7.8
Rate of self-financing (without stocks):				
$\dfrac{\text{Gross savings}}{\text{Investment}}$	57.9	59.4	65.9	68.6
$\dfrac{\text{Gross savings} + \text{investment aid}}{\text{Investment}}$	64.7	62.8	69.2	71.8

Source: Conseil National du Crédit, op.cit., note 2.

can now take deposits for more than two years, and the other groups of banks have been allowed to take on extra functions, making them much more like the German 'universal' banks. A major boost was given to expanding the availability of long term credit, and long term savings were encouraged. The banques de crédit à long et moyen terme have grown significantly as a result of the reforms; they are mostly subsidiaries of larger banks.

The savings bank sector, led by the Caisse des Dépôts et Consignations (CDC) acts as a central bank for all French savings banks. The Caisse is a state agency having many functions, e.g. administering pension and insurance funds. It is a very large buyer of bonds and equities on the Stock Exchange, and a big supplier of loans. It lends mainly to local authorities, national enterprises, and for social housing. It can lend to industry, but only when a programme is being subsidised by the State or when State funds have been guaranteed.

The Treasury and PTT (postal and telecommunications services) collect savings. The Treasury undertakes lending, mostly to local authorities, but also to public and private enterprises. It grants long and medium term advances through the budget mechanism in the form of 'Fonds de Développement Économique et Sociale'. FDES makes direct loans to public enterprises, accounting for about two-thirds of funds lent to this sector, and it supervises lending by specialised public credit institutions to private industry. FDES has flexibility in the manner in which it extends credit, e.g. capital subsidies.

There are some 400 'Établissements Financiers' which are governed in the same way as banks, but may not receive deposits from the public. They lend in very specialised ways, e.g. to particular industries, or for particular services like mortgage lending.

More important for companies are the 'Établissements de Crédit à Statut Légal Spécial', specialised financial institutions providing medium and long term credit to the private and public sector. The major ones are the 'Crédit National' (an industrial development bank), the 'Caisse Centrale de Crédit Hotelier Industriel et Commercial', the 'Crédit Foncier de France', the 'Sociétés de Developpement Regional', the 'Banque Français du Commerce Extérieur', the 'Caisse Nationale des Marchés de l'État' and the 'Institut de Développpment Industriel'.

In 1979, banking and financial institutions' loans to all companies (except self-employed) totalled FF765.3 billion, an increase of 8 per cent over 1978; 45.5 per cent of this went to finance working capital, and the rest to fixed capital. Mainly because of a financial strengthening of companies, the demand for finance for fixed capital increased more strongly. In the case of working capital, the Banques Inscrites supplied 78 per cent in 1979. In the case of loans for fixed capital, the banks as a group (Inscrites, à Statut Légal Spécial, and Établissement Financiers) lent 63 per cent of the total, and non-banking institutions most of the remainder. The overwhelming maturity of banking loans for investment were medium term.

Government and local authority financing

French central government financing is undertaken by the Trésor which, apart from current financial transactions, has an important role in lending and borrowing under annual guidelines set by the Government's budget. In the French system, a forecast deficit/surplus for the annual budget is debated in Parliament at the end of each calendar year. Authorised spending is often different from actual spending (out-turn), and supplementary budgets are sometimes used to cover this.

Budget spending includes operating subsidies to the nationalised industries, and loans for the capital operations of the nationalised industries via the FDES. But most nationalised industry loan finance is raised from the market by loans under a government guarantee. This is not incorporated in the borrowing requirement or the balance of Treasury operations since the nationalised industries are not in the public sector in France. Also public and semi-public financial intermediaries raising money in the capital market or from private banks — even when on-lending to nationalised industries or other public bodies — are not included in any definition of public borrowing. By contrast, some large items of capital spending are excluded from the central government accounts, e.g. most of the road building programme does not appear in the Loi de Finances; joint state/private sector companies raise loans independently on the capital market. Certain types of Government capital spending are excluded from the budget, e.g. low cost apartment and housebuilding by the CDC.

In France, local authorities have separate budgets and are in principle self-financing. They borrow, not from the central government, but from savings banks, semi-public credit institutions, or the capital market. Central government spending throughout the year, 'l'exécution des lois de finance', is published on a cash basis.

At the end of 1978, the total size of the public debt in France was FF355.90 billion; the rate of increase has been rising annually since 1971. The breakdown is shown in Table 2.4.

Table 2.4
French public debt (FF billions)

Internal debt		External debt	
perpetual debt	48.56	Subscriptions to international	
Treasury bills	45.04	agencies	9.33
Current public bonds:			
banking sector	47.79	external debt:	
other (CDC)	33.03	in foreign currency	0.26
liabilities towards Banque		redeemable in France	—
de France	12.14		
Totals	186.56		9.59
Debt of Treasury correspondants			
PTT	69.88		
local authorities	35.18		
financial institutions	8.09		
public and semi-public			
organisations	8.94		
various	20.95		
Total	142.84		
Budget debt due to PTT	16.91	Grand total of public debt	355.90

Source: *Bulletin Trimestriel*, Banque de France, no.33, December 1979.

The size of the public debt has been increasing annually, with corresponding impact on servicing the debt (although inflation reduces the
real burden), and has been accompanied by continuing increases in the
size of the budget deficit. In addition, although public receipts have
kept their share of gross domestic product fairly constant in recent
years, the percentage taken by public spending has been high and is
forecast to increase strongly (see Table 2.5).

Table 2.5
Public expenses and gross domestic product

Percentage GDP	1959	1971	1975	1978	1979	1985 (projected)
Expenses	35.3	36.6	41.5	42.7	43.0	46.8
Advance payments.	32.3	33.8	36.0	38.0	39.4	43.2

Source: Rapport du Comité du Financement, Commissariat Général du Plan, *Préparation du
Huitième Plan*, 1981–85, la Documentation Française, Paris 1980.

The Loi de Finance Initiale for 1979 brought out a deficit of FF15.1
billion, compared with FF8.1 billion for the 1978 budget. The Loi de
Finance Rectificative, at the end of 1979, raised this to FF37.5 billion.
This law is in the nature of a supplementary budget, brought out in
December of each year with the intention of reviewing the economic
situation. After a lapse it has been recently re-established. In that year,
for example, many supplementary credits were raised. There are various
ways of measuring budget balances in France. The one already
mentioned is the 'situation de l'exercise' – anticipated balance of
budget. Another useful measurement is the 'solde effectif d'exécution
des lois de finance' (International Monetary Fund transactions
excluded) – this is a management measurement of the deficit. The
'solde effectif' showed an increase in the deficit from FF27.4 billion in
1978 to FF29.3 billion in 1979. However, the 'deficit d'exécution' as
a proportion of GDP is still one of the lowest in Europe; e.g. in 1979,
Germany reported –1.9 per cent, UK –4.5 per cent, compared with
–1.2 per cent in France. In the larger sense of the public debt (including
local authorites and social security), the French borrowing requirement
is falling (1.8 per cent of GDP in 1978, 0.8 per cent in 1979 (the 1980
budget was rather more expansionary and the proportion could rise
slightly).
In 1979, the budget deficit was financed 43 per cent by net capital
market borrowing, 40.6 per cent by money creation, and 16.4 per cent
by 'other resources' (CDC current account, Treasury bills, and deposits

of correspondants). Financing by money creation has been encouraged
in recent years. In 1977 by contrast, money creation was only 5.4 per
cent of GDP, compared with 69.5 per cent of 'other resources' and
25.1 per cent of net capital market borrowing. Table 2.6 shows a
detailed breakdown of sources of finance for the Government's budget.

Table 2.6
Sources of finance for the State budget: cumulative variations
(gross FF billion)

	Dec. 1978	Dec. 1979
Financing needs:		
(Operations of the IMF deducted)	−27.4	−29.3
Resources:		
Fixed interest resources (net)	+9.0	+12.6
Capital market issues	+13.5	+15.0
Amortisement	−4.5	−2.4
Monetary resources (M2)	+3.5	+11.9
Other resources	+14.9	+4.8
Treasury bills bought by non-banking organisations	+2.0	+2.4
Treasury bills in CDC portfolio	+8.0	+9.0
Correspondant deposits	+4.4	+2.1
Guaranteed bonds	+0.1	−2.9
Various (+ adjustments)	+0.7	−5.4

Table 2.6 shows heavier reliance on money creation (mainly through
the Banque de France) in 1979 compared with 1978, while 'other
resources' fell. Consequently, the Trésor was obliged to cover a greater
part of its 1979 deficit by capital market borrowing. This rose from
FF13.5 billion in 1978 to FF15 billion in 1979. After deduction of
repayments on bonds, the bond market provided the Government
with FF12.6 billion in new money in 1979, compared with FF9 billion
in 1978, an increase of 38 per cent.

It is not the Government's intention to 'crowd out' the stock market,
and make it more difficult for private sector borrowers to raise equity
or fixed interest loans. Various voices have been raised in official and
unofficial reports on the undesirability of this sort of development for
private sector investment. In consequence the Trésor issued the 1979
bonds in tranches, and gave no favourable fiscal advantages to bondholders. In all, three loan issues were made in 1979. Over the whole

year, on the capital market, the State issued FF15 billion or 21.9 per cent of the total value of issues, the local authorities FF3.5 billion (5.1 per cent), PTT FF1.7 billion (2.6 per cent), financial institutions FF30.8 billion (45 per cent), nationalised industries FF10.4 (14.5 per cent) and foreign issues FF0.8 billion (1.2 per cent). The remaining FF6.3 billion (9.7 per cent) was taken up by private sector issues of bonds and equities.[5]

As far as local authorities are concerned, current spending is financed by the sale of goods and services, grants, etc. and local taxes. Capital spending is financed by loans, grants and self-finance. Self-financement and loans are the major categories, amounting to around three-quarters of total borrowing in the mid-seventies. In more recent years, local authority borrowing has tended to stabilise, owing to a slowdown in the rate of growth of their operating and capital expenditure. Since 1977, net borrowing has varied around FF21–22,000 million. Most local authority borrowing on medium and long term is from the official credit institutions (over 80 per cent in 1977) on preferential terms. This group includes the CDC, Caisse d'Épargne, Crédit Mutuel Agricole and Non-Agricole. The remainder comes from the capital market. Local authorities are discouraged from borrowing on short term by not being granted preferential conditions. Foreign borrowing is usually approved only for large authorities contemplating big infrastructure investment projects; little of this has occurred in recent years. The official credit institutions' loans are actually organised by the Central Government, and CDC normally accounts for one-half of this lending.

Structure and practice of the French stock markets

Organisation

There are seven stock exchanges in France: Paris, Bordeaux, Lille, Lyons, Marseilles, Nancy and Nantes. All have been created by an arrête (order) of the Ministry of the Economy. Their respective sizes are very different. In 1979, Paris accounted for 98 per cent of the capitalisation of all types of securities, and if anything, its proportion of the total seems to be growing against the six provincial exchanges. However, the provincial exchanges rank better when numbers of new listings and existing lines of quotations are considered. At the end of 1979, the provinces accounted for 22 per cent of all new listings, and for 14.6 per cent of all existing lines of quotations.[6]

The creation (or suppression) of French stock exchanges requires approval from the Chambre Syndicale des Agents de Change (the Executive Council of Stockbrokers), and the Commission des Opérations de Bourse (the Committee for Stock Exchange Transactions). But the major role of these two bodies is to carry out specific legal duties with regard to the stock exchanges.

All 'agents de change' (brokers) are members of the 'Compagnie des Agents de Change' (CAC). Although this is a private company, its powers are officially recognised: the règlements générals of the CAC have legal endorsement by the Minister of the Economy. The executive body of the CAC is the Chambre Syndicale des Agents de Change which is elected annually by members. The Chambre comprises a chairman ('syndic') and seven governors. The 'syndic' is represented on the provincial exchanges by a 'syndic délégué'. The main functions of the Chambre Syndicale are to ensure the smooth running of the market according to the rules, to enforce regulations governing 'agents', to arbitrate, and to manage the guarantee fund. Its administrative functions include examining all documents filed by prospective listing companies, publishing the daily official list, and managing the electronic data processing of stock market information.

The Commission des Opérations de Bourse was established in 1967, its chairman and members being elected for four years at a time. COB has a supervising role, under the direct scrutiny of the Minister of the Economy, as follows: ensuring listed companies provide all the information required, preventing 'insider trading', and registering and investigating complaints. It can also suggest modifications to the rules governing Stock Exchange organisation and procedures, as it frequently has done in the past in its annual report, or by special report.[7] With advice from the Chambre Syndicale, it also decides on the admission of securities to the official list.

Types of markets and securities

The Cote Officielle (official market) is divided into two: the 'marché au comptant' (cash or spot market) and the 'marché à terme' (delayed payment and delivery or 'forward market').

The marché au comptant is uncomplicated. All officially listed securities — equities and bonds — are negotiable on the cash market and can be bought and sold in any quantities for immediate payment and delivery.

On the 'marché à terme', the most active French and foreign securities, mostly bonds, are negotiable for future payment and delivery. The system obliges bargains struck to be firm in price and quantitiy, but payment and delivery take place on the next settlement day, i.e. seven work days before the end of the month in which the transaction is made. Table 2.7 shows the settlement schedule for à terme transactions.

On the marché à terme, securities may be traded only in large

Table 2.7
Settlement schedule on the forward market

Declaration day	1st day	2nd day	3rd day	4th and 5th days	6th day	7th day
Buyers of 'prime' and 'option' dealings make decision	Settlement day	Contango day (first day of the new account)	Sellers deliver registered certificates	Internal operations between brokerage firms	Sellers deliver bearer certiciates	Last working day of the month: payment

Source: The Paris Stock Exchange, 'A Guide for Foreign Investors', Chambre Syndicale des Agents de Change, Paris, January 1980.

parcels, valued at around FF10,00 a deal. If investors want to buy smaller amounts of a particular share, they must deal on the cash market, at higher prices. The margin which clients must provide on forward dealings is as follows: cash or Treasury bonds 20 per cent of dealings, French fixed yield securities or gold 25 per cent, other securities 40 per cent.

The marché à terme itself is subdivided into a marché des reports, and the marchés conditionnels. In the former, dealers in the marché à terme can carry over a bargain to the second settlement day to the marchés à reports (contango markets). The market operates once a month, and allows for rebuying by bulls and reselling by bears. There is a contango rate for bulls when the buying position exceeds the selling position, and a backwardation rate for bears when the selling position exceeds the buying position. On the marché conditionels, where most securities on the à terme market can be traded, dealings may be divided into operations 'à prime' and 'à options'. There are also 'stellage' operations (put options) and 'operations du double' (put and call options), but these are less popular. On the marché à prime the buyer can cancel his bargain before settlement day on payment of a fixed forfeit (prime). Transactions can be made for up to two months ahead. There is not yet a fully-fledged options market in Paris, in the sense of a market for negotiable options, but on the marché à options as it exists at present, buyers may purchase à option de vente (put), i.e. the right to sell at fixed prices any time within nine months, or à option d'achat (call), i.e. the right to buy a given number of securities at fixed price within the same period.

Finally, there is a market for unlisted securities (marché hors-cote) where securities are traded by agents de change under much the same rules as for the official market, except that transactions are for cash only, and the agents de change are responsible only for prices quoted and their publication, but not for the validity of the securities traded.

There are sub-divisions of the marché hors-cote: the 'special compartment' made up of companies which publish full information required for official listing, and agree to apply for official listing within three years; and the 'ordinary compartment' covering all other securities. Securities on the marché hors-cote are eligible for the tax advantages of the Loi Monory subject to certain conditions, which include a minimum number of transactions undertaken within a certain period. In general, companies on the unlisted market are considered to be in the first stages of listing officially.

The size of these various markets differs. Table 2.8 shows the division in value of transactions between the two major modes – à terme and au courant – between the official and unofficial markets, and between Paris and the provinces for 1979.

The unequal division in the value of transactions between Paris and the provinces is immediately apparent. On the Paris bourse, the value of transactions on the au comptant market is nearly twice that on the à terme market. The unlisted market is not large and accounts for only about 2 per cent of cash transactions in securities. The same sort of picture recurs in the provinces, except that the à terme markets are even smaller in relation to the au courant markets, only 15 per cent compared with nearly 50 per cent in Paris. The provincial unlisted markets are quite small. Bonds and equities are turned over on about the same scale in Paris and in the provinces on the official market, but the unlisted market in all the exchanges is mainly for equities.

Securities which may be listed on the Paris Exchange are fonds d'État (Government bonds), obligations émises par des collectivités publiques ou semipubliques (bonds issued by public or semi-public institutions), actions (equities), parts (management shares), obligations de sociétés/collectivités privées (preference bonds) and obligations convertible en action (bonds convertible to equities). In addition, bearer depository receipts (e.g. certificats d'actions) permit the trading of foreign shares deposited outside France. Most French securities are in bearer form. There are only two basic types of companies eligible for listing on the Stock Exchange – the société anonyme, and the sociétés en commandite par actions (limited partnerships). In the sixties, investment funds (sociétés d'investissement à capital variable) were allowed to list, and these have shown very rapid growth in recent years.

Membership

Agents de change have a legal monopoly to trade in securities on the Exchange. They are appointed by the Minister of the Economy after having fulfilled certain conditions, and buy their places in the Exchange from retiring agents. Whether in limited partnerships or limited companies,

Table 2.8
Division of transactions: French stock markets, 1979 (in 1,000 FF)

(1979 transactions)	PARIS			PROVINCES			TOTAL
	Official market	Unlisted market	Total	Official market	Unlisted market	Total	Paris + provinces
à terme	33,825,821	–	33,825,821	228,488	–	228,488	34,054,309
au comptant	60,965,340	1,305,368	62,270,708	1,470,328	107,345	1,577,668	63,848,376
Total	94,791,161	1,305,368	96,096,529	1,698,811	107,345	1,806,156	97,902,685

Source: *L'Année Boursière, 1979*, Compagnie des Agents de Change, Paris.

their firms are strictly private. Agents are Government nominees, but not Government employees. They are not allowed to act as 'market makers', but may deal directly with clients under certain conditions. Although this function was originally fairly strictly forbidden, a law in March 1973 modified the position of 'contrapartiste'. It did not bring the role of the agent de change nearer to that of the British jobber, for instance, but allowed the agent to provide a service for clients outside the official hours of the bourse. He may now deal directly with a client for his own account, and so may the banques inscrites, banques populaires, and financial institutions registered as investment houses.

In sum, (i) agents de change may deal with clients only 'out-of-hours', (ii) deals must be carried out on the basis of the last price quoted on the official market (taking into account a commission), (iii) any securities bought by agents must be resold as quickly as possible. In 1980 there were around eighty agents de change, a number that has fallen over the years.

Commission charges and listing costs

There are no listing fees as such on the Paris Stock Exchange although there are costs involved in legal fees and commercial and bank publicity. The total is not easy to work out. There are also issuing costs for certificates. Commission charges, which are not high, are shown in Table 2.9.

Agents de change are allowed to grant a part of their commission to authorised individuals or institutions which collect Exchange orders from investors. The maximum amount an 'agent' may receive for any one transaction is FF40,000.

Stamp duty (impôt de bourse) is payable on all securities except those traded on regional exchanges, and on bonds and debentures which will be fully redeemed within the next seven years; the rate is 0.30 per cent of transactions up to FF1 million and 0.15 per cent thereafter. VAT is 17.6 per cent of the brokerage commission.

Quotations and settlement

Convertible bonds, indexed bonds and foreign currency bonds are quoted in francs and centimes with accrued interest included in their price. Minimum fluctuations in their prices are graded by size of quotation, e.g. FF1.00 for securities from FF500 to FF5,000. All other bonds and debentures are quoted as a percentage of their par value excluding accrued interest. The daily *Cote Officielle* publishes the amount of accrued interest as a percentage of the nominal value. Only one price is quoted on all the French exchanges for any given security at any given time, and it is binding on both buyers and sellers.

Table 2.9
Commission charges
Cash and forward transactions — French and foreign securities

	Paris Stock Exchange		Provincial Stock Exchange	
	Rate %	Minimum FF	Rate %	Minimum FF
Basic cash and forward transaction rates				
(i) Transactions in shares, paid and scrip, capital increases, convertible, exchangeable, participating and indexed bonds	0.65	1.00	0.75	1.00
(ii) Government stock and other bonds	0.50	1.00	0.50	1.00
Scaled rates for cash and forward deals				
(a) For securities included in section (i) above:				
from FF600,001 to FF1,100,000	0.43		0.50	
from FF1,100,000 to FF2,200,000	0.325		0.375	
over FF2,200,000	0.215		0.25	
(b) For securities included in section (ii) above:				
from FF600,001 to FF1,100,000	0.33		0.33	
from FF1,100,000 to FF2,200,000	0.25		0.25	
over FF2,200,000	0.165		0.16	
Contangoes	0.10–0.15		0.10–0.15	
Premium and option transactions				
for premiums and options given up	4.00	4.00	4.00	4.00
for premiums and options taken up, commission is calculated on total amount of transaction or total amount of capital involved in deal on rates shown in sections (i) and (ii)				

Agents de change therefore attempt to match the largest number of buyers and sellers in each security. There are three types of quotation: 'par casiers', 'à la criée' and 'par opposition'. The first is a cash market quotation, using pigeonholes for each brokerage firm. A commissaire collects all buying and selling orders and establishes a price which maximises bids and offers. The second is a forward market quotation where dealings are carried out orally and by auction. A balancing price is found by the auctioneer in each security. The third is a cash market quotation for securities traded on the forward market. 'Par opposition' limits arbitrage between cash and forward prices to a maximum of 2 per cent.

Settlement is centralised by computer, except for very small turnovers of securities. Briefly, either securities are delivered and settled physically (if they are 'titres vifs') on a two-weekly basis via the accountancy department of the Stock Exchange, or else (for securities admitted) they are cleared through SICOVAM (Société Interprofessionelle pour la Compensation des Valeurs Mobilières). SICOVAM is by far the most important clearing system in France, and now operates nationally and internationally at a sophisticated level. It was created in 1949 as a société anonyme with a conseil d'administration made up the same way as its equity holders: members of the banking and stockbroking profession. The Ministry of the Economy fixes the conditions of its operations. SICOVAM's essential achievement is to execute change of ownership of securities quickly and efficiently. To this end, its brief is as follows:

(a)   to open current accounts for securities on behalf of stockbrokers and banks who are members of the scheme,
(b)   receive for deposit French bearer securities,
(c)   register foreign nominative securities,
(d)   link with foreign clearing systems wherever possible,
(e)   register all securities deposited with it, and arrange for transfer of ownership without physical transfer of paper.

In order to carry out these functions SICOVAM benefits from privileged legislation, established in 1949:

(a)   the transferability of current account securities, and therefore unnumbered securities,
(b)   the deposit of a security with SICOVAM is equivalent to a concluded bargain, and cannot be reversed,
(c)   no forfeitures are allowed on SICOVAM current accounts,
(d)   exemption from detaching dividend coupons, paying interest, or issuing representative certificates,
(e)   exemption from paying on fully amortised bonds.

Depositors with SICOVAM remain owners of their securities, not creditors. SICOVAM itself has the right to decide on the admission of securities to its depository. The following French securities are eligible: officially listed securities, bonds and convertible bonds officially listed, other securities approved by the Ministry of the Economy, e.g. oil certificates, equities negotiated on the marché hors-cote, SICAV equities, and bonds eligible for trading on the money market. Foreign securities which are registered are also admitted and, in exceptional cases, those in bearer form.

SICOVAM's operations are simply deposit, withdrawal and transfer of securities deposited with it. It administers the securities in the sense of arranging payment of dividends whilst preserving anonymity, issuing certificates representing application and allocation rights to bonus issues, and avoiding the physical detachment of rights coupons. It has established links with the Centrum voor Fondsenadmistratie (CF) in Amsterdam, the Caisse Interprofessionelle de Dépôts et de Virements de Titres (CIK) in Belgium, the Japan Securities Clearing Corporation (JSCC) in Tokyo, and expects to extend these links further in time to other clearing systems as they emerge. In effect, SICOVAM operates as a 'mutuelle' (friendly or mutual benefit society) with profits limited to those necessary to pay its statutory dividends on the securities which make up its capital, making provisions and keeping minimum reserves.

The advantages of SICOVAM are clear in terms of the management of securities. Its efficiency has been demonstrated both by the speed with which its work is handled, and by the reducing cost of its services. SICOVAM has not ceased growing for thirty years, and almost all securities quoted on the stock market are eligible for membership (the exception is 'obligation à lots'). The number of French and foreign securities deposited with it has grown consistently from some FF540 million in 1969 to FF1.28 billion in 1979. It holds about 70 per cent of all French securities quoted on the Stock Exchange. The form of title 'au porteur vif' has become quite insignificant. In terms of accuracy, not taking into account 4,277 cases of insufficient information on the part of depositors, the number of errors made by SICOVAM was 103 or 0.016 per cent, i.e. one error per 62,888 entries. This accuracy improves year by year, despite increases in the quantity of business.

Supervision

The Chambre Syndicale has general responsibility for controlling and regulating rules of the Compagnie des Agents de Change. One of these concerns control over prices. All prices quoted on the Main Exchange and the hors-cote market must be approved by the Chambre Syndicale.

On the cash market, the Chambre Syndicale keeps opening prices for French bonds within 2—3 per cent of yesterday's closing price. In the case of French equities, the margin is 4—5 per cent. Any excess of opening price is reduced by the Chambre Syndicale. If this adjustment causes less than 20—25 per cent of buying or selling orders to be carried out at the price set, trading is suspended for the day.

On the forward market, the Chambre Syndicale does not permit the opening price of securities to differ by more than 8 per cent from yesterday's closing price. If this occurs, trading is stopped. On the other hand prices of foreign securities are free to move in accordance with their home market prices.

In the matter of take-overs (offres publiques d'achat ou d'échange) and mergers (fusions), the general principle is that such manoeuvres must equally affect all the shareholders. The same is true of block trading. The rules for these are to be found in the 'Règlement Générale de la Compagnie des Agents de Change'. In the case of a take-over bid, the Chambre Syndicale must approve the offer submitted by one or two banks on behalf of the bidder. The application must contain:

(a) minimum and maximum (if any) number of equities to be purchased;

(b) offer price and means of payment. The offer can be for cash (achat) or exchange of securities (d'échange).

An offer is not permitted involving more than 10 per cent of the capital of the bidding company. The Ministry of the Economy can veto any offer within three days; once an offer is approved, it is published in the *Cote Officielle* and must remain open for a minimum of one month. Equity holders in the company under offer may withdraw their acceptances at any time up to, but not later than, ten days before the expiry of the offer. Only if there is a competing offer can the bidder cancel. Also, while an offer remains open, a 100 per cent margin must be provided with any order on the forward market for equities in the company taking over; conditional dealings are suspended.

The Chambre Syndicale also has rules on block trading. Approval for this to take place is given only if the Chambre is persuaded that the trade in blocks of equities does not amount to a controlling interest in the company concerned. If this is the case, the buyer must either formally request a take-over bid, or obtain from the Chambre permission to acquire the block under certain conditions: (a) complete information on the transaction to be published in the *Cote Officielle*, (b) the buyer offers to purchase, at the same price, every equity in the block offered for sale during the fifteen following trading sessions. If equities are traded in block on the forward market, transactions are suspended for two sessions on both the forward and cash markets. Securities sold on the forward market must be deposited before the transaction takes place.

The elaborate rules concerning offres publiques d'achat, d'échange et de vente are contained in the Arrêté of 7 August 1978, instituting a committee of surveillance of public offers on the Paris Stock Exchange.[8]

Evaluation

The Paris Stock Exchange has been subject to a good deal of critical examination over the years, beginning with the Commission Baumgartner, set up by M. Giscard-d'Éstaing, then Minister for Economics and Finance, and more recently the Commission Perouse, set up in 1979, which reported in the Autumn of 1980. The recommendations of the Perouse Commission are detailed and evaluated later in this chapter,[9] so comment here is confined to weaknesses in the present structure and practice of the Bourse, and some general observations.

In its 1971 Report,[10] the Commission Baumgartner pointed out several deficiencies in the economy affecting savings and investment, and some structural and procedural weaknesses in the Paris Stock Exchange. It then proceeded to make ambitious recommendations to improve both the financial environment and the stock market itself. Many of the points made by the Commission were still true eight years later when the Commission Perouse took up the study. In the first place, as now, there was excessive liquidity in the economy, caused by the strong tendency of French households to prefer cash, or at the best short term investments, to longer term ones. Partly this has historical roots in the fears of prewar hyperinflation lingering in French savers' minds. The stock market in 1971 was not favoured by households or institutions, each group holding only small proportions of their savings in the form of equities. Also, only a small part of the total saving population invested in equities or bonds at all. Consequently, the stock market was small, turnover slight, and offered relatively few different types of paper in which to invest. Only the Sociétés d'Investissement à Capital Variable (SICAV or investment trusts) offered investing instruments which were attractive, and reasonably strongly taken up. Agents de change, in 1971, worked on small margins and on small scale, much as they did when the Commission Perouse made its investigation eight years later. The Paris Stock Exchange, being small and trading thinly, with taxation discriminating against non-residents, did not attract foreign investors, neither were many French securities listed abroad.

The reforms recommended by the Commission Baumgartner were

extensive: they included lowering taxes on dividends, increasing brokers' commissions to make their business more remunerative, and allowing them to act for their own accounts; and reducing tax discrimination against foreign investors on the Paris market. Since the weaknesses of 1971 persisted into the late seventies, many of the Commission Baumgartner suggestions were reaffirmed by the Commission Perouse in 1979–80. The most important of the Commission Baumgartner recommendations to be put into practice were rules introduced in 1972 and 1973 concerning take-over bids and block trading, and in 1972 the removal of restrictions from agents de change in acting as 'contrapartistes' (market makers), although their new role was more narrowly defined than in the UK or USA.

In 1979, although French industry still sought funds for investment in the face of recession, the stock market supplied only a fraction of those needs. Table 2.2, (p.54) shows the small proportion raised by (net) security issues in the balance sheets of all French companies' uses and sources of funds for that year.

The Paris Stock Exchange can claim credit for a growing market capitalisation as a result of attracting savings, a sophisticated clearing system in SICOVAM, and methods of listing and quotation that are sometimes considered to be reasonably efficient.[11] But at the same time companies frequently appear to be lacking in knowledge about the techniques, costs and general procedures concerning issues on the stock market. Procedures for issuing securities on the unlisted market also seem difficult. Once issued, companies are not able to assist in keeping the secondary market lively by dealing in their own securities. French legislation is much stricter on this than in other countries. Insurance companies, in their turn, are disallowed from holding securities of unquoted companies.

As far as financial intermediaries are concerned, agents de change do not enjoy high morale. Their work is complex in the Paris Stock Exchange structure, and their commissions often not related properly to the amount of work they have to undertake. Meeschaert[12] points out that the number of agents de change fell from 187 in 1950 to 77 in 1975. Most of the reduction is accounted for by mergers. But whereas, over a long period, the Paris Stock Exchange enjoyed considerable growth in capitalisation (particularly in bonds), volume of transactions, and speed of circulation of all securities, this has not been accompanied by healthy growth in the financial affairs of agents de change. The level of commissions for agents de change has been so low as to allow them small remuneration in the face of rising interest rates. In 1973 commissions in Paris were three times lower than those in London or New York. In 1979, they were relatively just as low for small transactions, in fact five times lower than in New York for deals of £5,000. Since most deals on the Paris stock market are small (more than 80 per cent of cash orders for equities are for less than FF10,000, and 50 per cent less than FF2,500), earned commissions are kept to a low level.

There are too many ways of holding securities, both bonds and equities. The three principal modes are bearer ('vif'), bearer securities held in SICOVAM, and registered securities. There are other variations. Those securities not cleared by SICOVAM are slow and expensive to manage. Even in one issue there may be a multiplicity of types of securities to manage. Agents de change have extensive functions apart from their main one of carrying clients' instructions. Some of these are paid, e.g. holding registered title, and sending out annual reports; others are not paid, e.g. tax payments and advice, calculating capital gains on securities, recovering taxes paid by foreign investors, and establishing tax credits. Since not all securities are transferable, agents are obliged to use three systems of delivering them: (i) bimonthly through SICOVAM − accepted securities, (ii) weekly for equities and bonds in series not admitted to SICOVAM, (iii) for most bonds, a non-compensatory system under common law.

Despite what has been said before about the efficiency of quotations, the actual methods of quotation are inconvenient. First, the trading hours of the stock market are too short, and coincide with lunch-time. This short time prevents those giving orders from making contact with others when the market for a security quickens up. Also the single price system is resented by foreign investors. Second, it is necessary to be physically present at the bourse to follow the market. Anyone else knows only yesterday's closing prices, or at best the prices when trading starts. But even physical presence is not enough. Information about quantities of securities changing hands and orders waiting, is largely unavailable. The 'criée' method of quotation is generally too fast for even professionals present in the bourse to make all the deals they would wish. Third, the concentration of dealings on the first price quoted does not prevent questionable practices. The 'criée' system of quoting often leads to impulsive and erratic dealing and price movements. Agents giving orders can consult the book of the agent de change who specialises in securities quoted 'par casiers', and this can sometimes lead to an artificial change in offers and bids.

The market for block trading has acquired a certain notoriety. Blocks of securities can be exchanged at exceptional prices where industrial securities are concerned. Dealers in blocks of securities can choose between public offers and controlled block matching. Nothing prevents them from picking and choosing throughout the whole market ('ramassage') and this has occurred more recently in the market for public offers for sale. They can also use other procedures like options for those who have bonds, or deal after bourse trading hours.

Securities on the marché à terme are quoted at two parallel prices each day — one on the marché à terme, and one on the marché au comptant. The spread of prices between the two markets has no rational basis in financial standing of the securities, seeming to depend more on payment delays than anything else. It is another contribution to market fragmentation.

The system of supervising stock market practices, although greatly improved in recent years, is not as rigorous as in some other financial centres. For example, although article 10-1 of legal order no. 67-833 of 28 September 1967 censured 'opérations d'initiés' (insider trading), it is not clear how widespread the practice is or whether it is penalised sufficiently by existing legislation. In 1979 the Commission de la Bourse conducted inquiries into several cases of alleged operations d'initiés. The Commission was aided in this task by a more recent legal order of 23 December 1970 which attempts to define the 'délit d'initié' (insider trading offence). This covers all persons who 'use their profession or function to make use of privileged information'. Two legal judgements were made in 1979 against insider traders, resulting in imposition of fines by the Tribunal de Grande Instance de Paris.

The French bond market has been subjected to criticism.[13] We must recall that it is relatively recent in origin; not until 1968—70 was significant capital tapped. Even now, with FF65 billion francs issued in 1979, the market is still modest in comparison with other Community States; although this figure excludes loans of local authorities which may not be counted in the market properly defined. The market is correctly placed under the control of the 'Pouvoirs Publics' (Public Works Department), but this control is excessively bureaucratic in arranging the calendar of issues, and fixing rates of interest which do not reflect accurately the maturity of the loan or the standing of the borrower. Some borrowers have had imposed on them maturities and procedures for depreciation which they would not have wished. The reforms of M. Leca,[14] which in 1968 considerably rejuvenated the bond market, are becoming increasingly ignored. The lucrative issue market for bonds is now fairly clearly delineated from the secondary (stock) market, since French banks are much more interested in the former, abandoning interest in the secondary market and therefore in the continuity of the market and any regularity of quotation of bonds. This, of course, makes the next issue more difficult. Issuers are classed into first and second category. A finer grading is required if there is to be correct definition of notes.

Some idea of the crudeness of the bond market can be given by the fact that 5 or 25,000 securities are on the same circuit at the same price. The fixing of bond interest rates is anachronistic in France, partly as a result of the small size of the market: less than thirty dealers operate permanently in the market for French bonds, and four or five of these account for 35–40 per cent of total business transacted. The French bond market turns over completely at a rate of once every ten years; the bond market in New York turns over completely once every year. Thus, financial institutions managing FF5 or 10 billion of bonds are faced with a market which, in 1979, represented less than FF50 billion in volume. In addition, the traditional clients of the bond market, Compagnies d'Assurances and Caisses de Retraite, are also hindered by regulation of their reserves and bear tax burdens.

Performance and efficiency of the Paris stock market

In 1979, issues of securities, in gross values, reached FF82.1 billion, an 11.5 per cent increase over 1978 (FF73.6 billion). The increase is smaller in net terms (after amortisation on loans, subscriptions by State, local authority and nationalised enterprises, and certain sub-scriptions to capital increases)[15] − from FF58.4 billion in 1978 to FF62.9 billion in 1979, an increase of 7.7 per cent. However, this followed two years of strong net growth.

Certain traits in the stock market appeared in 1979:[16] (a) a slight increase in bond issues over 1978 (+13.3 per cent), (b) a weak increase in the total of new equity issues (+5.1 per cent), (c) a fall in the level of equity issues by already quoted firms (−31.8 per cent) and (d) stagnation of net stock market contribution to the finance of investment. In terms of the savings and investment environment in 1979 and 1978, it is worth noting that 1978 was characterised by a big reduction in the need for funding by private industrial and commercial enterprises, accompanied by rising household savings. Industry's demand for investment picked up slowly in 1979, more strongly in the case of public enterprises.

The equity market

Table 2.10 shows the growth of gross and net issues of equities on the Paris Stock Exchange, 1976–79.

Several features are worth noting. The year 1978 saw a big rise in issues of equities by quoted companies, helped by strong equity prices and by Loi Monory savings. But the effects wore off in 1979. Increases in capital by companies were particularly weak. But although 1979 was generally a weaker year than 1978 for issues of equities, the level of issues by listed companies was still three times that of the years shown preceding 1978. In terms of current francs, however, this is not very satisfying. In current values, the figures attained have changed little for

Table 2.10
Issues of equities, Paris Stock Exchange

		Amounts in FF billions					Variation in %		
		VI Plan	1976	1977	1978	1979	77/76	78/77	79/78
GROSS:	By call for public savings	14.5	1.6	2.7	5.3	4.8	+68.8	+96.3	− 9.4
	(of which quoted firms)	(7.6)	(0.9)	(1.1)	(4.4)	(3.0)	(+22.2)	(+300)	(−31.8)
	Without call for public savings*	37.2	9.9	10.8	10.5	11.8	+9.1	−2.8	+12.4
	Total equities	51.7	11.5	13.5	15.8	16.6	+17.4	+17	+5.1
NET:	By call for public savings	12.1	1.2	1.6	4.6	3.2	+33.3	+187.5	−30.4
	Without call for public savings*	31.9	7.3	8.3	8.4	9.8	+13.7	+1.2	+16.7
	Total equities	44	8.5	9.9	13	13	+16.5	+31.3	−

Structure of total issues (%) (equities + bonds)

		VI Plan	1976	1977	1978	1979
GROSS:	By call for public savings	6.8	3	4.2	7.2	5.8
	(of which quoted firms)	(3.6)	(1.7)	(1.7)	(6)	(3.6)
	Without call for public savings*	17.5	18.4	16.6	14.3	14.4
	Total equities	24.3	21.4	20.8	21.5	20.2
NET:	By call for public savings	7.5	2.9	3.3	7.9	5.1
	Without call for public savings*	19.7	17.7	17.1	14.4	15.6
	Total equities	27.2	20.6	22.3	22.3	20.7

Source: Commission de la Bourse, douzième rapport au Président de la République, année 1979.

*Primarily consisting of increases in capital.

the ten years up to 1979. It is interesting to see the large sums of money raised by unquoted companies in each year. Also, the bulk of net equity raised has been without call on public savings. Growth in both gross and net issues of equities over the period 1976—79 has been unimpressive, especially if one considers calls on public savings by quoted companies, which is the mainstream business of the Stock Exchange. The record looks a little better if equity issues as a proportion of gross domestic fixed capital (GDFC) are considered. Between 1976 and 1979, the percentages are as follows (source, as for Table 2.10):

		1976	1977	1978	1979
(a)	ratio of equity issues to GDFC of private companies	5.6	6.1	7.6	6.9
(b)	ratio of equity issues of industrial companies to GDFC of industrial companies	5.4	5.4	7.4	6.5

Since 1970, the total capitalisation of equities on the Paris Stock Exchange has been very variable. The year 1970 itself represented a new plateau of equity market capitalisation, of the order of FF127 billion. Not for the preceding ten years had this level been reached. But in 1974, total market capitalisation fell to FF117 billion, a level only just above that reached in 1962 (FF112 billion). The years 1976 to 1979 are also erratic: 1976 FF134 billion, 1977 FF129 billion, 1978 FF188 billion, 1979 FF222 billion.

The index of equity prices is similarly erratic over a long period. Table 2.11 shows the behaviour of the index of French equity prices since 1969.

Table 2.11
Index of French equity prices on the Paris Stock Exchange
(INSEE, base 1961 = 100)

end year		end year		
1969	92.6	1974	73.2	1979 (September) 133.8
1970	88.4	1975	93.7	
1971	83.2	1976	78.2	
1972	100.6	1977	74.7	
1973	96.3	1978	109.0	

Source: *Bulletin Trimestriel*, Banque de France, December 1979.

It is worth mentioning the performance of the SICAV's separately, since over the same ten-year period their progress has been strong. In 1969, these investment trusts numbered 30; in 1979, 114. In 1979 they were managing FF7,472,525 million in French equities or 3.96 per cent of market capitalisation, and their total assets amounted to FF36,990,097 million.

The yield on equities bought on the Bourse (including avoir fiscal) has shown a similar erratic trend since 1969. INSEE calculations show the following yields on equities bought on the Bourse (end of year, percentage per annum):

1969 3.95, 1970 4.47, 1971 5.28, 1972 4.55, 1973 5.40, 1974 7.82, 1975 6.17, 1976 6.96, 1977 7.68, 1978 5.84, 1979 (September) 5.25.

As will be pointed out later, these yields are much lower than those obtainable from public or private sector bonds bought on the Bourse over the same period.

The bond market

Table 2.12 shows gross and net issues of bonds on the Paris Stock Exchange, 1976—79.

By comparison with Table 2.10, it becomes clear that bond issues are the major part of the stock market in each year. In 1979, they made up just under 80 per cent in gross terms and yet, as Chatillon points out,[17] this bond market is still small compared with many countries of the European Community. But Table 2.12 shows the steady growth in the total value of bond issues, gross and net, in the four years 1976 to 1979. Only when the components of the table are examined does it become apparent that convertible bonds (an almost negligible type of paper in value terms) have fluctuated in annual issue values over the period in a marked fashion.

As with equity issues, public industrial and commercial companies dominate the bond issue market. Nine companies account for one-quarter of the total liabilities of the bond market (in 1978, FF15.6 billion). The largest by far are EDF and Caisse Nationale de l'Énergie with FF6,300 million, followed by SNCF with FF2,520 million and the Caisse Nationale des Télécommunications with FF2,200 million in 1978. But it is still true that such bond financing is only a small source for even these nine large borrowers on the market. EDF and Caisse Nationale de l'Énergie for example, borrow only 12.4 per cent of their total funds this way. Loans of private industrial borrowers are much smaller than those of the public industrial borrowers. For example, in 1978, Rhône-Poulenc SA borrowed FF400 million, CII Honeywell Bull

Table 2.12
Issues of bonds, Paris Stock Exchange

		Amounts in FF billions					Variation (%)		
		VI Plan	1976	1977	1978	1979	77/76	78/77	79/78
GROSS:	Convertible	5.6	1.1	1.8	0.7	0.8	+63.6	−61.1	+14.3
	Straight	155.2	41.1	49.6	57.1	64.7	+20.7	+15.1	+13.3
	Total	160.8	42.2	51.4	57.8	65.5	+21.8	+12.5	+13.3
NET:	Convertible	5.4	1	1.6	0.5	0.6	+60	−68.7	+20
	Straight	112.5	31.7	36.9	44.9	49.3	+16.4	+21.7	+9.8
	Total	117.9	32.7	38.5	45.4	49.9	+17.7	+17.9	+9.9

		Structures of total issues (%) (equities + bonds)				
		VI Plan	1976	1977	1978	1979
GROSS:	Convertible	2.6	2	2.8	0.9	1
	Straight	73.1	76.6	76.4	77.6	78.8
	Total	75.7	78.6	79.2	78.5	79.8
NET:	Convertible	3.3	2.4	3.3	0.8	0.9
	Straight	69.5	77	76.3	76.9	78.4
	Total	72.8	79.4	79.6	77.7	79.3

Source: Commission de la Bourse, douzième rapport au Président de la République, année 1979.

FF300 million, and la Compagnie Française de Pétroles FF382 million. The public financial institutions are more important and raised FF24.9 billion in 1979, (FF21.7 billion in 1978), i.e. they tapped the bond market for 30 per cent of its total resources in 1979, although the VIth Plan envisaged about 38 per cent. In 1979, la Caisse Nationale de Crédit Agricole raised FF5 billion, and la Caisse Centrale de Crédit Hotelier, Commercial et Industriel FF1.8 billion. The *private* financial institutions have also borrowed heavily from the bond market (FF7 billion in 1979 and FF5.1 billion in 1978). Finally, the 'administrations' (Trésor and Collectivités Locales) tapped FF20.4 billion in the market in 1979, compared with FF19.6 billion in 1978. The 1979 total represented about one-quarter of the market's issue of bonds.

The role of domestic bond financing in enterprises investment is two to three times as important as funding by equities, but it is not growing fast as a proportion of GFCF spending. Between 1976 and 1979 the percentages are as follows (source as for Table 2.10):

		1976	1977	1978	1979
(a)	ratio of bond issues to GFCF of enterprises and the administrative authorities	13.2	14.3	15.3	15
(b)	ratio of bond issues to GFCF of enterprises only	15.1	13.6	12.7	13.1

There are two trends discernible in bond financing. The Government is borrowing on an increasing scale for budget purposes (line (a) above), and industry is both being somewhat crowded out of the bond market and not increasing its borrowing on the market at any appreciable rate.

Since 1970, when the level of total market capitalisation of bonds stood at FF113 billion, it has grown uninterruptedly and accelerated in current money terms to reach FF410 billion in 1978 and FF456 billion in 1979. The INSEE index of prices of French bonds shows a similar steady rise from 1969, as shown in Table 2.13.

The accelerating growth in the index is apparent after 1977 following steady rises in the preceding eight years. This price acceleration is also apparent on the equity market (Table 2.11, p.76).

Table 2.13
Index of French domestic bond prices on the Paris Stock Exchange
(INSEE, base 1961 = 100)

end year		end year		end year	
1969	99.7	1974	113.8	1979	184.5
1970	100.8	1975	120.5		
1971	104.2	1976	123.1		
1972	108.5	1977	134.6		
1973	108.2	1978	150.7		

The calculated yield on bonds bought on the Bourse, whilst showing increase over the whole period, does not rise so steadily. The INSEE index shows the following yields on bonds bought on the Bourse, taking account of purchase costs and credit taxes (end of year, percentage per annum):

	Public and semi-public sector	Private sector
1969	8.63,	8.91
1970	8.26,	8.81
1971	8.28,	8.65
1972	8.28,	8.39
1973	9.65,	9.83
1974	11.21,	11.90
1975	10.18,	10.89
1976	11.04,	11.39
1977	11.07,	11.70
1978	9.94,	10.27
1979 (September)	11.56;	11.88

In general terms, the performance of the Paris Stock Exchange over the last ten years, measured by various indicators, appears somewhat better than steady in equities, and quite commendable in bonds. The whole role of the stock market in industrial and commercial financing is not strong, however, and this experience appears to mirror that of the other member states of the Community.

Another method of measuring the performance of the stock market and its ability to transform savings into investment efficiency is to consider, in rather more depth, real values in the market. Peyrard[18] in a 1976 study of French equities, basing the cost of capital concept on that of Gordon—Shapiro (dividend model), came to the conclusion that the cost of equity capital to French companies (up to 1976) was high.

The cost of bonds was a good deal lower, helped by tax relief. The relative attraction of companies to debt is explained, and Peyrard points out that this had been the case for the preceding ten years. The falling volume of new equity issues, noticeable over several preceding years, was due partly to the sluggishness of the secondary market, and partly to the cost of equity capital.

Up to approximately the same period, Boisivon[19] examined reasons for the deficient performance of new issues. An index of the volume of new issues (1970 = 100) fell to 23 in 1977. The total value of new issues fell from FF1.37 billion in 1970 to FF0.57 billion in 1977. Using a method similar to Peyrard, but examining a wider range of borrowing instruments, Boisivon concluded that, between 1966 and 1975, issues of equities and convertible bonds cost (after tax) approximately twice as much as loans outside the Bourse.

Finally, Balin and Chedebois[20] calculated the real earnings of equities, bonds and bank loans over the period 1950–79 in France. This extensive and sophisticated study concludes that, over the thirty year period studied, bonds barely protected the purchaser from negative returns, taking good years with bad. Equities, on the other hand, returned real earnings which exceeded inflation over a long period (though not always over a short period), but experienced large fluctuations in prices. Short term loans (from banks etc.) offered 'security', but returned negative real earnings. These findings are weaker for the period from 1961 owing to stock market optimism in the 1960s. But towards the end of the sixties, earnings on all types of borrowing had become weaker.

Efficiency tests

Numerous statistical tests have been made of the Paris Stock Exchange to establish its 'degree of efficiency', many following the model originally proposed by Eugene Fama and others, which basically measured the speed with which the market responds to new information, under various conditions.

In 1974, Hamon[21] published a paper on the application of the moving average technique to French equities. The technique seeks to demonstrate whether investors, by using the moving average method, can obtain higher earnings than those who use the classical 'buy and hold' method. Put simply, the investor's strategy is to buy an equity when the curve of its price cuts the moving average of its price from below, and sell in the reverse case. By simulation, Hamon found that for 18 out of 28 equities studied, the moving average strategy gave better gross profits and yields than 'buy-and-hold' (65 per cent). But the performance of the model gave very unequal results, security by security. When risk is taken into account, it is at a minimum (the co-efficient of variation is weakest) for an investor applying the moving average method security by security. The reduction of risk is an important element in the choice of strategy. It would appear that the Paris stock market is largely imperfect. Security prices adjust to new information so slowly that there is room for techniques like the moving average to beat the naive strategy of 'buy-and-hold'.

McDonald and Jacquillat[22] have made a number of studies of the efficiency of initial equity issues or introductions on the French Bourse. In their study of the French sealed-bid auction for initial equity issues (a modification of the competitive auction system), the authors found that, between 1968 and 1971, using a sample, mean offering price was only slightly below mean market price in early trading. The efficient market hypothesis requires fairly rapid price adjustment to equilibrium value, and this was satisfied. Initial price adjustment was rapid in terms of the available information, and market-adjusted returns following the close of first-day trading were small in the subsequent four weeks.

In his doctoral thesis, Hamon[23] examined the efficiency of the Paris Stock Exchange over a period 1957–71. The company CEREFIA was selected for special treatment. In tests for 'weak-form efficiency' Hamon uses tests of serial correlation, and discusses the use of spectral analysis and non-parametric tests. He also discusses methods of strategic intervention in the market, e.g. graphical techniques like filter systems, moving average, 'points et croix', and strategies of intervention at the level of portfolios, e.g. redistribution, and 'relative force'. For tests of semi-strong efficiency, he considers the speed of reaction of equity prices to capital increases, mergers, changes in accounting rules, dividend announcements and tax modifications. For the strong-form test, only the performance and behaviour of the SICAVs are studied. Hamon establishes for the weak-form test of efficiency, that when information taken into account includes only past prices, there is an almost instantaneous adjustment. No sophisticated strategy of inter-vention can bring superior results to the naive 'buy-and-hold' strategy. Coefficients of correlation are significantly different from zero, but very weak, especially over any long period of time. In testing for semi-strong efficiency, and considering all information, results appear contradictory. Adjustment of prices followed forty weeks after announcements of increases of capital, and an adjustment of 3 per cent was realised on average during this period. Adjustments following dividend announcements were of the order of 4 per cent in twenty weeks. No tests were undertaken for strong-form efficiency, but Hamon refers to the study by McDonald[24] in which the superiority of the SICAVs is demonstrated over the naive strategists, largely by virtue of their privileged information. Thus the Paris Stock Exchange on this test alone cannot be considered strong-form efficient.

Finally, the major work by Bertonèche[25] should be mentioned. Testing for weak-form efficiency on the Paris Stock Exchange by use of the random walk hypothesis, Bertonèche calculated coefficient of autocorrelation on daily and twice-weekly series of observations of equity prices. For the period 1966–74, using daily data, the French data showed an average coefficient of autocorrelation of –0069. Since the random walk hypothesis specifies autocorrelation should be zero, it can be rejected for French data within the limits of 95 per cent confidence. The efficient market model is basically about systematic and individual security risk. Central to the theory is the concept of β – a parameter which indicates the relation between fluctuations in prices of the security and fluctuations in the market index. In effect, it measures the volatility of the security. The return on a security is a linear function of its market risk in an 'efficient market'. Bertonèche demonstrates that the efficient market model does not constitute a valid predictor for France (and other Community countries examined). For one thing, the presence of heteroscedasticity during the period contributes to the instability of β, which is fundamental to the EMM.

New legislation and stock market reform

As early as 1971, weaknesses in the Paris Stock Exchange were perceived as serious, and in that year M. Giscard d'Estaing, then Minister for Economics and Finance, set out the terms of reference of a Commission chaired by M. Baumgartner. Its function was to suggest 'means of improving the operation of the stock market so as to meet the needs of savers and satisfy more easily the requirements of business'. The Minister was also conscious of the then prospect of the enlargement of the EEC and of competition from other European financial centres.

Although the proposed reforms were touched on earlier in this chapter, it is worth considering them in detail at this point. Among its recommendations the Commission pointed to the lack of public interest and understanding of the stock market in France, and suggested greater media coverage might correct this, as well as the inclusion of stock market matters in university economics curricula. Information in company annual reports and accounts was inadequate and should be upgraded. Consolidated group accounts should be mandatory. With equities suffering discrimination from competing forms of investment (like bonds, or bank loans), it was recommended that they should be allowed tax relief at least for smaller portfolios. New types of bonds should be introduced and an 'after-market' built up for them.

Although SICAVs were considered successful, it was believed that the banks (who operate them) generally inhibited direct equity ownership, and that they should take greater interest in the stock market. The work of agents de change would be improved if they were allowed to form companies with or without external shareholdings. Information should be spread more speedily and widely. Sales of SICAV units could be broadened by linking them to life assurance. The commission rates of agents de change should be increased so as to increase the quality of service. Government tax on transactions should be reduced.

To encourage new investors, investment restrictions in SICAVs should be liberalised. Even stock options for employees could be used with advantage. Take-over offers should be on equal terms to all eligible shareholders. Foreign investment on the Paris Bourse should be encouraged by relief of taxation on dividends, and restrictions on French investment overseas lifted. A system of underwriting, or of placing with institutions at a published price, was recommended.

It was also recommended that agents de change be permitted to act as principals in the cash market, and have recourse to outside capital for this purpose. Block trading rules should be formalised, and rules for take-over bids established. Market practices were considered complex and little understood by the general public. It was recommended that dual pricing on the terme and comptant markets should cease, as an instance.

Finally, dealing methods were criticised as anachronistic in a lively market. No information was made available on unfilled orders. Trading hours were too short, and the electronic processing of settlements should be encouraged.

This long list of suggested improvements gives some idea of the kind of 'malaise' the Stock Exchange was experiencing at the beginning of the seventies. But in fact introduction of the Baumgartner recommendations began at a fast rate and then stopped completely. In 1972, the investment dollar pool was abolished, and in 1972 and 1973 new laws laid down instructions for the control of 'special operations' by the Chambre Syndicale of the Compagnie des Agents de Change. They concerned two major problems pinpointed by the Baumgartner Report: take-over bids and block trading. Rules on take-over bids were further tightened up by legislation in 1978. The law of July 1972 authorised agents de change to act as principals on their own account, i.e. as 'contrapartistes' or market makers and, as a consequence, modified their functions. Agents de change were allowed to form either 'sociétés en commandite simple' or 'sociétés anonymes' to allow them to acquire sufficient resources to carry out their role as market makers more effectively. A law in December 1972 brought in new rules for controlling the functions of 'remisiers' and portfolio managers.

In February 1973, a décret loosened the conditions surrounding renunciations of preferential rights to subscribe to capital increases. In August 1973, the position of 'contrapartie' was changed — it was allowed on the marché hors-cote; but in other respects correspondants or 'collaborateurs' of agents de change were not allowed to take orders or manage portfolios — these functions remaining the sole preserve of the agent de change. The legal changes of 1972 and 1973 were a direct consequence of the Commission Baumgartner, and are extensively covered in a study by the Chambre de Commerce et d'Industrie de Paris.[26] But these reforms were not followed up by implementation of the remainder of the Baumgartner recommendations. It was not until the Barre/Monory administration had come into power in 1978 that the remaining numerous weaknesses of the Paris Stock Exchange were again examined.

In the years between, French industry did not noticeably increase its borrowing from the stock market. On the contrary bank borrowing, self-financing, and direct or indirect State assistance were still the main means of raising funds. Between 1973 and 1976, equities never accounted for more than 7 per cent of total financial resources (see Table 2.1).

The next measures were taken in 1978. One relieved the penal tax on high value, long term investments. The second was the law to encourage savings towards financing industry, introduced by M. Monory, Minister of the Economy. It consists of a tax rebate granted to those tax payers buying equities of French companies. The rebate is substantial, and offers to every French man or woman, domiciled in France, the chance to deduct from his or her taxable income a sum up to FF5,000 a year, if this sum is devoted to the purchase of French equities. If the individual is head of a family, the sum may be increased by FF1,000 for two children and FF2,000 for three children. So the deduction can go as high as FF7,000. It is available on an annual basis, assuming the investment takes place, until the year 1982 (1981 revenue) when the scheme will terminate unless renewed.

Since the scheme began in 1978, the French Ministry of Finance believes that the average amount of tax savings per investor is in the region of FF1,000 to FF2,500. The tax rebate is a powerful incentive to invest. The example given by M. Bruno de Maulde[27] is as follows: if a taxpayer is married with two children, and has a total income of FF100,000 in 1978, his tax bill in 1979 will be FF1,500 lower. The return on investment is improved sharply. This taxpayer paid only FF3,500 for shares having a market value of FF5,000 since he obtained a tax rebate of FF1,500. If the current dividend on the equities he bought were 7 per cent, the actual return this taxpayer would get would be 10 per cent. Another way of looking at it is to point out that the tax rebate sharply reduces the risk of capital loss. If the market value of the equities bought were to decline, the taxpayer in the example would still get positive real earnings from his investment as long as his equities did not fall further than 30 per cent.

The conditions of the rebate are (i) there must be *new* investment in equities, (ii) there must be durable investment — the equities bought must be kept or arbitraged against other equities of French companies for the same amount — for four years, (iii) the investment must be in French shares, either directly, or indirectly through SICAVs.

Clearly the 'Monory Act' was designed to increase the equity capital of French firms, i.e. to allow them to raise *new* money for investment. The French Government believes that the very low level of equity capital of French firms leaves them vulnerable to downtrends in their markets, and unable to borrow for investment purposes. The other purpose of the Monory reform was to convert the high level of short term deposit savings in France (some 17 per cent of disposable income) into investment orientated savings. The Government also attempted to improve firms' profitability, and therefore to increase their equity capital through retained earnings, by dropping price controls.

The results of the Monory Act appear to have been dramatic so far. During the second half of 1978, it was estimated that 850,000 tax-payers bought new equities, about 80 per cent through the SICAVs, and the rest directly from the market. M. de Maulde estimated that about half the total of investors had come to the stock market for the first time. New funds brought to the market in just one half of one year are estimated at FF3.5 billion to FF4.0 billion. The upsurge in new equity issues by French firms is noticeable. In 1977, the total value of new issues was FF1.5 billion, in 1978 FF4.5 billion. But the situation is complicated. Although in the first eleven months following the introduction of the scheme, the CAC equities rose 16 per cent, it has been suggested[28] that some of the new money raised by equity issues was used, at least at first, to reduce excessive short term borrowing rather than for investment in fixed capital.

The Monory concession was extended to the marché hors-cote and, under certain conditions, to the SICAVs and pension funds. For this purpose, and to diversify the new investment as much as possible, new borrowing instruments were created — actions à dividend prioritaire sans droit de vote (priority dividend shares without voting rights), and prêts participatifs (participating loans).

In 1978, an arrêté defined more clearly the conditions under which take-over bids could take place. Firstly more information is required under the Act concerning the objective of the take-over. Secondly, publication is required of all transactions affecting at least 5 per cent of the capital of the company which is the subject of the take-over. The Commission des Opérations de Bourse felt that the four take-overs occurring in 1979 did so in a much more informed and egalitarian atmosphere.

Among other recent legislation affecting the stock market is the law of 21 December 1979 which exempted from stock market tax all transactions in securities quoted on the provincial stock markets. This measure was taken under the encouragement of a Commission presided over by M. Mayoux to decentralise financial markets. Also in 1979, six décrets and arrêtés were introduced to follow up a law of 3 January 1979 relating to SICAVs. This legislation was designed to simplify rules regarding contributions, and to ensure protection and information for the equity holder. Among many modifications are: modernising the definition of capital of the SICAV by abolishing the notion of nominal capital, making it easier to value take-overs, mergers and stock splits, lowering from 90 to 85 per cent the proportion of the net assets of SICAV in securities, control of SICAV to be solely in the charge of a 'commissaire aux comptes', SICAV credits to be allocated according to a list established by the Minister of the Economy, all 'special operations' of SICAV (e.g. mergers) must be authorised by the Minister and Commission des Opérations de Bourse. COB itself is given greater powers over SICAV for the protection of savers.

Also in 1979 (October), Parliament passed a law allowing for the creation of mutual funds (fonds communs) open to the general public under certain conditions. Fonds communs are now defined as co-ownership bodies not subject to the same conditions as companies. The law separates clearly managers and depositors. The liquidation of fonds communs can be achieved only by buying back *all* its shares, not a proportion; liquidation is compulsory if the credit of a fond falls below FF1 million. Publicity and canvassing of shares is forbidden. Also, fonds communs should have minimum assets of FF2.5 million, and maximum FF100 million. By insisting on more, and regular, information, and regular auditing, savers are protected better; and shareholders benefit from certain tax exemptions. Fonds communs investments are limited to French securities, and also limited to 10 per cent of assets, except for investment in SICAV and other special cases. Finally, the COB controls certain administrative aspects of the fonds communs like commission rates and managers' remunerations.

In 1978 and 1979 employees of industrial and commercial companies were given priority in purchasing fond commun new issues under certain formulae, but little advantage has been taken of the scheme by employees so far.

The latest, and most important, initiative in quite a long line of studies of the stock market came in July 1979, when M. Réné Monory, Minister for the Economy, commissioned M. Maurice Perouse, Dirécteur-Générale de la Caisse des Dépôts et Consignations, to chair a working party of six, with a brief to examine internal practices of the Paris Stock Exchange considered to be in need of urgent reform. The Commission's deadline was short, and in fact it worked very hard to produce the final report for approval in the autumn of 1980. Three sub-committees were established, approximately corresponding to the three main areas of its study, although there was invariably overlap and joint work. The sub-committees, chaired respectively by M. Chatillon, M. Plescoff and M. Dantresme, considered the legal position of securities and means of settlement; quotations and the question of a 'continuous market'; and the level and structure of commissions.

These three areas of study were the main brief for the Commission, although a number of smaller matters were included, such as stock market taxes.

In the field of 'régime des titres' or settlement of securities, the Commission favoured a move from the existing practice of 'dépôt facultatif des titres' (depositing securities with brokers) to a much wider but simpler system, 'inscription en compte' (credit accounts). This move would effectively demonetise securities when they were out of circulation. It is the system applied already in Treasury bonds in current accounts. The system suggested has four main features:

(i) establishing a single means of holding securities, the 'inscription en compte', in place of the present multiplicity of systems;

(ii) the best system, in the Commission's view, is one actually in operation already, the 'inscription dans les comptes de SICOVAM', which it recommends to be extended to all securities;

(iii) although the Commission favours a centralised system of depositing and clearing securities, it nonetheless recommends a choice for the security holder, to use either a centralised depository, or else a financial intermediary which would conserve anonymity;

(iv) the system should include all quoted securities listed in the 'compartiment spécial' of the unofficial market.

In the second area of study, quotations and the question of a continuous market, the Commission was motivated by the following considerations. First, to open the stock market to the outside world and attract foreign investors by establishing a system they were familiar with. Second, recognising that the first objective could not be achieved with the present system of quotations, which was concentrated on the first price quoted. The recommendations therefore were:

(i) hours of trading should be extended, particularly for the benefit of non-residents;

(ii) continuous quotations should be encouraged, and supported by technical information systems wherever possible (such as the present Autiope-Bourse and Investdata electronic systems);

(iii) the system of dual quotation, on the marché à terme and the marché au comptant, should be discontinued, as it is only confusing to the general public; this should naturally be accompanied by a unification of the two markets. In addition, quotations should be based on the 'à terme' market;

(iv) agents de change, as they are currently constituted on the Paris Bourse, should have their 'market-making' powers extended more in line with 'jobbers' in the UK or 'specialists' in the USA;

(v) securities should continue to be quoted either on the Paris Bourse, or the provincial ones, but not on both at the same time.

In the third field, modernising and restructuring the present system of brokers' commissions, the Commission was very aware of the low level of remuneration received by brokers, the fragmentation of orders and, together with tax considerations, the financial burden on investors. Consequently, the Commission recommended the following:

(i) a degressive structure of commissions — to discourage un-economical small orders;

(ii) an increase in the minimum level of remuneration of brokers;

(iii) establishing a base commission which would have the advantage of applying equally to all dealers;

(iv) a reduction in tax on stock market dealings.

As well as these points, the Commission pronounced itself in favour of a negotiable options market in securities, based on Paris. It favoured abolishing the actual techniques of simple and double options, and also spoke against the idea of an indexed options market. The Commission favoured the continuation, at least for a time, of 'opérations à primes' and 'stellages'. 'Opérations à primes' work only in a buying direction;

'stellages' are 'put' options. It did not support the idea of the sale of uncovered options.

In April 1981 the COB tightened up on the rules governing large scale buying of equities on the official market. The objective is to force equity holders to disclose within five days any buying activity which takes a holding over between 10 and 35 per cent.

The new COB ruling reduces the period a buyer can build up a large equity stake from one month to five days. The buyer must now declare a large stake, and the COB has obliged concerted action involving a buyer and a number of proxies to be declared.

Other prescriptions for reform

More information could be given to equity and bond holders by companies. The Commission des Opérations de Bourse noted in its 1979 report the considerable delays in publishing quarterly and half-yearly information required by French law. This should be tightened up. Similarly, when the COB made its annual examination of annual reports by companies quoted on the official exchange, it saw no improvement in 1979 over previous years. The proportion which the Commission judged as satisfactory was 42 per cent.

In the case of take-over bids, there is an excessive delay between the announcement of quotations which mark the beginning of the operation, and equity holders' receipt of the necessary information about the companies concerned, the motives involved, and the appreciation of prices which is proposed. The COB has suggested various ways of overcoming this delay, including notifications in the press.

Although the Commission Perouse suggests a strengthening of the role of 'market maker' for the agents de change, this may not be enough. Unless agents de change can really act on their own accounts, making prices and matching buying and selling orders, the chances of a strong system of continuous trading being set up are reduced. Freeman[29] makes the point that a sequence of price fixings throughout trading hours does not constitute a 'continuous market', neither really does the hybrid New York Exchange System, where a new price fixing is made when a security which one may call 'foule' (popular) brings a sufficient crowd of buyers around a specialist for him to make a price.

The Report of the Commission Perouse does not mention the disadvantage caused by imbalance between bonds and equities. This problem of 'crowding out' is common to all the European bourses, but no corrective action appears to have been taken *within* the market mechanism to encourage equities. This is not forgetting the valuable encouragement given to household savers by the Loi Monory. The

French Government is in conflict in this respect; whilst it is tapping the bond market for the first time in recent years, it is clearly aware that it reduces the liquidity of the market for equities and possibly reduces their relative earnings.

Finally, the needs of small and medium sized companies appear to have been omitted from the calculations of the various reform groups. In the case of the Commission Perouse, it is only fair to say that its brief was restricted. The Government has set up 'établissements de crédit spécial' (special credit institutions lending to small and medium sized companies) e.g. the Caisse Nationale de Crédit Agricole, and the Crédit Foncier de France, but their volume of lending does not seem to be increasing. At the same time, if commissions or listing rates are raised, borrowing from the Stock Exchange may become prohibitive.

Fiscal and savings/investment incentives

Industry, agriculture, households, administrative institutions, and non-residents all enjoy low rate credits from Government (or more correctly its public credit institutions), but it must be observed that, between 1969 and 1979 export and investment activities of industrial and commercial enterprises in France have fared less well in terms of total borrowing than the other categories. Table 2.14 shows this. The trends

Table 2.14
The importance of privileged-rate credits by receiver

Receiver	1969 % of total	1973 % of total	1979 % of total
Companies:			
export	6.7	7.3	6.9
investment	27.3	22.5	15.6
(of which agriculture)	(12.6)	(11.9)	(8.0)
non-agriculture	(14.7)	(10.6)	(7.6)
buildings	23.6	23.6	16.1
Households:			
housing	21.4	23.6	31.7
Administration:			
collective equipment	20.8	21.6	19.4
Non-residents	0.2	1.4	10.3
	100.0	100.0	100.0

Source: Place des Crédits à Taux Privilégiés dans le Financement de l'Économie, internal document, Banque de France.

are clear. Company investment has received less and less low rate credit over the ten-year period, compared with other major sectors. The favoured sectors have been households (accommodation) and non-residents.

However, small and medium sized industrial and commercial enterprises do receive fiscal assistance. They are allowed exemption of 33 per cent of taxable profits during their first four years of life, as well as installation loans from the Government. They also receive financial aid in the form of a premium granted by the Government to Sociétés de Développement Régional (Regional Development Companies) which acquire holdings in these companies. In addition, Établissements Publics Régionaux (Regional Public Agencies) may contribute to guarantee funds (cumulative total FF43 million in 1978). Also, a National Guarantee Fund was set up in 1978 with a capital of FF40 million. Similar measures have been taken to encourage exporting by small and medium sized firms — a Special Guarantee Fund established, and loans for export-orientated industry.

As far as tax treatment of equities and companies is concerned in France, the system is one of partial imputation of tax credits. The rate is 50 per cent of dividend received. There is no withholding tax as such, but the tax credit is effectively similar. Thus, the treatment of share dividends is more favourable for equities than for bonds or other forms of investment. France, like other countries, has special tax exemptions for the income received on some fixed interest borrowing instruments; in this case, interest from national bonds, equity dividends (a FF3,000 annual tranche of dividends received is exempt from tax), income from securities purchased from long term savings accounts.

French equities and SICAV units are, of course, eligible for the deduction of capital invested in equities from taxable income, as has been described earlier (the Loi Monory) and this has proved a significant stimulant to investment in the stock market. The Monory concession cannot be used together with the FF3,000 dividend exemption from tax mentioned above. Capital gains are taxed more favourably than total income, on an optional basis. France also practises a form of complete tax exemption if equities are held for a long period, i.e. beyond a 'speculation limit'. With these sorts of tax exemption available, there are restrictions on holdings of foreign equities by institutional investors not listed on a national stock exchange. There are other institutional restrictions. Insurance companies must invest at least 30 per cent of reserves in bonds, and not more than 5 per cent of one company's securities, but SICAV securities are admitted to their portfolio if foreign shares represent under 50 per cent of SICAV assets. For SICAV, at least 30 per cent of their assets must be in French bonds, and at least 85 per cent of SICAV assets must comprise transferable securities, Treasury bills and cash. SICAV are restricted to 5 per cent of their investment in one company, 5 per cent of one company's securities, and 5 per cent of voting rights in one company. The Caisse des Dépôts et Consignations is confined to investing in securities issued by the Government or under Government guarantee and securities listed on a French Stock Exchange; it cannot invest in foreign securities not listed in France. Special Social Security Schemes and Friendly Societies are limited in their investments to 20 per cent of assets in domestic securities on a list drawn up by the Government. The Supplementary Scheme for Employees in the distributive trades and industry is restricted to holding 50 per cent of its assets in Government or Government-guaranteed securities. Finally, collective investment funds must hold 80 per cent of their assets in transferable securities, Treasury bills and cash, and not more than 10 per cent of a single company's equity or more than 10 per cent of their own assets in the same company's securities (except for public authorities).

The French Government has been sensitive to the encouragement of savings and investment in general, and to re-animation of the Stock Exchange in particular, and nearly every year several measures designed to do this were introduced. In June 1979, for instance, tax allowances and accelerated depreciation were introduced for 1978 and 1979 in the case of net increases in investment compared with the year preceding, at a total cost of FF3 billion over two years, equivalent to 1.5 per cent of private productive investment. Also in 1979, to encourage investment in building and civil engineering, the Government released a FF2.55 billion appropriation for the construction of new buildings and energy-saving equipment.[30]

Summary

French postwar economic performance has been relatively impressive in the Community. Even in the recession beginning 1979/80, its economic policy has been reasonably well designed and successful in most aspects, but inflation and unemployment are nowhere near solved.

In recent years, French companies have suffered from lower profits and therefore less self-financing, relying more on fixed interest borrowing. The companies have responded to this higher debt by improving marketing and modernising equipment. Bank loans are important.

French Government public debt has been rising uninterruptedly since 1971, financed partly through money creation, and partly by carefully managed stock market gilt issues. The Government's budget deficit has never been very large, and it is not the Government's intention to 'crowd out' equities.

The structure and practice in the Paris Stock Exchange are complex, in the opinion of several investigating Commissions excessively so, but there are some efficient features, notably the SICOVAM and introductory procedure. The Commission des Opérations de Bourse is a keenly interested supervising body. Unfortunately, the Stock Exchange still supplies only a small fraction of industry's needs. Internally, there are many weaknesses; low commission charges, a multiplicity of types of securities to manage, anachronistic quotation methods, and so on.

The equity market in Paris has been thin and variable. Most net equity has been raised without call to public savings. On the other hand, the bond market, especially Government bonds, has grown steadily, and now accounts for the bulk of new issues. However it still remains true that, over a long period, only equities (as a group) have beaten inflation.

Several tests of efficiency, along the lines of the efficient market model, have been made of the Paris market. None shows the market to be more than 'weak-form' efficient.

There have been two major and several minor Commissions investigating reform of the Paris Bourse. The first major one (Baumgartner, 1971) brought some changes — on 'market making', take-overs and block trading. The Commission Perouse reported late in 1980, and pin-pointed several weak areas, recommending a continuous trading market, restructured and new levels of commissions, and a modernised clearing system. But it is too early to see implementation. The only other major change was the 1978 Loi Monory, encouraging savings, with noticeable effect.

The French Government has been forward in establishing low interest credits, and tax relief and exemptions for French industry and commerce.

With the advent of the new Socialist Government in May 1981, the Paris equity market has been thrown into a melting pot, the results of which will take some time to emerge.[31]

Notes and references

1   Dubois, Paul, 'Le Financement des Sociétés Industrielles et Commerciales au Cours des Dix Dernières Années', *Économie et Statistique*, (revue mensuelle), Institut National de la Statistique et des 'Études Économiques', no.99, Paris, April 1978.
2   Conseil National du Crédit, Rapport Annuel, no.39, 1979.
3   Fayolle, Jacky, 'Le Comportement d'Investissement depuis 1974', *Économie et Statistique*, INSEE, no.127, Paris, November 1980.

4   Elstoh, Mayer (ed.), *Banking Structures and Sources of Finance in the European Community*, 3rd edition, Banker Research Unit, London 1979.

5   *France*, OECD Economic Survey, May 1980.

6   *L'Année Boursière, 1979*, Compagnie des Agents de Change, Paris.

7   For example, *Recommendations concernant l'Information des Actionnaires et la Rémunération des Apports en Nature dans les Opérations du Fusion, Scission, ou Apport Partiel d'Actif*, Commission des Opérations de Bourse, September 1977.

8   The official documents dealing with these supervisory matters are: (a) *Règlementation des Cessions de Blocs d'Actions Conférant le Contrôle d'une Société faisant Publiquement Appel à l'Épargne*, Commission de la Bourse, September 1975; *et la Rémunération des Apports en Nature dans les Opérations de Fusion, Scission on Apport Partiel d'Actif*, Commission de la Bourse, September 1977; (b) *Textes conçernant les Offres Publiques d'Achat, d'Échange, et de Vente*, Commission de la Bourse, October 1978; (c) see also note 7 above.

9   A rather fuller account and analysis of the Commission Perouse Report and its recommendations can be found in the author's paper, 'Reforming the Paris Stock Market', *The Investment Analyst*, March 1981.

10   *Le Marché des Actions*, Rapport Présenté au Ministre de l'Économie et des Finances par la Commission chargée d'Étudier le Marché des Actions, juin 1971, La Documentation Française, Paris 1971.

11   McDonald, J.G., Jacquillat B.C., 'L'Efficacité de la Procédure Française d'Introduction en Bourse', *Banque*, no.325, January 1974; Commission Perouse (draft report) 1980.

12   Meeschaert, Emile, 'La Bourse en Question', *Banque* no.356, November 1976.

13   Chatillon, Jean-Paul, 'Pour un Véritable Marché Obligataire', *Banque*, no.397, July—August 1980.

14   Described in detail in de Feuilhade de Chauvin, T., 'La Réforme du Marché Français des Obligations', *Banque*, no.274, May 1969.

15   Net issues also include issues effectively realised during the course of the year, e.g. calls on funds in previous years now realised, etc. The definition of 'net' and 'gross' issues is fully detailed in Commission de la Bourse, Annual Report 1979, p.117.

16   *L'Année Boursière, 1979*, op.cit. (note 6).

17   Chatillon, op.cit. (note 13).

18   Peyrard, Josette, 'Coût des Actions des Enterprises Françaises', *Banque*, no.356, November 1976.

19   Boisivon, Jean-Pierre, 'Le Coût des Fonds Propres Externes des Sociétés Cotées, 1966—1975', *Analyse Financière*, 3ième trimestre, 1978.

20   Balin, Jacqueline and Chedebois, Marc, 'Rentabilité Comparée des Actions, des Obligations et des Placements à Court Terme, en France, sur la Période 1950–1979, face à l'Inflation', *Analyse Financière*, 2e trimestre, 1980.

21   Hamon, Jacques, 'Application d'un Modèle de Moyennes Mobiles au Marché Français des Valeurs à Revenue Variable', *Revue de Science Financière*, July–September 1974.

22   McDonald, John G. and Jacquillat, Bertrand C., 'Pricing of Initial Equity Issues: the French Sealed-Bid Auction', *Journal of Business*, January 1974; with J. Rolfo, 'l'Introduction en Bourse des Sociétés', *Banques*, June 1979. See also note 11.

23   Hamon, Jacques, 'l'Éfficience des Marchés Boursiers; Étude du Marché Parisien (1957–1961)', thèse pour le doctorat d'état ès sciences de gestion, Université de Rennes 1978.

24   McDonald, J., 'French Mutual Fund Performance: Evaluation of Internationally-Diversified Portfolios', *Journal of Finance, XXVIII*.

25   Bertonèche, Marc, 'Les Marchés Européenes de Valeurs Mobilières: Éfficience, Diversification Internationale et Perspectives d'Intégration', thèse de doctorat ès sciences de la gestion, Université de Bordeaux, September 1978.

26   Chambre de Commerce et d'Industrie de Paris, Direction des Études, Études et Documents Sérié Générale 1973, no.10, *Les Récents Aménagements des Pratiques Boursières*, December 1973.

27   'The Monory Act and the French Stock Market', speech delivered unscripted by M. Bruno de Maulde, Deputy Director of the French Treasury Department, at the Stock Exchange, London, 13 September 1979 (in the series, The Chairman's Lectures).

28   Brittan, S., *Financial Times*, 11 February 1980.

29   Freeman, Peter (J.M. Finn and Co.), 'Étude', Bourse, no.2, 1er trimestre, 1980.

30   *France*, OECD Economic Survey, May 1980.

31   First results of the Socialist victory on the Paris Bourse were an 18 per cent fall in the CAC General Index, and a 12 per cent drop in equity values by December 1981. Clearly, nationalising many leading French companies, including banks, is going to radically affect the structure of French financial markets. The nationalised companies will be quoted on the bond market in future, and some 17 per cent of equity capital moved to the State sector.

3 Germany

Company financing

The economic performance of German companies in the seventies was highly successful. In 1980, such a dramatic change took place that it is difficult to choose a typical date to examine the structure of company financing. However, 1980 is chosen here as a representative year on the grounds that oil prices are likely to remain relatively high, and competition in overseas markets, especially from Japan and the newly industrialising countries, will remain strong.

The growth of the German economy between 1973/74 and 1980 was fuelled by high levels of company spending on fixed capital. An index of gross fixed capital formation calculated by the Deutsche Bundesbank shows it increasing (irregularly) from 85 in mid-1975 to around 133 in mid-1978 (1974 = 100). An index based on the same year of pre-tax profits for the period shows a close correlation, rising from 98 in mid-1975 to 136 in mid-1978. The fit is better for small and medium sized companies than for large ones, possibly because the latters' capital investment plans are determined on a fairly long term basis, rather than on short run anticipated profitability or current earnings. But this may be too facile an explanation, since there appears to be an inconsistency. In the first six months of 1980, companies' total spending rose by 15.5 per cent compared with the previous twelve months, to reach DM107 billion. In the whole of 1979, spending was DM92 billion.[1] Yet company profits were under pressure in 1980:

they did rise slightly in the first half of the year compared with 1979, but not at the same rate as national income by any means. Although exact figures for company earnings are not known for the early 1980 period, it appears that the growth rate was well down. The Deutsche Bundesbank explains this apparent anomaly by attributing the rise in GFCF to (i) companies investing more to streamline their productive processes, and (ii) greater innovation to become more competitive by modernising and extending production plant. But a more convincing explanation is the existence of lags in investment programmes, and an unwillingness by firms to alter their plans in the face of what they believe may be only short term pressures.

In the first half of 1980, companies greatly increased their spending on stocks. By June 1980 it reached DM19 billion compared with DM4.5 billion for the first half of 1979. Although this can be characteristic of the initial stages of a boom, i.e. stocking up in anticipation of large sales, it was not the case in early 1980. This was confirmed by the general performance of the economy and companies in the second half of 1980 and the first quarter of 1981. Clearly, companies were building up stocks to beat rising prices of imported raw materials. Some of the stock building was involuntary in the sense that orders were growing less rapidly (eventually for some industries, like metal-making, they fell in late 1980 and early 1981).

Companies' earnings fell in early 1980 as a result of higher negotiated wage and salary costs, higher import prices (with oil leading the rise) and higher VAT. The Bundesbank[2] estimated that of the 6.3 per cent average price rise in retail goods in the first half of 1980, 46 per cent was due to domestic causes, and 54 per cent to higher import prices.

Consequently, the proportion of their own funds which companies could devote to financing their capital spending fell. In the first half of 1980, it was 84 per cent which, although high, was lower than the previous year (88 per cent). Historically, as a result of continuing high profits, German companies have been able to finance most of their capital investment with their own money. From 1969 to 1972 it averaged just under 70 per cent, from 1970 to 1974, 73.5 per cent. A detailed discussion on the merits or otherwise of a high proportion of self-financing is not appropriate here, but it has been undertaken by Samuels and McMahon[3] in a comparison of company financing in Germany and the UK. These authors see the comparatively higher self-financing of British companies as a disadvantage, contributing towards a higher cost of capital. The question is complicated, and depends partly on different definitions of self-financing. No research appears to have been done on the role of expectations in the choice of gearing, and in the case of the German companies, Samuels and McMahon implicitly assume that they have achieved an optimum gearing for growth. But the events of 1980 and 1981 may eventually demonstrate that greater dependency on fixed interest borrowing is a handicap in a period of high interest rates and falling profits.

In the first half of 1980, German companies were obliged, by market conditions, to seek greater external finance to achieve their investment strategies. As Table 3.1 demonstrates, investment spending in 1979 was maintained by increased liabilities, especially the issue of equity and increased short term borrowing from banks. Companies' financial assets were down, and within the structure of assets there was a transfer of funds from short term bank investments to higher yielding Government bonds and to equities. In 1979, of gross capital formation of DM200.5 billion, DM176.7 billion was financed internally. In 1978, internal finance completely covered gross capital formation at DM158.6 billion. In 1980 (first half), of gross capital formation of DM107 billion, DM90 billion was financed by internal resources. From 1978 onwards, the share of internal financing in gross capital formation has been falling, and 1981 is undoubtedly set for a further fall.

In Germany, the banks are closely involved in company financing. As Table 3.1 shows, of external liabilities incurred, in 1978 70 per cent were domestic bank liabilities, mostly long term; in 1979, the percentage was 82 per cent, equally divided between short and long term; and in 1980 (first half) the percentage was 35 per cent, again equally divided between short and long term but, within the structure of total external borrowing, showing a swing from domestic bank borrowing to short term borrowing abroad. In 1979, for instance, 80 per cent of total German bank lending went to non-bank enterprises and individuals. In terms of equity ownership, it appears that the banks in Germany own around 7.4 per cent of domestic equities outstanding. But since the banks generally own the investment funds as well (which held 3.1 per cent in 1979), the total proportion of ownership is rather higher. The Gessler Report on the Banking Industry released in 1979 concluded that 336 banks and credit institutions it surveyed held 662 individual stakes in non-banks. Some 285 of these holdings were of between 25 and 50 per cent of equity and included Daimler-Benz and Preussag.

In addition, individual banks have greater or less participation in companies, and within the structure of the complex banking system some, like the credit co-operatives and savings banks, are able to expand their lending quickly if necessary, owing to their wide range of customers. In general, the banking system in Germany has a much closer involvement with industry than most of its European Community partners, certainly more than in the UK. A feature of the German banking system is that the commercial banks engage in all sorts of banking operations, irrespective of whether they are private, co-

Table 3.1
Companies' external financing and acquisition of financial assets compared with internal savings and investment (excluding housing and financial institutions) (DM billion)

Item	1978	1979	1980 (1st half)
1 Gross capital formation	158.6	200.5	107.1
(a) internal resources	158.6 (100%)	176.7 (88%)	90.0 (84%)
(of which, consumption of fixed capital)	(105.3)	(114.2)	(62.0)
Financial deficit (1 – a)	–0.0	–23.8	–17.1
2 Liabilities incurred	47.9	63.5	30.1
(a) Bank liabilities:	33.5	52.7	10.7
short term	9.9	27.1	5.7
long term	23.6	25.7	5.1
with other domestic agencies and in the market for securities	10.6	7.3	5.5
abroad	3.7	3.5	13.9
(of which short term)	0.2	–0.2	12.6
(b) Equity issues	3.6	3.8	3.2
Total (a + b)	51.5	67.3	33.3
3 Financial assets acquired			
with banks	33.4	14.7	–5.2
(of which):			
currency and sight deposits	17.8	0.1	1.2
time deposits	15.2	14.9	–5.9
with other domestic agencies and in the security market	6.0	13.2	7.9
(of which):			
acquisition of bonds	2.1	5.3	1.8
acquisition of equities	2.2	5.9	4.6
abroad	11.5	17.1	13.5
(of which trade credits)	6.0	9.6	7.6
Total	50.9	44.9	16.2

Source: *Bundesbank Monthly Reports*, vol.32, nos 5 and 10.

Note: Discrepancies due to rounding.

operative or public in nature. They are truly 'universal' (or multi-purpose) banks, dealing with not only credit, deposit and payment transactions business, but also investment banking and securities. The other main branch of the banking system is that of the 'specialist' banks. In the capital market, the commercial banks also own a large proportion of DM bonds of the specialist banks and therefore finance their lendings. The commercial banks also place new issues and bonds of the mortgage banks with their customers.[4] These statistics do not reflect fully the control which the universal banks have over companies in Germany, but whether control benefits the companies is a contentious issue. In the UK, a strong body of opinion maintains that bank funding and management has been a major factor in the industrial growth of Germany. However, sharply falling bank profits in 1980 in Germany have led a number of them, e.g. Dresdner and Commerzbank, to sell part of their equity in Hochtief, Kaufhof and Metallgesellschaft in early 1981.

Government and local authority financing

It is difficult in Germany, because of the federal system of government, to define central government debt and public sector debt. The position of the Laender is the most difficult to place statistically. Although the term 'public authorities' deficit' refers to the total operations of the Bund (Federal Government) Laender (States), Gemeinden (local authorities) and the social security system, the Statistische Bundesbank (Statistics Office) publishes separate statistics for the Bund, Lastenausgleichfonds (equalisation of burdens), ERP Sondervermoegen (Marshall Aid), Laender, Gemeinder/GV and Zweckverbaende (Community ventures). It seems reasonable to take the definition of the public sector (public authorities) used by the Bundesbank, as follows: Bund, Lastenausgleichfonds, ERP Sondervermoegen, Laender Governments, and Gemeinden.

Table 3.2 shows the total indebtedness of the German public authorities at June 1980, for categories of authority, and type of debt. It is clear that the Federal Government and the Laender Governments are the major borrowers in the public sector. Clearly, too, the banks are the biggest channel for borrowing — the proportion of funds borrowed this way has not changed much in the seventies. This is the most striking feature of Government borrowing — the large part played by the banks in lending directly to the Federal Government and the Laender: in most years of the seventies around one-third of total outstanding debt in the case of the Federal Government, and two-thirds of total outstanding debt in the case of the Laender Governments. The

101

Table 3.2
Indebtedness of the German Public Authorities* (DM million, June 1980)

	Total	Bundesbank Book Credit	Discountable Treasury Bonds	Tax Reserve Certificates	Medium Term Notes	Federal Bonds	Federal Savings Bonds	Bonds	Bank Advances	Loans of non-banks		Commutation and compensation debt	Equalisation claims	Covering claims	Foreign debt
										Social Security Funds	Other				
Public authorities, total	442,431	95	6,558	—	21,010	5,836	25,487	57,879	280,295	10,510	17,213	216	17,032	69	32
Federal Government	224,808	—	6,558	—	20,610	5,836	25,487	45,944	93,963	2,487	12,604	216	11,011	69	24
Lastenausgleichsfonds	2,750	—	—	—	—	—	—	1,686	537	24	424	—	—	69	10
ERP Sondervermoegen	2,468	—	—	—	—	—	—	—	2,218	—	250	—	—	—	—
Laender Governments	122,755	95	—	—	400	—	—	11,695	98,478	3,623	2,442	—	6,021	—	2
Local authorities	92,200	—	—	—	—	—	—	240	85,636	4,400	1,918	—	—	—	6

Source: *Deutsche Bundesbank Monthly Report*, vol.32, no.10.

*Excluding local authorities' mutual indebtedness.

next largest single item is bonds (including Federal savings bonds): for the Federal Government about one-fifth of total debt and for the Laender about one-tenth. The structure of the debt reflects the nature of Government financing in Germany, and to some extent, the smaller importance of the capital market compared with, say, the United Kingdom.

In the first half of 1980, an increase in public indebtedness became apparent, as both the Bund and Laender borrowed more heavily on the bond market, and built up non-bank loans. Since about the middle of the seventies, in terms of sectoral financial balances, the private sector's savings were large, and Germany also had a large balance of payments surplus. The Government was induced to correct this by high public sector borrowing to prevent inflation. In 1978, the Government introduced a 'Programm für Zukunftsinvestitionen' (programme to encourage demand and growth). It consisted of tax concessions, and was intended to promote business investment. But in 1980, not only did the public sector deficit remain high (it shot up in 1981), but the private sector deficit increased with increasing investment and a weakening in companies' earnings. The situation deteriorated rapidly late in 1980 when the Deutsche Mark fell against leading currencies, and investors on the German bond market were not attracted by the historically high rates of up to 10 per cent.

Structure and practice of the Stock Exchange

Organisation

There are eight Stock Exchanges in Germany: Berlin, Bremen, Düsseldorf, Frankfurt, Hamburg, Hanover, Munich and Stuttgart. Although some of the exchanges were operating in some way before this, it can be said that they were originally created, or unified, by the Stock Exchange Act ('Börsengesetz') of 1896. They are legally special types of public corporation. The 1896 Act, which applies to all eight Exchanges, has been revised several times, the major revision being in 1975. The Law of that date applies also to the commodity exchanges and the foreign exchange markets.

Frankfurt is the largest Stock Exchange in terms of turnover, with DM31,700 million, or 46 per cent of the turnover of all the German Stock Exchanges in 1979. Second largest was Düsseldorf, with a turnover of DM23.5 million, or 34 per cent of total turnover. Together, the two Stock Exchanges accounted for 80 per cent of total turnover of the German Stock Exchanges in 1979. However, Frankfurt has other claims to premiership. In foreign securities, it turned over 67 per cent of all foreign equities, and 80 per cent of foreign bonds.[6] The remaining six Stock Exchanges are quite small.

Although each Stock Exchange operates within a Land, e.g. Düsseldorf in Rheinisch-Westfalia, and its opening requires the approval of the Land authorities in whose territory it operates, in legal terms all the Exchanges are linked together. Prices on each Exchange are known instantly on the others, and in practice, since the rules and regulations of securities trading are common, the various City Stock Exchanges can be thought of as separate trading floors of one centralised Stock Exchange, and referring to the 'German Stock Exchanges' is entirely correct. Both the Statistische Bundesamt and the Deutsche Bundesbank publish statistics on an aggregated basis for all the Exchanges.

Control of each Stock Exchange by the Land in which it is located is formal and restricted. According to the terms of the Stock Exchange Act of 1975, the Laender have the following functions:[7]

(i)   to approve the establishment or the suspension/abolition of a Stock Exchange,

(ii) to approve the rules and regulations issued by the Stock Exchange Board (of Governors),

(iii) to appoint the Kursmakler (officially appointed market-maker),

(iv) to nominate a State Commissioner (Staatskommissar der Börse) who supervises the application of the rules and regulations governing the Exchange, but may directly intervene in its operations,

(v)   to issue, by way of a statutory order, regulations concerning the creation of an honorary committee which can impeach Stock Exchange members admitted to trading who have acted unethically. Penalties include fines up to DM2,000, or temporary suspension from the Exchange. (Kursmakler and their deputies are exempt.)

The Stock Exchange Law delegates management to the Exchanges themselves. Each Exchange has its own regulations (Börsenordnung), although these are virtually identical for each. The Börsenordnung require a Board of Governors (Börsenvorstand) to be set up, which is responsible for the direction of the Exchange. It issues the regulations, which deal with organisation of the Exchange, rates and commissions. It decides on the admission of companies and individuals to the Exchange (independent dealers, deputies and 'freie makler'; briefly, independent intermediate dealers for their own account). The Börsenvorstand also lays down trading conditions and rules, e.g. trading days and hours; the opening, suspension and cancellation of the official quotation (for example, when there is an imbalance of offers and bids so that rationing is called for, or when the opening price for equities is 1 per cent different for bonds from the day before, or 5 per cent for equities); and decides on special quotation terms like scrip issues. The Börsenvorstand itself consists of between 19 and 22 members; 19 members elected as follows: (a) 13 representatives of admitted credit institutions, (b) two Kursmakler, (c) two freie Makler, and (d) two deputies. Members are elected for three years. In addition, three more members may be elected from issuers of admitted securities and investors.

Other organs of each Stock Exchange are the Listing or Admissions Committee (Zulassungsstelle), and the Association of Official Brokers (Kursmaklerkammer). The former is a partly independent body, licensing securities before they are admitted to official quotation. It examines documents and ensures adequate information is given. The latter is a public body representing the official brokers, is responsible for supervising the Kursmakler and allocating securities among them, for controlling the settlement of prices, and editing the Official List. The two large Exchanges also have a plethora of other committees, whose functions are fairly self-explanatory, or will be explained later. For example, the Supervisory Committee (Börsenaufsichtausschuss), the Quotation Committee (Kurskommission), the Foreign Exchange Committee (Devisen-Ausschuss), the Committee for Fixed Interest Securities (Ausschuss für Festverzinsliche Werte), the Committee for Unlisted Securities (Ausschuss für Geschäfte in Amtlich Nicht Notierten Werten), the Arbitration Tribunal (Schiedsgericht), and the Committee for Insider Trading (Gebildete Prüfungskommission für Insider-Fragen).

Types of markets and trading

As Dr Hartmut Schmidt points out,[8] the distinction between official and unofficial trading on the German Exchanges can be confusing, because 'in both cases dealings take place on the floor of the Stock Exchanges, the participants being almost identical, and even if one takes the German Stock Exchanges together, the issues traded are the same to a large extent'.

There are three main trading markets, and some subdivisions.

1 The official market This is the 'Amtlicher Markt' for bonds and equities which includes all bonds and equities admitted to official listing by each Exchange's Listing Committee. In addition, it includes securities which may be admitted to official trading with admission procedure, including issues by the Bund and Laender. The official trading market is defined by the official price fixings for its securities by the Makler. Dr Schmidt correctly distinguishes two sub-markets within the official trading market:

(a) *Single quotation (non-continuous trading)* The single quotation price (Einheitskurs) is established for every Stock Exchange session for each security listed. The Einheitskurs is fixed by the Makler by comparing buy and sell orders in his order book, and fixing a price which clears the maximum number of bids and offers for each security — what the Commerzbank has termed the 'principle of maximum turnover'.[9] The market includes all small orders for equities admitted to continuous dealing. Trading takes place once a day (at around 1145 hours), and only securities with a nominal value of at least DM500,000 outstanding may be traded. Sometimes, the Makler may be assisted by the Bundesbank where Bund bond issues are involved.

(b) *Continuous quotation market (Variabler Kurs)* In each Exchange, the Börsenvorstand may approve requests from companies issuing a large volume of equitics that they be traded both at the single quotation, and subsequently continuously at the variabler Kurs. Consecutive prices are established throughout the trading session from 1130 hours to 1330 hours, but there is a minimum bargain size. It is fifty for equities, and DM500,000 for convertible or option bonds, or any multiple.

On both the Einheitskurs and Variabler Kurs markets, the Makler collects bid and offer prices at the beginning of each session. The principle in both cases is the same. The Makler fixes the opening and closing prices as part of the consecutive quotation price in the same way as the single quotation price. In practice, only small amounts of bonds are traded on the official market, and these are mainly Bund bonds. The remainder, a considerable number, are traded out-of hours between banks on the 'OTC market'.

2 The unofficial exchange

(a) *Regulated unofficial dealing* Strictly speaking, this is a hybrid, a 'regulated free market' or 'semi-official market' ('Geregeter Freiverkehr'). Securities may be traded (on the same Exchange floors) in unofficial dealings, either regulated or unregulated. The legal basis for unofficial trading is provided for in the German Civil Code, the German Code of Trade and Commerce, and practices established by the Standing Commission of the

Federal Association of German Banks for Affairs related to Unofficial Dealings. Securities may be traded on this basis if they are not suitable for listing because they are in small lots, or if they are already listed on another German Stock Exchange. Some short maturity bonds, e.g. Bund bonds and debentures of large banks are also traded this way. The regulated unofficial market is subject to supervision by the Committee for Unlisted Securities mentioned above, which also regulates admission to the market. Admission to this market is easier than to official trading. Admission fees are about one-half, and the prospectus required is abbreviated. But only the freie Makler and banks are permitted to deal unofficially. Unofficial Exchange trading takes place sometimes continuously, but mainly at individual prices. No investor has the right to have his order executed by the freie Makler, or even of market order to buy or sell at the offer or bid. In this sector, quotations are called 'preis' rather than 'kurs', and are published daily in the Stock Exchange Gazette (Kursblatte) within the quoted spreads of actual bids and offers.

(b) *Unregulated unofficial dealing*   Securities traded under these terms have not been admitted to the official listings or approved for regulated unofficial dealings. Such securities are usually not ready for trading in these other markets or for listing. But dealings take place at official hours, i.e. 1130 to 1330 hours; and supervision is undertaken by the Committee for Unlisted Securities not the Stock Exchange Board, as in the case of the Regulated Official Trading Market. As in that market, investors have no right to have their orders executed.

The market is characterised by ease of access. Banks may apply to admit securities at any time with no special procedures to follow. All trading is undertaken by the Freie Makler and credit institutions only.

But the biggest part of the market is over-the-counter sometimes referred to as 'Telefonverkehr' (the telephone or telex market). This way, officially listed securities may be bought and sold as well. Dealers are the freie Makler, and participants are banks and financial institutions. Arbitrage with foreign stock markets with different trading hours is possible. Execution of orders on the OTC market is on a net basis, i.e. prices agreed between two contracting parties are not subject to any additional charges (courtage or bank commissions). Bonds are also traded on the OTC market in the following ways: (a) trading of officially listed bonds, (b) trading of unlisted issues,

(c) direct placing of new issues, (d) placing of underwriting participations, and (e) trading of new issues. Category (b) includes registered bonds (mortage and communal bonds), DM private placements, and certificates of indebtedness (Schuldscheindarlehen). These can only be traded OTC.

3 Options trading The options trading market is not large in Germany, and is concentrated on Frankfurt and Düsseldorf. Puts and calls with three different contract periods are traded. Approved traders are Stock Exchange members recognised by the local options clearing association, the 'Lombardkasse' or 'Liquidationskasse'.[10] A few securities are traded heavily. Approval for trading is given by the Federal Finance Minister and the Börsenvorstand, and supervision is by the Committee for Options Dealing.

Types of securities

Equities admitted to the Stock Exchange are issued mainly by industry, banks, transport companies, insurance companies, and foreign companies. Equities admitted are primarily in bearer form (Inhaberpapiere). Registered equities (Namenspapiere) which are obligatory for insurance equities, are the exception. There is a variety of bonds issued. The Bund issues certificates of indebtedness, and the local authorities borrow communal loans to finance their budget deficits from mortgage credit institutions, which in turn refinance by issuing communal bonds. Credit institutions issue bank debentures. Company debentures are rare. Convertible and option bonds are also rare. But there has been fast growth in recent years in issues of foreign DM bonds.

The public authorities in Germany are heavy borrowers on the capital market: they include the Bund, Federal Government agencies like the railways, the Laender, local communities, and cities. The fixed interest instruments they use to borrow are: bonds (bearer debt certificates), notes (Kassenobligationen — medium term debentures), certificates of indebtedness (Schuldscheindarlehen — interchangeable loans), federal savings bonds (Bundesschatzbriefe — untraded, no-price risk) and federal obligations (Bundesobligationen). At the end of 1979 on the German exchanges, bonds of domestic and foreign issuers totalled DM574.6 billion (nominal value), equities of domestic issues DM85.0 billion, and units of domestic investment funds 1,139.3 millions. Clearly, the German Stock Exchanges are dominated by bonds, in the proportion of about 7:1.

Membership

This has been covered to some extent. Two main groups are admitted

108

to membership of the Exchanges: (i) the banks, savings banks, credit institutions and (ii) the Makler, who act as intermediaries in securities trading. The banks play a leading role in the Exchanges since they are authorised to deal. Orders must be placed with the banks, who handle all stock market transactions and behave in all respects as brokers. They can deal directly with each other or indirectly through the Makler, who effectively play the role of 'jobber' or 'specialist'. The banks make loans on margins, deliver, clear, and safe-keep securities, and undertake security analysis. The dominant role played by the banks in the German Stock Exchanges and their direct involvement in German industry has been the subject of much comment and analysis.

Listing and trading fees and taxes

The costs and charges for listing are made up of the admission fee, cost of publishing the application for admission and the listing prospectus, and commission charged by the banks for arranging the listing. These are non-recurrent expenses as follows:

(i) *Bank commisions:*
   for bonds 0.50 per cent for private customers, 0.25 per cent for credit institutions
   for equities 1.00 per cent for private customers, 0.25 per cent for credit institutions.

(ii) *Stock Exchange admission fees:*
   for bonds DM150 on each million up to DM300m. of issue's nominal value
   for bonds DM75 on each million above DM300m.
   for bonds DM1,000 minimum fee
   for domestic equities, DM300 on each million up to DM20m. of listed capital
   for domestic equities, DM200 on each million DM21–DM50m.
   for domestic equities, DM100 on each million above DM50m.
   for domestic equities, DM500 minimum fee
   for foreign equities, the admission fee may be reduced on application, to two fifths; minimum fee DM500, maximum fee DM50,000.

(iii) *Maklers' fees (courtage):*
   (a) On equities Calculated on the value of the transactions (including rights issues) at 1.0 per cent; minimum commission DM0.50.

(b) On bonds   The calculation is based on the par value (or nominal value):

	%
Up to nom. DM50,000	0.075
Up to nom. DM100,000 (minimum DM37.50)	0.050
Up to nom. DM250,000 (minimum DM50.0)	0.035
Up to nom. DM500,000 (minimum DM87.50)	0.0325
Up to nom. DM1,000,000 (minimum DM162.50)	0.020
Up to nom. DM2,000,000 (minimum DM200)	0.015
Up to nom. DM5,000,000 (minimum DM300)	0.010
Above nom. DM5,000,000 (minimum DM500)	0.0075

All transactions are for cash, so there are no charges for forward transactions. Contangoes do not apply.

(iv) *Stock Exchange turnover tax (Börsenumsatzsteuer):*
Levied on capital transactions and on the trading of securities (defined as debentures, equities, and mutual fund units). The transaction must be undertaken in Germany or abroad with the participation of at least one German resident. Depending on the type of securities traded, the tax rates vary between 0.0 and 0.25 per cent.

Bonds issued in the form of a collective debt register claim since mid-1972 are exempt together with Federal Savings Bond, notes issued by the Bund, the Federal Railways, and the Federal Post Office. The rate of turnover tax is reduced to one-half if one of the parties to the contract is a foreigner residing abroad.

(v) *Withholding tax:*
The rate is 25 per cent on convertible bonds and option bonds. There is no withholding tax on bonds held by German residents. The rate for foreign holders of debentures of domestic issues, including convertible and option bonds is 25 per cent. No tax is levied on DM denominated bonds issued by foreign borrowers. Foreigners living in Germany do not have to pay capital gains tax.[10]

Clearing

At the present time, securities are rarely delivered physically. Custody of securities has always been with the banks, but nowadays most banks use the clearing facilities of the Land Central Banks (Landeszentral-banken), branches of the Deutsche Bundesbank and the institutions acting as central depositories for securities (Kassenverein).

The basis for the Kassenverein depository system is provided for by the law governing the custody and transfer of securities, the Depositories Act.[11] The notion of collective deposits of securities and transfer of ownership shares in these collective deposits goes back to the 1880s. Today, the stage has nearly been reached where all the German Exchanges have computerised their securities transactions and the processing of Stock Exchange business is centralised. The Stock Exchanges, depositories and EDP centres are nearly combined in a system of transacting and clearing that is swift, cheap and free from error. The system now operates basically in a credit/debit account way.

In addition to the domestic Kassenverein, in 1970, following suggestions by the German commercial banks active in the international and underwriting and securities business, the depositories set up the 'AKV German Foreign Depository' in Frankfurt. Its function is to act as trustee for foreign securities held by foreign banks, to encourage foreign registered equities to official trading on the German Exchanges, and to participate in the international clearing of securities.

The collective depositories centralised on Frankfurt have been very successful in attracting security clearing into the system. At the end of December 1979, there were 13,882 separate security lines in the computer system, compared with 12,994 at the end of 1978. Between 1970 and 1979, the value of German bonds cleared by the central Kassenverein increased from DM19.2 billion to DM156.5 billion; in numbers of securities from 80 million to 630 million. Equities rose from DM85.3 billion to DM185 billion, or in number from 82 million to 180 million.[12]

For the AKV Foreign Depository, the results have been equally good: from 1970 to 1979, a rise in value of foreign securities cleared from DM0.04 billion to DM4.538 billion. Eighteen countries were represented in 1979, not including CEDEL (for Eurobonds). The annual turnover in foreign securities has increased from 14,255 in 1971 to 160,140 in 1979.[13]

Already, the Kassenverein at Frankfurt has begun exploring the possibilities of EDP clearing link-ups with automated clearing systems in other countries. The first link is likely to be made with SICOVAM in Paris in 1982. The Max Planck Institute has studied the technical procedures necessary for this to take place and has found no insurmountable barriers.[14] After that links with CIK (Belgium), a special section of the Österreichische Kontrollbank AG, Wien, or Schweizerische Effekten-Giro, A.G, Zurich (SEGA) etc. would be entirely possible.

Supervision

The German Stock Exchanges' authorities have come in for some criticism on grounds of supervision. In spite of their combined size and ranking among Community Stock Exchanges, the degree of protection afforded to savers and investors is less than in some of their smaller counterparts. Reasons for this include the dominating role in the Exchange of the banks which, through their size, strength and ethical standards, provide a protection of their own; and a continuing sympathy for market liberalism in Germany. As in other countries, Stock Exchange Boards are not in control of all activities of companies; for example, take-overs of listed companies can occur outside the Stock Exchange altogether, but prices of listed securities will be affected. In Germany, as elsewhere, there is legislation outside the Stock Exchanges controlling some of the activities of companies.

As far as company law is concerned, the Federal Cartel Office, by virtue of the Act against Restraints of Competition, must be notified of any major plans for takeovers or mergers, and can condemn them in the interest of fair competition. For example, any group of companies acquiring 25 per cent of a third company's capital must notify the office of their intention. Voting rights and dividend rights are suspended until such notification is given. The company approached must, if it is a listed company, publish any subsequent statements. A breach of these rules is a breach of law. Similarly, German company law requires that a company's capital ownership be published, and therefore any major change in shareholdings should be known and made public. A company's prospectus must set out details of any connections with other companies, and shareholders with more than 25 per cent of the company's capital must be named. Finally, by way of example, the Bund can, by virtue of the Foreign Trade Law of 1961, require companies to notify it of any intended acquisition of their securities by foreign investors. It must be said that there is not very much contact between the Börsenvorstanden and the Federal Cartel Office in their separate consideration of transfers of control of companies.

Part of the German Stock Exchanges' problem in controlling company ownership activities in order to keep equity holders fully aware of events, is that they have no legal powers to oblige listed securities to be dealt with on the Exchanges (although in practice most transactions go through the market). Although German banks will pass all their transactions through the Stock Exchanges on the grounds of good ethics, clients wishing to bypass the Exchanges for reasons of anonymity, especially when dealing with blocks of securities, can insist that the banks comply. In short, the German Stock Exchanges do not have a monopoly of dealing in listed securities, and this calls for special care in supervision.

The rules governing transactions in securities are mainly derived from the professional body representing Stock Exchange members (in this case, the elected Börsenvorstand). In turn, this body is under the administrative control of the Laender. In addition to the Börsenvorstand and Laender, and the internal committees of the Stock Exchanges mentioned already, The Special Committee on Stock Exchanges at the Ministry for Economic and Financial Affairs has set up a Control Commission to report to the relevant Federal Minister on any infringements of good conduct (with the permission of the parties concerned).

Control by the Börsenvorstand is tighter when company take-overs are foreshadowed by the acquisition of existing shares — usually by dealing in blocks of equities. There are no Stock Exchange rules calling for the buyer of a controlling interest to ensure all equity holders get equal treatment. But minority equity holders are protected, to some extent, by the Company Law (Aktiengesetz) of 1965, under which they may receive compensation. Take-overs are not so widespread in Germany now as they were in the sixties. The early operations of a take-over bid can be carried out within the framework of the general Stock Exchange rules, and if they appear unethical, the Börsenvorstand can suspend dealings.

In the case of proposed mergers, a draft merger contract must be available to equity holders of the companies concerned before a general meeting is called. In the related case of capital increases, the capital cannot be increased without three-quarters of equity holders (in value) approving.

On the question of the abuse of inside information to gain unfair advantage in purchasing or selling securities, the Special Stock Exchange Commission on Stock Market Reform set up in 1968 recommended rules to prevent 'insider trading'. The Commission published 'Guidelines Governing Insider Dealings' ('Insiderhandels-Richtlinien') and 'Rules for Dealers and Security Counsellors' ('Händler und Beraterregeln') at the end of 1970, and the German Trade Associations ensured their implementation. The rules adopted are voluntary, not statutory, and depend on the goodwill of the parties concerned. For each Stock Exchange, a Supervisory Commission (Prüfungskommission') has the task of identifying and disapproving insider trading. In 1973, for instance, a take-over bid was commenced on the Stock Exchange in Düsseldorf with an offer by August Thyssen-Hütten AG (ATH) for 51 per cent of the equity capital of Rheinstahl AG. In the negotiating period leading up to the take-over, Rheinstahl equities rose markedly in price on the unofficial market, suggesting insider dealing. As a result of an inquiry, it was revealed that there had been no ATH purchases of Rheinstahl equities in the negotiating period, and that the rules on insider dealings had not been infringed.

113

Evaluation of structure and practice
of the German Stock Exchanges

The general impression given by the organisation of the German Stock Exchanges is rather liberal and loosely controlled. All the interest in terms of real activity lies in Frankfurt and Düsseldorf, although the much smaller Stock Exchanges in other Laender do not seem to be as regionally oriented or interested as perhaps the provincial French Exchanges. Frankfurt is undisputed in terms of transactions in foreign securities.

In organisational terms, each Stock Exchange has a panoply of committee surveillance, both internal (by professionals) and external (Federal and Land supervision). But this has not prevented supervision of practices from being modest, and may even have caused fragmentation. Rules, regulations, and practice, have established guidelines about the transfer of control of companies, but since the Stock Exchanges have no monopoly in the transactions of listed securities, and since the banks are powerful dealers in securities, they can be circumvented. This is not to say that standards of ethics are not high, but the Stock Exchanges can suffer (in their public image) from deals made outside the Exchanges. For example, in 1978, when the Federal Cartel Office disallowed the proposed take-over of Sachs AG by the British company Guest Keen Nettlefold, the latter disposed of its 25 per cent holding, bought in anticipation of a majority equity holding, to Commerzbank, not offering them to the public on the Exchange. On other practices, such as insider trading, rules are voluntary and weak.

The mixture of single quotation and continuous quotations is probably not desirable. There appear to be no complete statistics on the distribution of equities and bonds between the official and unofficial markets, and none of deals done over-the-counter. As in other countries, the equity market probably tends to suffer from the size of the bond market, and it is a particular feature of the German bond market that it tends to fluctuate closely with bank liquidity, as banks are the major holders and non-Government issuers involved. In general, the banks are unusually heavily involved in the German Stock Exchanges both as intermediaries and investors.

The fees on the German Stock Exchanges are relatively high, for both listing and dealing. Bonds tend to be favoured, and foreign investors put somewhat at a disadvantage.

The clearing system is efficient, and generally considered to be a model for other countries. In part this is due to the banks' wish to place their security settlements on the same credit/debit accounting system as the rest of their business. But whatever the reason, the success of the system is undoubted.

114

A more detailed evaluation will be undertaken in considering reforms of the Stock Exchanges in a later section.

Performance of the German Exchanges

1   The equity market

In general, the German equity markets have performed less well than German companies, and the performance of equities has not compared well with that of bonds. Table 3.3 shows the rather lack-lustre and irregular behaviour of equities between 1975 and mid-1980.

The number of listed companies has fallen steadily since 1975 (and earlier), and although the value of their gross capital has increased slowly but steadily over the period, the market value of company equities has fluctuated. This is reflected in the price of shares. Whilst the dividend and yield (including tax credit) are generally up on previous years, if the credit had not been introduced, the trend would have been very static, and reducing in real terms. As will be seen later in this section, the level of equity yields is well below that on bonds. An 8 per cent gain over six years in the total market value of equities is a poor performance.

Table 3.4 shows the sales of equities by German residents from 1975 to 1979, on the listed and unlisted markets. Over this period nominal value is down, and market value and average issue price erratic, but generally weak in total. Performance on the unlisted equity market is surprisingly poor, and for both markets 1980 and 1981 were much weaker years.

Finally the index of equity prices (for all equities) from 1975 (29 December 1972 = 100) is not impressive:

Year	1975	1976	1977	1978	1979	1980 (first 9 months)
Index	93.7	101.5	101.4	108.9	105.5	99.0

(Source: Deutsche Bundesbank, Statistische Beihefte zu den Monatsberichten, Reihe 2, *Wertpapierstatistik*, no.10, October 1980.)

The Commerzbank index (1953 = 100), figures of which are available for 1980 and early 1981, tell an even sorrier tale: January 1979 825, December 1979 720, January 1980 700, December 1980 690, February 1981 670.

Only around 20 per cent of the country's public limited companies are listed on the German Stock Exchanges, and about 50 per cent of their nominal capital is represented there. Of those companies listed, it is estimated that about 38 per cent of securities are firmly held, and

115

Table 3.3
Capital of officially listed public limited companies — price, dividend and yield of equities

End of year or month	Capital		(of which)	Market value	Price	Average values			
	Public limited companies	Total	Listed ordinary equities			Dividend		Yield	
						Including	Excluding	Including	Excluding
						Tax Credit*			
	Number	DM million				DM		Percentage	
1975	471	39,177	34,553	134,405	389		13.67		3.52
1976	469	40,551	35,724	125,959	353		12.77		3.62
1977	465	42,019	36,280	136,478	376	15.28	13.87	4.06	3.69
1978	459	43,075	37,334	151,892	407	19.07	12.20	4.69	3.00
1979	458	44,500	38,592	137,481	356	19.38	12.40	5.44	3.48
1980 (August)	458	45,280	39,154	145,095	371	21.42	13.71	5.78	3.70

Source: Deutsche Bundesbank, Statistische Beihefte zu den Monatsberichten, Reihe 2, *Wertpapierstatistik*, no.10, October 1980.

*From 1977 there was a modification in the taxation system. The equity holder from 1977 gets a tax credit set off against his income tax liability.

Table 3.4
Equity issues by residents — sales

Period	Total sales			Listed			Unlisted		
	Nominal value	Market value	Average issue price	Nominal value	Market value	Average issue price	Nominal value	Market value	Average issue price
	DM million		%	DM million		%	DM million		%
1975	3,531	6,010	170.2	1,888	3,659	193.8	1,641	2,349	143.0
1976	2,667	6,081	228.1	1,245	2,743	220.4	1,424	3,341	234.8
1977	2,598	4,368	168.0	1,023	2,004	196.1	1,578	2,364	149.8
1978	2,645	5,550	209.9	1,506	3,972	263.6	1,138	1,578	138.8
1979	2,542	5,513	217.1	1,433	3,635	253.5	1,107	1,880	169.8

Source: Deutsche Bundesbank, Statistische Beihefte zu den Monatsberichten, Reihe 2, *Wertpapierstatistik*, no.10, October 1980.

not traded.[15] This has the effect of making the secondary market much thinner and more volatile. Generally speaking, equities of foreign issues have done rather better than domestically owned equities since 1975 (from DM2,256 million in 1975 to DM4,173 million in 1979 for the former — steady increase, compared with DM27,466 million to DM25,663 million for the latter — irregular behaviour).

In terms of German companies, Table 3.5 for selected German equities shows the major set-backs experienced by the largest German companies between 1979 and 1981 for various indicators.

At least three major companies were in trouble by early 1981 — AEG Telefunken, Commerzbank and Volkswagen. The last two saw their equity prices drop from highs of 187 and 192 in 1980 to 127 and 135 respectively in 1981. Other companies' equity prices also saw dramatic falls: BASF from 150 to 118, Deutsche Bank from 302 to 227, and Thyssen from 91 to 53. Only five out of the sixteen companies shown managed to increase their earnings per share, and Commerzbank declared a nil dividend in 1980. Company profits are clearly under pressure.

The options market has not built up into any size as yet, and appears to be somewhat irregular in its growth, and not growing very fast. There is no information about its profitability. Table 3.6 shows the position since 1975.

The opening of option contracts does not seem to have increased greatly (even less in real terms), and the proportion not exercised is

Table 3.5
Performance of selected German equities, 1979–81

Equity	Recent price DM	Equity market capitalisation DM billion	High 1980	Low 1981	Earnings per share 1979	Earnings per share 1980	Historic PER (%)	Last dividend declared	Yield (%) Net	Yield (%) Gross
BASF	118.10	4.66	150	118	24.00	21.00	5.6	8.00	6.77	10.58
Bayer	107.90	4.60	129	105	18.00	16.50	6.5	7.00	6.49	10.14
Commerzbank	131.60	2.22	187	127	–	–	–	Nil*	–	–
Daimler Benz	264.50	7.19	234	225	49.65	52.50	5.0	10.00	3.78	5.91
Deutsche Bank	276.50	6.33	302	227	–	–	–	9.00	3.25	5.08
Dresden Bank	156.00	2.77	205	158	–	–	–	6.00*	3.85	6.01
GHH	186.00	1.81	224	183	32.00	30.60	6.1	7.00*	3.76	5.88
Hoechst	114.10	4.17	127	106	22.50	18.50	6.2	7.00	6.13	9.59
Karstadt	190.50	1.37	258	189	7.39	8.75	21.8	6.00	3.15	4.92
KHD	173.50	0.92	231	174	16.00	17.00	10.2	7.00	4.03	6.31
Mannesmann	123.50	2.36	139	112	21.00	20.50	6.0	5.50	4.45	6.96
RWE	174.30	6.27	197	163	19.74	20.48	8.5	8.00*	4.59	7.17
Siemens	250.20	9.01	286	238	25.55	28.20	8.9	8.00*	3.20	5.00
Thyssen	65.80	1.71	91	53	8.50	6.00	11.00	4.00*	6.08	9.50
VEBA	123.30	4.15	160	123	19.40	18.50	6.7	7.50	6.08	9.51
Volkswagen	138.00	3.31	192	135	58.65	39.00	3.5	10.00	7.25	11.33

Source: *Investors' Chronicle*, 27 February 1981, compiled by Laurence Amboldt of Galloway and Pearson.

*for 1980.

Table 3.6
German Stock Exchanges' options dealings (DM million, base price)

	Options to buy				
	Increase	Decrease due to			Memo item:
Period	New contracts	Exercise of option	Expiry of terms (non-exercise of option)	Options un-exercised at end of period	Option costs paid during period for contracts concluded
1975	344.9	183.1	92.6	135.9	26.4
1976	420.3	179.8	254.0	122.6	26.8
1977	259.8	162.9	132.3	96.4	13.6
1978	382.5	185.9	127.8	165.3	18.7
1979	315.0	126.6	261.0	92.9	15.0

	Options to sell				
	Increase	Decrease due to			Memo item:
Period		Exercise of option	Expiry of terms (non-exercise of option)	Options un-exercised at end of period	Option costs paid during period for contracts concluded
1975	110.6	18.1	59.0	47.7	4.5
1976	119.4	80.2	58.5	28.2	4.2
1977	96.6	24.3	65.1	38.4	2.9
1978	145.2	45.1	84.0	54.5	4.6
1979	158.0	112.8	60.0	39.4	6.1

Source: Deutsche Bundesbank, Statistische Beihefte zu den Monatsberichten, Reihe 2, *Wertpapierstatistik*, no.10, October 1980.

quite high. Similarly, options to sell seem to have moved little from their 1975 position.

Finally, the investment companies (Kapitalanlagegesellschaften) in Table 3.7 have a chequered history of sales receipts from the general public. They are a force in the market, but only the bond-based funds have any size, accounting in most years for the bulk of sales. The whole market for investment funds has peaked several times, in 1969 (DM5,509 million), 1972 (DM4,043 million) and 1977 (DM7,616

Table 3.7
Investment companies — sales receipts, DM millions

| Period | Total | Sales receipts of German funds open to the general public | | | | Net purchases of foreign investment fund units by residents | Memo item: |
		Total	Equity-based funds	Bond-based funds	Open-end real estate funds		Sales receipts of German specialised funds
1975	1,690	1,650	975	511	163	41	1,407
1976	4,475	4,512	1,489	2,783	242	−36	1,333
1977	7,616	7,635	1,080	6,263	292	−17	2,105
1978	6,283	6,294	613	5,170	511	−10	2,284
1979	2,225	2,264	−163	2,236	191	−40	2,189

Source: Deutsche Bundesbank, Statistische Beihefte zu den Monatsberichten, Reihe 2, *Wertpapierstatistik*, no.10, October 1980.

million). Since 1977 total sales have fallen.

If we were to compare domestic bonds, domestic equities, and units of domestic investment companies' funds *outstanding*, we would find the bulk of outstanding securities were accounted for by the investment companies; e.g. in 1979 in outstanding values, bonds of domestic issuers = DM504.5 billion (nominal value), equities of domestic issuers = DM85.0 billion (nominal value), units of domestic investment companies' funds = 1,139.3, and DM bonds of foreign issuers DM70.1 billion (nominal value). Again, in terms of outstanding value, the growth of investment companies' funds since 1975 has been rapid (from DM554.1 billion n.v. to DM1,139.3 n.v. in 1979).

2 The bond market

It was pointed out earlier that the market for bonds is the largest part of the market in terms of turnover, partly because of the rapid increase in Federal Government and local communities' borrowing, and partly also because of the highly liberal character of the German Stock Exchanges which has attracted foreign DM borrowers. (The previous strength of the Deutsche Mark has added to the attraction.) The German Capital Market Committee is technically responsible for the timing and volume of new Public Debt issues under the direction of the Bundesbank.

Between 1968 and 1979 the debt of the Bund quadrupled from DM47 billion to DM202 billion. Debt of the Laender rose over the same period from DM24 billion to DM116 billion, that of the Gemeinden from DM34 billion to DM91 billion. The sector on foreign DM bonds tripled from DM19.3 billion at the end of 1970 to over DM70 billion at the end of 1979.

The main issuers in the bond market are the Bund which includes the Railways and Post Office (about 25 per cent of outstanding bonds of domestic issuers, by nominal value, at the end of 1979) and the banks and credit institutions (74 per cent). Industrial companies borrow very little by way of debentures, around 1 per cent of bonds outstanding in 1979, although companies accounted for something like 15 per cent of the market just after World War Two. They have replaced expensive debentures with certificates of indebtedness. The statistics tend to underrate the importance of company fixed interest borrowing for this reason. Also, some of the banks' fixed interest borrowing is re-lent to industry by way of long term loans. The Bund borrows partly through listed bonds, the Laender by certificates of indebtedness and bank loans, and local communities by loans from mortgage credit institutions.

Investors are private individuals, accounting for an average of some 18 per cent of total sales of fixed interest notes over the period 1969–79, but fluctuating considerably with interest rates; corporate investors 4 per cent average over the period, again fluctuating; banks and credit institutions 41 per cent over the period, and the most important group of buyers — again fluctuating with monetary policy and corporate investment activity; insurance companies 12 per cent, fairly steady; investment companies 6 per cent; and foreign investors — wide fluctuations according to exchange rates and interest rates.

Table 3.8 shows the performance in gross and net sales of bonds by domestic borrowers.

The annual new issue volume of bonds has been growing at a rate faster than total outstanding volume, as a result of shorter maturities, producing a quicker rate of capital turnover. Table 3.8 shows the rapid growth in bank bonds over the period, especially 'other bank bonds' and communal bonds, and the reducing volume of sales by the Bund and its agencies. The 'fall' in public bonds was technical only in 1979. Sales of Bund bonds were as strong as ever, but the other public borrowers redeemed more bonds than they sold. Gross sales of public bonds still remained high. Foreign DM bond sales were well down in 1979 as yields fell below those on domestic bonds, and the Mark came under pressure.

The apparent decline of the bond market in 1979 in terms of public borrowing is also partly due to the omission of the very popular certificates of indebtedness (Schuldscheindarlehen) which are nowadays a major means of financing the public and private sectors. In 1979 the

Table 3.8
Sales of fixed interest bearing securities by domestic borrowers
(par value, DM billion)

GROSS SALES

| End year | Total | Public bonds | Bank bonds | | | | Industrial bonds | DM bonds of foreign issuers |
			Mortgage bonds	Communal bonds	Bonds of specialised banks	Other* bank bonds		
1975	76.1	18.6	8.0	30.9	4.0	14.2	0.3	7.5
1976	73.7	20.6	6.2	28.6	4.3	13.9	0.2	8.7
1977	80.5	25.7	10.0	26.4	3.5	14.6	0.3	13.2
1978	95.4	22.7	14.9	33.2	5.5	18.8	0.1	15.3
1979	118.1	19.9	10.7	39.7	5.5	30.5	0.0	11.6

NET SALES

End year	Total	Public bonds	Mortgage bonds	Communal bonds	Bonds of specialised banks	Other* bank bonds	Industrial bonds	DM bonds of foreign issuers
1975	48.9	13.5	5.4	23.9	2.3	3.9	0.0	6.0
1976	48.4	16.9	3.7	21.4	2.0	4.8	−0.5	6.6
1977	50.5	21.2	7.2	16.6	1.3	4.5	−0.4	10.3
1978	44.6	14.2	8.2	16.3	2.4	4.4	−1.0	10.3
1979	49.1	5.3	3.6	16.0	2.0	16.5	−1.1	6.9

Source: Commerzbank, *The German Bond Market*, 1980.

*E.g. central giro institutions.

Table 3.9
Volume and types of borrowing by public borrowers
as at December 1979 (DM billion)

	Total	Federal Government	Railways	Post Office	Federal States	Local Authorities
Bonds	74.0	40.6	13.8	7.5	11.8	0.3
Notes (medium term debentures)	21.9	20.8	0.6	–	0.4	–
Schuldscheindarlehen	271.1	84.2	12.0	7.2	85.7	82.0
Federal Savings Bonds	26.6	26.6	–	–	–	–
Discountable Treasury Bonds	8.5	8.1	0.4	–	–	–
Bundesobligationen (legally fixed interest bearing securities)	0.6	0.6	–	–	–	–

Source: Deutsche Bundesbank, *Form, Trading, and Administration of Securities*, 1976.

Commerzbank estimated these to total DM400 billion outstanding. Medium term notes and non-marketable Federal savings bonds are becoming very important (see Table 3.9).

The popularity of Schuldscheindarlehen can be easily seen. They can have maturities ranging from short to long term and are completely transferable.

As far as ownership of bonds goes, domestic banks and non-bank companies (e.g. insurance, investment) normally hold the bulk, but individuals rank high. In 1979, private investors' purchases rose strongly, together with those of non-bank institutions, at the expense of the banks. This was in line with the Government's tighter monetary policy.

In 1980, the Federal Government and Laender increased their borrowing significantly to meet a high PSBR, and the volume of new issues rose to record heights. Bund borrowing rose to DM8.5 billion at the end of the first half of 1980, already three-quarters of total 1979 borrowing.

Yields on fully taxed newly-issued bonds have tended to fall over the period 1970 to 1979 as follows:

1970	1971	1972	1973	1974	1975	1976	1977	1978	1979
8.3	8.0	8.0	9.3	10.2	8.6	7.9	6.3	6.0	7.5

But during 1980 the fluctuations became greater, between 7.9 per cent at the beginning and 9.6 per cent towards the end of the year. Nonetheless, private investors are increasingly turning to the fixed interest market, and away from equities, as the bond market plays a steadily increasing role as an investment medium. The equity market is not making real returns as the bond market is. In comparative terms, the par value of new listings of fixed interest stock on the German Exchanges was far and away the highest among the EC countries in 1979, the next highest being the UK and Eire Exchange at two-thirds the value. Also in 1979 the German Exchanges led in total par value of fixed interest listed stock, again the nearest to it being the UK and Eire Exchange at two-thirds the value. But Germany had only one-seventh the (market) value of bond turnover of the UK and Eire; the secondary market is by no means so lively.[16] The verdict on the performance of the German bond market is that it is reasonably flexible, but tending to react in a volatile fashion to changes in internal and external determinants, after a long period in which the market has been decidedly sluggish.

Efficiency of the German Stock Exchanges

Only three statistical studies of the efficiency of the German Stock

Exchanges have been made that are known to the author. Efficiency in these studies is defined as security prices which are generated by the Stock Exchanges and reflect information contained in the sequence of past price changes (the random walk hypothesis).

In the early study by Solnik,[17] the distribution of serial correlation coefficients of 35 separate equities (for Germany) was calculated. They were then tested for deviations from the random walk, and also the degree of stability over time investigated. No evidence was found of negative serial correlation, and the deviation from the random walk became less significant for longer time intervals. The serial correlation coefficients for individual equity lines were fairly stable over time. Solnik concluded there were some inefficiencies in the German market, certainly more than in a similar statistical comparison of random walk behaviour of US equity prices.

In a further paper by Conrad and Jüttner,[18] the authors demonstrated that German equity prices did not fluctuate randomly; that dependent price changes were present. The statistical techniques applied were runs and serial correlation tests. The daily closing prices of fifty-four German equities provided the basic data. The hypothesis of randomness was not proved, by demonstrating that successive price changes were dependent. To measure the degree of dependency, the authors applied serial correlation tests for daily changes in equity prices. Correlations were generally high, i.e. prices were generally dependent, and the Stock Exchanges could not be called efficient by this criterion.

Finally, James Guy[19] examined monthly price and dividend data for ninety German companies from 1960 to 1970. In contrast to the two studies outlined already, Guy found that, except for high positive serial correlations for equities of larger companies, German equity prices generally conformed to a weak-form test of market efficiency by testing for serial correlation of investment returns.

New legislation and Stock Exchange reforms

There have been no large scale changes or reforms of Stock Exchange practice or conditions, apart from revisions to the Stock Exchange Law of 1896, like that of 1975. But these did not radically revise the basically liberal nature of the German Stock Exchanges or give them monopoly powers. Changes have been piecemeal, and some changes in economic policy have indirectly affected the positions of savers and investors in the markets. These will all be examined.

For example, in early 1980, the Bundesbank agreed to allow foreigners to hold domestic fixed interest securities with a maturity of more than two years. This move to relax capital imports was a consequence of the falling value of the Deutsche Mark and rapidly rising capital outflows. In addition, the Bundesbank agreed to relax the rules governing the sale of Schuldscheindarlehen of over two years' maturity by German banks to foreign investors.

In 1975, several reforms were framed as a result of the amendment to the Law of 1908, 'Gesetz zur Änderung des Börsengesetzes vom 28 April 1975'.[20] The programme included concentrating all equity transactions within the Stock Exchanges, increasing Stock Exchanges' information through publishing full statements of listed companies, requirements for admission to membership of the Exchanges, the manner in which quotations in equities should be made, the reintroduction of futures trading in the form of traded options, and the regulation of insider trading. Certain other problems were also considered: institutional investment companies, tax on equities, the admission of securities for listing, earlier publication of companies' prospectuses according to the rules of listing, improved statements of dividends, the closer supervision of parallel markets, and how borrowing for capital investment could be encouraged.

Not since this date has there been any official discussion of Stock Exchange reforms. The reforms of 1975 have made little impact on actual practice in the market, and the Börsensachverständigen-kommission, set up in 1968 to investigate the improvement of practices in the Exchanges, has not made a significant impact on their efficiency. There has, however, been a good deal of unofficial discussion and debate about reform, and some of the arguments are set out in the next section.

But the Government made a major change to the environment of savings and investment in 1977 by taxation changes contained in the 1977 Company Law Act (Körperschaftsteuerreform). Until that year, taxation had been a major burden to the Stock Exchanges in Germany. Dividend income was taxed twice — first companies paid tax on distributed profits, and then equity holders paid tax on income. The new rules abolished double taxation of the distributed profits of companies, and equity holders could obtain tax credit certificates from companies to compensate their own income tax liabilities.

Under the new system, the general rate of corporation tax on undistributed income from equities is 56 per cent (with reductions for some organisations like banks) and on distributed income 36 per cent. For resident companies with income up to DM20,000 there is an exemption of up to DM5,000. Non-resident companies with a permanent establishment in Germany pay a flat rate of 50 per cent (rebates for West Berlin companies).[21]

The 1977 Act had an immediate effect on the differential in yields between equities and fixed interest securities. Between 1970 and 1977, the dividend yield on equities moved between 3.1 and 4.4 per cent, putting equities at an investment disadvantage compared with bonds whose yields moved between 8 and 11 per cent over the same period. By 1979, for example, the yield on equities had risen to an average 5.4 per cent for the year, with an effective annuity interest of 8.5 per cent. At that time, the yield differential between bonds and equities had fallen to around 3 per cent compared to around 4.5 per cent before the tax reform.[22]

In 1978, the first year after the reform, the total sum of dividend paid came to DM3.9 billion. Tax-paying equity holders increased their real dividends in the year by 37.5 per cent. Table 3.10 shows the difference in costs of capital for bonds and equities as a result of the tax reform.

The relatively improved position of domestic investors as a result of the tax reform does not apply to foreign investors. Thus, for example, foreign investors not receiving a tax credit on top of their dividend payouts are still benefiting from the yield advantage of bonds. Even investment in a convertible bond with a low premium or none may still be a better purchase than equities.

There were some other side effects. The tax reform enabled some enterprises, which were previously organised in the form of sole proprietorships or partnerships, to convert themselves into private limited companies. This was attractive to owners since trade tax on earnings was saved if the amounts previously shown as profits now appeared in the profit and loss account under 'staff costs' and 'managers' salaries'. This may account for the large quantity of new issues in 1978 (DM6.5 billion). The Statistische Bundesamt estimated that the number of private limited companies rose by 21,200 (or 14 per cent) in 1977, and by 27,400 (or 16 per cent) in 1978, compared with an average increase of 11,100 (or 10.5 per cent) between 1971 and 1976.

Other prescriptions for stock market reform

There is a large amount of literature on improvements which could benefit the German Stock Exchanges. This is partly due to the lack of official initiatives in the last few years, and partly because, in many respects, the liberal character of the Exchanges has tended to cause practices not in the best interests of savers and investors. The role of the banks is an important element in the situation. As long as they remain major lenders to industry, and participate in the stock markets themselves, there is a tendency for the markets to compare unfavour-

Table 3.10
Comparative burden of taxes before and after
reform, bonds and equities (DM)

Expenses	Industrial bonds	Equity issues	
		Before tax reform and lower capital tax	After tax reform and lower capital tax
1 Cost, including provision for capital replacement:		Cost for equity listings of comparable size remains allowed for.	
(a) non-recurring costs:			
listing and bourse introduction costs	0.50		
(b) recurring costs:			
coupon detachment, renewal of coupon sheets, 0.25 per cent interest/dividend	0.02	0.02	0.02
Trustee fees 1 per cent per DM100 (bonds)	0.10		
2 Cost of capital utilisation	8.0	8.0	8.0
3 (a) Tax on equity holder before reform		2.6	
(b) Capital tax 1 per cent before reform lowered to 0.7 per cent		0.95	0.66
(c) Corporation tax on capital		1.05	0.84
(d) 0.6 per cent trading capital tax	0.57	0.57	0.57
(e) 15 per cent trading revenue tax	1.2	1.89	1.42
Total cost	10.39	15.08	11.51
Cost on capital of 100 DM	10.39	15.87	12.12

Source: M. Bierich, 'Die Finanzierung nach der Körperschaftsteuerreform', *Zeitschrift für das gesamte Kreditwesen*, January 1977.

ably with bank borrowing. However, to be fair, the banks in Germany would generally like to see the equity market flourish. Household savings rates are high in Germany, around 13–14 per cent of gross income. But although the State encourages saving and capital formation, the bulk of personal savings goes into bank accounts for security. The German people, despite the experience of the past, do not seem inflation-minded. Much saving is directed to property purchase – apartments and housing – and there are tax incentives to invest in building societies and insurance companies. This does not assist the equity market. It is also believed that in securities the Germans are interest-sensitive, so the relative earning abilities of bonds and equities are important to savers.

It has been pointed out that there is too little long term investment in the stock markets.[23] Investors tend to treat the markets too speculatively, holding securities for short periods only, or else hold securities unimaginatively. Even for the banks, investment in securities is 'ersatzdebitoren' (not real investment). This is in spite of Government concessionary premiums on saving in equities. It is believed that these premiums should be raised.

On the question of supervision of company information, the only State approval required for a public quotation of securities is the owner's name and written undertaking, according to articles 795 and 808a of the Code of Civil Law.[24] In other countries, there are supervisory agencies involved, e.g. Commission des Opérations de Bourse in Paris. It is a weakness of the German system. There are no rules for the first offering of public sales of securities, whereas for example in Belgium the Commission Bancaire examines prospectuses and dossiers and their integrity. For admission to listing, although the Börsenzulassungstellen requires a prospectus to be delivered, it does not examine the contents or validity of the statements made. Again this contrasts with the Comité de la Cote in Belgium, the Commission des Opérations de Bourse in Paris, and the Comissione Nazionale de la Società e le Borse in Milan. Internal control of the information concerning Exchange admissions in Germany could be tightened up for the benefit of investors.

Similarly, the extent of external supervision and control of company information in Germany is weak in comparison with other Community countries. Germany alone has no form of external control. On the other hand, there are rules on the publication of company turnover values, although the details and regularity required are rather less than among its Community partners (with the exception of Belgium, which has no general rules).

As for bourse trading and the oversight of bourse orders, the German Stock Exchanges exercise supervision through the Stock Exchange Acts, through the Laender Börsenkommissar, with no Bund authority involved, and generally this is satisfactory. On the regulation of the OTC market (ausserbörslichen Wertpapierhandels), there is little control. The Vermögensanlagengesetz (law relating to capital investment) oversees general conditions governing the issue of public securities, but not effectively. In the USA and France, control is more effective, and certainly Germany should move in this direction in view of the large volume of bonds traded OTC. On 'insider-trading', there is voluntary control, although the Prüfungskommission has powers to investigate and report. There is a general movement among the European Stock Exchanges to tighten up on the abuse of insider information in purchasing and selling shares: witness the strong recommendations of the FIBV and the European Commission's draft directive of 1976. The UK has incorporated stringent rules in its 1981 Company Law Act. It would be to the advantage of the German Exchanges to increase confidence of savers and investors by bringing in rules for closer scrutiny and penalties for insider trading and related practices.

The German Exchanges are stronger on the regulation of investment companies (mutual funds), which is fortunate, since their number and strength in the markets are formidable. Through the Bundesaufsichtamt für das Kreditwesen (BAK, Federal Office for Mutual Funds) registration is closely controlled, and BAK also requires half-yearly and yearly statements from the Funds. Also, through the Gesetz über die Kapitalanlagegesellschaften (KAGG, law relating to investment companies) and the BAK, as well as the Auslandsinvestmentgesetz (AIG, foreign investment law), there is good control of the investment companies' trading transactions.

Finally, it has been pointed out that companies' dividend policy could be improved.[25] There has been a tendency in the seventies to treat equities almost like bonds in terms of the inflexibility of dividends, and to 'secrete' rises in dividends within the company by stock capital adjustments and increases in equity capital. It increases the 'self-financing' power of companies, and is to some extent the result of poor information given out to holders of equity. A more flexible dividend policy, supported by Stock Exchange encouragement or legislation for listed companies, would be desirable.

Fiscal and other savings/investment incentives

The 1977 Corporation Tax Reform has already been described in detail, and its results seen to be favourable for the Stock Exchanges. In addition to this Act, Germany treats bonds more favourably than equities, e.g. there is a withholding tax on dividends (25 per cent) which acts against foreigners holding shares. But at the same time, the State allows concessions when the withholding tax is levied, ('Nicht-veranlagungsbescheinigung') (exemption voucher). Also it exempts income from capital as follows: DM300 plus DM100 exemption for expenses per year per person.

The Government, which encourages a wide range of savings instruments, gives premiums for saving in equities. They are subject to an annual savings ceiling of DM800 for single people and DM1600 for a married couple, and to a ceiling on the recipient's income (DM24,000 and DM48,000 respectively) and are graded according to the number of the recipient's children. To qualify, the equities must be held for either six or seven years. There is also a system of additional premiums, reserved for employees. In these cases, the employer makes payments to assist this investment in equities in the company. The premiums are available only to German residents. Income from equities held by employees in their own companies are not taxed as fully as ordinary income.

The Bund has produced statistics on the impact of the concessionary fiscal and subsidy measures it has taken to encourage savers to invest in equities. The proportion of premiums paid by the State relating to equities is between DM20 million and DM40 million a year, corresponding to DM50—100 million worth of equity purchases.

There are however some small restrictions on investment in Germany. By law, insurance companies may not hold more than 20 per cent of their actuarial reserves and 25 per cent of other technical reserves in investors' assets. They may not hold more than 5 per cent of the capital of a single company, and more than 4 per cent of actuarial reserves or 5 per cent of other technical reserves in equities listed on a foreign country's Stock Exchange.

Summary

The German economy enjoyed a relatively prosperous decade in the seventies. Even with the onset of recession, in 1979/80, its problems were not so intractable as most of its Community partners. It has an industrial structural problem, but Government policy is proving to be as sensitive in this crisis as it was in the earlier and easier years of high growth.

Typically, German company financing is high-geared and favours bank borrowing. This form of financing, which does not help strengthen the Stock Exchanges, becomes expensive and difficult in a recession. The German banks play a big role in the finance of companies, and even in their management, though some maintain this has been one reason for the high rate of Germany's economic growth.

The Federal and State Governments are major borrowers in the public sector, and the main lenders are the banks. In the Stock Exchanges bonds have been heavily favoured until the 1977 Company Law Act reduced some of their fiscal advantage.

The Stock Exchanges are elaborate in organisation, with a variety of sub-markets and borrowing instruments. Frankfurt and Düsseldorf together account for 80 per cent of the total turnover of the eight Exchanges. Fees on the Exchanges are not low. The clearing system is advanced and is anticipating international links. Supervision comes in for some criticism on a number of points, some of them structural, and some legal. The Exchanges seem liberally-orientated and managed, with the ethical standards of the banks providing much of the necessary integrity.

The performance of the equity markets has not been very impressive, less so than the general performance of the economy in the seventies would have led one to expect. Numbers of listed companies have fallen, and yields compare poorly with bond yields. The equity price index 1975 to 1980 is unexciting. The options market is still modest in size. The bond market (which is larger) has been more bullish, but is still small by international standards. According to a small number of statistical tests of efficiency, the Stock Exchanges are no better than 'weak-form efficient'.

Official innovations in structure and practice on the Exchanges have been timid. Only the 1977 Company Law Act and fiscal incentives outside the markets, technically speaking, have assisted savings and investment. But unofficial discussion of reforms has been widespread, particularly regarding the paucity of information available to investors, lack of strong surveillance of trading practices within the bourses, and the ambivalent role of the commercial banks in the markets. Nonetheless, the Government can point to a good record of fiscal and monetary assistance to savers and investors, which compares well with its Community partners.

Notes and references

1   *Deutsche Bundesbank Monthly Report*, vol.32, no.10.
2   Ibid.
3   L.M. Samuels, P.C. McMahon, *Savings and Investment in the United Kingdom and West Germany.*
4   Stein, Juergen, *The Banking System of the Federal Republic of Germany*, Bank-Verlag-Köln, 1977.
5   Stonham, Paul, *Study of Central Government Statistics in Member Governments of the European Community*, Report to the Statistical Office of the European Communities, Luxembourg 1978.
6   Frankfurt Stock Exchange, *1979 under Review.*
7   Frankfurt Stock Exchange, *History, Organisation, Function*, June 1980.
8   Schmidt, Hartmut, *Advantages and Disadvantages of an Integrated Market compared with a Fragmented Market*, Collection Studies, Competition—Approximation of Legislation Series no.30, Brussels, March 1977.

9   Commerzbank, *The German Bond Market*, Equity Research Department, Frankfurt, July 1980.

10   Information from Commerzbank, *The German Bond Market*, 1980; Deutsche Bank, *Form, Trading, and Administration of Securities*, 1976; Frankfurt Stock Exchange, *History, Organisation, Function*, 1980; Fédération Internationale des Bourses de Valeurs, *Commission Fees on FIBV Member Stock Exchanges*, 1979.

11   Delorme, Hermann, *Automation of Securities Transfers*, Frankfurt Stock Exchange, 1979.

12   Frankfurter Kassenverein Aktiengesellschaft, Wertpapiersammelbank, *Geschäftbericht für das 31 Geschäftsjahr 1979*.

13   Deutsche Auslandskassenverein Aktiengesellschaft, *Geschäftsbericht fur das 10 Geschäftsjahr, 1979*.

14   Delorme, Hermann, 'Mitglied des Vorstandes der Frankfurter Kassenverein Aktiengesellschaft', Die Deutsche Wertpapiersammelbanken, Knapp 1974.

15   Commerzbank, *Rum und die Börse*, 1977.

16   *A Survey of European Stock Exchanges in 1979* – a supplement to the Stock Exchange Fact Book, UK Stock Exchange, August 1980.

17   Solnik, B., 'A Note on the Validity of the Random Walk for European Stock Prices', *Journal of Finance*, vol.XXVIII, 1973.

18   Conrad, K., Jüttner, D.J., 'Recent Behaviour of Stock Market Prices in Germany and the Random Walk Hypothesis', *Kyklos*, no.26, 1973, pp. 576–99.

19   Guy, James, 'The Behaviour of Equity Securities on the German Stock Exchange', *Journal of Finance and Banking*, 1977, pp. 71-93.

20   Eichlet, Harald, 'Die Deutsche Börsen Reform', *Österreichisches Bank Archiv*, 1977, no.25, pp. 354–9.

21   Platt, C.J., *Tax Systems of Western Europe*, Gower Publications, 1980 (1st edition).

22   Report 1979, Rheinische-Westfälische Börse zu Düsseldorf.

23   Von Bargen, Malte, 'Strukturprobleme des Kapitalmarktes – Auswirkungen auf die Anlagepraxis', *Versicherungswirtschaft*, 1978, Jg.33, Heft 23, pp. 1442–6.

24   Much of the information for this section is contained in Schacht, Guido, *Die Deutsche Kapitalmarktaufsicht im Internationalen Vergleich*, Verlag V Florentz GmbH, München 1980.

25   Von Bargen, op.cit. (note 23).

4 Italy

Company financing

As early as 1975, the Banca Nazionale del Lavoro was writing about the weak balance sheet structures of Italian companies.[1] By 1977 corporate profits were still declining, a result, it was believed, of wages rising too fast and import-induced inflation adding to costs. At that time, rising wages were leading to the substitution of capital for labour, and loan-financed investment. As profits weakened, there was a tendency to seek other sources of external finance. Similarly, there grew a concentration of savings in the household sector as corporate profits dwindled. The result was increased bank lending, rising interest rates and higher company gearing. Table 4.1 shows some balance sheet ratios over the period 1968 to 1976 and indicates the general trend to greater indebtedness by the companies.

In all companies, average equity ratio (line 1) declined, and total debt to fixed assets (2) rose over the period, i.e. gearing increased steeply. Also, debt maturities shortened (3). Debt with the banks increased, reaching 46.5 per cent on average in 1976 (not shown in table).

OECD figures (Table 4.2) show how self-financing of total resources has fallen for all enterprises between 1967 and 1977 and how the share of resources devoted to investment has been falling too.

Retained earnings have fallen over the period (through lower profits), debt has increased steeply (especially short term to banks and other

Table 4.1
Italian corporations: trends in some relevant balance sheet ratios (figures in per cent)

Description	795 Corporations			Public sector			Private sector		
	1968	1972	1976	1968	1972	1976	1968	1972	1976
1 Owners' equity to total liabilities	20.7	15.3	14.5	18.1	12.9	14.6	22.5	17.4	14.5
2 Total debt to fixed assets	75.7	85.5	102.6	82.5	92.5	104.9	70.2	78.9	100.0
3 Funded debt to total debt	43.8	44.9	36.1	52.8	54.9	43.4	35.2	33.8	27.5
4 Cash flow to owners' equity	16.2	13.2	20.2	15.3	15.6	11.7	16.6	11.7	28.3

Source: *Italian Trends*, November 1977 (from Mediobanca, 'Dati cumulativi di 795 società italiane, 1968–76).

Table 4.2
Balance sheet sources and uses of funds of non-financial corporations (billion lire and per cent)

	1967	%	1972	%	1977	%
Sources	1,491		2,783		7,143	
1 Retained income*	677	45	990	35	1522	21
2 Short term debt (increase)	490	32	721	26	3169	44
3 Long term debt (increase)	261	17	723	26	1456	20
4 Bond issues	−31	−2	−33	−1	66	−1
5 Equity issues	94	6	383	13	931	13
Uses	1,491		2,783		7,143	
6 Investment in fixed assets and stocks	1,291	87	2440	88	4775	66
7 Increase in financial assets	199	13	623	22	2368	34

Source: OECD, Financial Statistics, 1979.

*Before depreciation and provisions.

Figures rounded.

credit institutions). Bond issues are negative (redemptions exceeded issues), and equity issues showed a small but noticeable increase. The picture on the use of financial resources is equally poor, showing a fall in fixed capital formation in 1977 (a year of cyclical upturn), and increasing 'financialisation' of companies.

It is useful to look in more detail at the source of external funds, and Table 4.3 does this.

Table 4.3
Structure of balance sheet liabilities and external financing
of companies (per cent)

		1965	1977 (year end)	1978
Debt:	short term	28.4	44.6	32.0
	medium and long term	21.1	30.7	36.1
(of which: special credit institutions)		(14.5)	(23.2)	(21.0)
Bonds		8.4	8.3	5.5
Equities and participations		37.8	10.3	11.0
Endowment funds (State groups' capital)		2.5	4.0	11.7
Finance by local organisations		0.9	2.1	3.7
		100	100	100

Source: Golzio, Silvio, 'Gli Investimenti in Italia — Loro Sviluppo e Finanziamento', *Bancaria*, June 1979; from Relazione del Governatore all'Assemblea dei Participanti, 1979, and Banca d'Italia, 1979.

The figures differ slightly from Table 4.2 since the breakdown is more detailed. Table 4.3 shows again the build-up in debt, but in 1978 there was a swing to longer term, a trend which has continued to date. Corporate borrowing by bonds (outstanding) has weakened, even in an up-turn year (1978), and borrowing by equities is low. Although still at low levels, borrowing from local 'Enti' is increasing.

To some extent, the mirror image of the trend in company borrowing can be seen in household saving patterns over the same period (Table 4.4).

The swing away from equity and bond investment to bank deposits is very noticeable, although 1978 saw an individual year's upturn. This has had the two-fold effect of reducing household savings and

Table 4.4
Annual household savings (per cent)

	1965	1977	1978
Cash	9.2	7.3	6.4
Cash deposits	30.0	55.4	50.7
Post Office deposits	9.8	9.3	9.8
Short-dated Treasury notes	–	2.8	7.3
Other deposits and interest bearing bonds	2.0	2.3	3.1
Fixed interest bonds	16.7	10.2	15.0
Equities*	17.5	0.7	1.3
Statistical residual	8.5	7.2	6.4
External assets	6.3	4.8	–
	100	100	100

Source: Golzio, Silvio, 'Gli Investimenti in Italia – Loro Sviluppo e Finanziamento', *Bancaria*, June 1979; from Relazione del Governatore all'Assemblea dei Participanti, 1979, and Banca d'Italia, 1979.

*In 1963, 24.6 per cent.

increasing the liquidity position of banks for lending to the corporate sector. Table 4.5 shows clearly the relationship between household savings and company debt and equity through coefficients, from 1970 to 1977.

The data in Table 4.5 show the ratio of M2 to household financial assets rising from 53 to 72 per cent between 1970 and 1977, the ratio of end-year total company indebtedness to total liabilities from 68 to 80 per cent, and that of equity issues to annual change in total liabilities from 15 to 8.5 per cent over the same period.

It is worth examining the State controlled companies separately, since the country's three largest — Ente Nazionale Idrocarburi (ENI), Istituto Riconstruzione Industriale (IRI) and Ente Particiipazione Finanziamento e Industria Manufattureria (EFIM) — employ some 0.7 million workers and account for around half the manufacturing output of large companies. Their special difficulties come from imported energy dependence, and following the oil price rises, inflation and high interest rates. Since 1973 none of these conglomerates has returned a profit, although EFIM (interests in aluminium engineering, defence

Table 4.5
Key ratios, financial situations of households and companies

Ratio	1970	1971	1972	1973	1974	1975	1976	1977
End-year company funds (M2) / Gross domestic product	28.7	30.8	34.3	35.1	31.4	31.6	30.7	30.8
Δ short term company debt / Δ company financial liabilities	37.0	22.2	32.9	29.2	49.4	39.1	53.2	45.8
Issues of equities / Δ company financial liabilities	15.4	11.1	12.6	12.3	6.6	8.7	9.0	8.5
Δ company indebtedness / gross domestic product	9.2	10.9	12.1	15.7	11.0	14.0	13.1	10.9
company indebtedness / company financial liabilities*	68.3	72.5	71.9	69.1	76.2	78.3	79.8	80.4
Δ household liquid assets (M2) / Δ household financial assets	65.1	59.3	63.6	75.7	94.9	76.8	82.6	80.5
household liquid assets (M2)* / household financial assets*	52.9	54.9	55.2	57.7	64.8	67.2	70.0	71.7

Source: Banca d'Italia, *Bolletino*, no.2−3, September 1978.

*End-year figures.

and tourism) is believed to have returned a small profit in 1980, and the group has forecast a surplus rising by 1983 to L135 billion. With IRI's interest primarily in shipping and steel, and ENI's in chemicals and textiles, their prospects are poorer.

After reaching a peak of investment in 1973, total fixed capital formation of these three groups fell by one-third in 1978. Since the 1979/80 rises in oil prices, the situation has worsened further. As a percentage of total industrial investment in Italy, this meant a fall from 34 in 1973 to 29 in 1981 (estimated), and as a percentage of

GDP, a fall from 3 in 1973 to 2 in 1981 (estimated).[2] Table 4.6 highlights some key financial information and coefficients for the three groups in 1978. The companies were suffering from low capitalisation and high indebtedness. In that year, for instance, interest charges on debt amounted to nearly 10 per cent of sales.

Table 4.6
Selected information on State controlled companies

Description	The three conglomerates			Consolidated totals
	IRI	ENI	EFIM	
1 *Major assets and liabilities in 1978*				
Fixed assets (bn. lire)	19.9	5.8	1.1	26.9
Owners' equity (bn. lire)	4.3	3.3	0.6	8.3
Total indebtedness (bn. lire)	21.1	7.6	1.4	30.0
2 *Results in 1978*				
Losses (bn. lire)	−1.1	−0.2	−0.1	−1.4
3 *Major coefficients in 1978* (%)				
Owners' equity to fixed assets	21.7	57.1	54.7	30.8
Interest charges to sales	n.a.	n.a.	n.a.	9.9
Losses to sales	−7.2	−1.1	−4.5	−4.4

Source: *Italian Trends*, December 1979; from Report of the Ministry of State Participations, November 1979.

Figures in lire rounded.

By early 1979, after eighteen months of relative boom, prime interest rates had fallen from 22 to 15 per cent, bank current and deposit accounts had contracted, and the Italian public was encouraged to invest in longer term bonds. Some companies borrowed on the Eurodollar market, and banks lent on variable interest, and leasing grew. Some large companies reduced debt by selling off property assets. The year 1978 saw new flows of money to quoted companies.[3]

Italy's financial system is complex, and the role of the banks, special credit institutions, and the Government in financing companies is important. In 1979 and 1980, there was strong though irregular demand for bank credit from companies, and some shift by households from bank deposits to Treasury bills. Lending by the special credit institutions and Government slowed down. Between 1978 and 1979 there was a 31 per cent increase in medium and long term lending by banks to enterprises. This was consistent with Government policy —

to reduce Treasury financing and establish a direct link with savers. Also, most banks were anxious to increase their high yielding loan business. But it is difficult to discover whether companies were borrowing to lengthen maturities or genuinely to finance new investment. The Banca d'Italia has kept ceilings on the banks' lending, not always consistently. Listed companies raised L11 billion more money in equity issues in 1979 than in 1977, but unfortunately, with issue prices above market valuation, most were taken up by underwriters. Unlisted State controlled companies also increased their issues. In 1977 and 1978, the Italian banks were persuaded by the Cossiga Government to form consortia to assist in refinancing and restructuring some large companies with intractable debt problems — Snia Viscosa, Società Italiana Resine, Liquigas, Montefiore (Montedison) and Pirelli. The banks' technique was to use their liquid assets to invest directly in equities of these companies in exchange for debt claims. There were some tax benefits. Some consortium rescue attempts have been successful, e.g. Pirelli and Snia Viscosa. Liquigas and Società Italiana Resine failed.

Although in 1979 funds flowing to the private corporate sector from special credit institutions and the bond market increased, the public sector still funded companies at a rate of about one-quarter of their requirements. Much of this latter funding was to loss making enterprises.

Government and local authority financing

In 1977 an Act of the Italian Senate legalised the use of a wider definition of the public sector in the publication of national statistics. This was to include, as well as the central government, all the many governmental and semi-governmental agencies within the public sector. For purposes of calculating the borrowing requirement, this 'enlarged public sector' (fabbisogno complessivo) is now in use, alongside three other less comprehensive measures of the public sector. Briefly, the definitions are as follows:[4]

1 General government cash borrowing requirement (central government, social security institutions, hospital and local authorities).

2 'Enlarged public sector', excluding financial operations (disavanzo), but including general government plus autonomous agencies, e.g. railways, electricity.

3 (2) plus financial operations (fabbisogno), i.e. grants to specialised credit institutions, State participations and local authority bank lending.

4   'Fabbisogno complessivo', i.e. (3) plus outstanding debts.

The Government has made retrospective changes in accounts to 1976, but there is still some confusion in the use of the statistics in the various publications emanating from Government and unofficial sources.

The Italian Government now tends to make more use of the concept of public sector borrowing requirement than deficit spending. It conforms with definition (2) above in terms of Italian budgetary statistics. The OECD definition of PSBR is the difference between actual cash payments and receipts of Government, autonomous agencies and social security, plus net debit and credit transactions of the public sector, including the purchase of equities and participations. Table 4.7 sets out the State sector borrowing requirement and its financing for 1977, 1978 and 1979, using data from the latest Banca d'Italia Annual Report (May 1980 for 1979). The borrowing requirement here includes autonomous agencies etc. and corresponds with definition (2) above.

The public sector borrowing requirement declined between 1978 and 1979, due mainly to trends in financial transactions — a reduction in the rate of growth of the sector's bank deposits, and reduction in transfers to public enterprises. The two years' PSBRs are closer when net debts are taken into account. During 1979, there was a change in the pattern of holding bills and bonds.

In 1980, the PSBR was estimated at L37,800 billion, the increase being expected to result from high current Government spending, particularly interest payments, indexed social transfers, and public consumption through indexed wage payments with high inflation. Public investment was expected to stagnate. The Italian Government's main financial problem is high public consumption and low investment spending. Tax revenue is difficult to collect, and the Government is torn between money creation and borrowing to fulfil its PSBR.

The Government borrows heavily in the domestic capital market. In 1978 and 1979, the gross totals of Government securities issued at nominal value were L173,562 billion and L198,209 billion, compared with equities at L31,234 billion and L40,885 billion. Net issues were both down between the two years, L31,383 billion to L23,910 billion for Government securities, and L2,984 billion to L2,732 billion for equities. The fall in bond issues resulted from companies' switch to bank loans, and the temporary slackening in PSBR. It is still true, however, even after the huge leap in secondary turnover of equities in the last half of 1980, that Government securities dominate the market for new issues. The switch in investors' preferences from long-dated to short-dated Government securities, observed in 1979, became more pronounced in 1980. The variable-coupon Treasury credit certificates

Table 4.7
State sector borrowing requirement and its financing
(calendar years, cash basis, lire thousand billion)

	1977	1978	1979	1980 (1st quarter)
Total borrowing requirement (net disbursements)				
Budget	-12.4	-33.4	-30.4	-0.1
Minor Treasury operations	.02	3.3	2.4	-4.0
Central PO fund, autonomous agencies, etc.	-10.0	-4.1	-2.0	-0.3
Total (PSBR)	-22.4	-34.2	-30.0	-4.4
of which: repayment of public agency debts in securities	-4.7	-1.8	-0.06	–
Requirement less repayment of debts in securities	-17.7	-32.4	-30.0	-4.4
of which: repayment of public agency debt in cash	-0.6	-3.4	-0.7	–
Financing of total borrowing requirement				
Medium and long term bonds excluding BI portfolio	8.0	14.4	12.1	-2.4
Treasury bills, excluding BI portfolio	15.2	9.5	10.1	5.1
PO savings	3.2	4.8	6.6	1.5
Borrowings from BI–UIC	-4.0	5.0	0.3	0.1
Borrowing abroad	–	0.2	0.6	-0.2
Other borrowing	–	0.2	0.3	0.9
Total	22.4	34.2	30.0	4.4
of which domestic financing: short term	14.4	19.6	17.2	6.8
(of which 'Treasury' monetary base creation)	-0.8	10.2	7.1	1.8
medium and long term	8.0	14.3	12.2	-2.4

Source: Banca d'Italia, *Report for the Year 1979*, 1980.

Figures rounded.

were particularly popular with non-bank investors, who acquired more than one-half of the certificates and straight Treasury bills in circulation. Yields on Treasury paper are tax free, and prime interest rates were raised in 1980; in May 1981 prime lending rate reached a record 19.75 per cent. Treasury bills are low risk, and clearly crowd out corporate paper; the rate in May 1981 was 20 per cent.

The expectation for PSBR in 1981 was originally estimated at over L40,000 billion, but with inflation running at over 24 per cent, and substantial public funds needed for State controlled industry, the Government followed the March 1981 devaluation of the lira and lift in interest rates with a L5,000 billion cut in PSBR to be financed by higher social security charges and cuts in public consumption spending. There is little doubt that the domestic capital market will be used even more fully by the Government in future to finance its way out of difficulty.

Structure and practice of the Italian stock market

Organisation

There are ten Exchanges in Italy: Milan, Rome, Turin, Genoa, Florence, Bologna, Naples, Venice, Trieste and Palermo. Milan handles the overwhelming volume of deals, around 70—80 per cent of securities traded through the Exchanges. In the future, Milan is likely to obtain even higher proportions of Stock Exchange business as the banks and other financial institutions are tending to gravitate there. Hence the Milan bourse will be taken here as synonymous with the Italian stock market.

The Milan Stock Exchange, like the others, is a public institution established by decree (decreto) of the President of the Italian Republic, under the Civil Code, and ultimately the administrative and political responsibility of the Minister of the Treasury, with the co-operation of the Interministerial Committee for Credit and Savings.

The main bodies concerned with the management and supervision of the Exchange are Camera di Commercio (Chamber of Commerce), Deputazione de Borsa (Stock Exchange Council), Comitato Direttivo degli Agenti di Cambio (Management Committee of Stockbrokers), Ordine degli Agenti di Cambio e Consiglio Nazionale degli Agenti (Association of Stockbrokers and National Council of Stockbrokers) and the Commissione Nazionale per la Società e la Borsa (CONSOB) (National Commission for the Stock Exchange).

The Chamber of Commerce has authority over the admission of securities to listing, the right to demand information on the financial solvency of listed companies, to stop or suspend the Stock Exchange, and to revoke the admission of a security to listing. These are legal duties defined by law. The Chamber of Commerce must provide an official for these purposes. With the establishment of CONSOB in June 1974, the Chamber has some other functions delegated to it: the right to obtain information on insolvencies etc. from agenti di cambio and keeping an up-to-date list of agenti. But in practice the important powers are becoming centralised on CONSOB.

The Council of the Bourse is responsible for policing the bourse, maintaining its rules and regulations, and other similar functions, some delegated by CONSOB. Members are appointed annually by the Minister for the Treasury and the Chamber of Commerce.

Members of the Management Committee of stockbrokers are elected for two years from among themselves. Between four and eight representatives are elected. The Committee is responsible for the correct technical functioning of the Stock Exchange, and more recently has been encouraged to promote the business of the Stock Exchange. The Management Committee has delegated to it by CONSOB the administration of the guarantee fund of the brokers, powers to intervene in cases of insolvency or liquidation to maintain continuity in the market, to keep the CONSOB informed on the situation in State bonds, and to deposit with CONSOB the books of defunct brokers. Other functions are to intervene in transactions when bond prices move by 10 per cent and equity prices by 20 per cent — such prices can be disallowed by the Management Committee. It also has certain disciplinary powers, e.g. deciding when a quotation is 'tel-quel' or ex-dividend.

The law setting up the professional association of agenti di cambio dates from June 1967, giving the brokers certain powers as intermediaries in the Stock Exchange. They are responsible to the Minister of the Treasury, CONSOB and the Consiglio Nazionale. Brokers are public officials, and their number is fixed by the Minister for the Treasury. They trade in 'recinto' (rings) by the method of 'la grida', calling out bids and offers on behalf of clients until an equilibrium price is reached. Stockbrokers must commit themselves exclusively to the business, and must trade on the floor themselves or through representatives. They may not be equity holders in clients' organisations, banks or companies, and they are obliged to maintain professional secrecy. In particular, they are not allowed to trade either on their own account or through intermediaries.

Other persons are admitted to the Exchange floor on certain payments, as observers with no trading privileges. This concession is taken up by banks and credit institutions. Apart from the 'mercato ristretto' (regulated over-the-counter market), which is dealt with in detail below, a good deal of trading in securities goes on between banks outside the Exchange, by telephone and interbank deals, and also 'in-house' trading. There is some control by the Stock Exchange, but it is limited. The Minister of the Treasury has extensive powers over the Stock Exchange. His primary powers are the right to close or suspend the Exchange, suspend forward deals and fix the cover required (either in securities or cash) for these transactions, and for options and contango deals.

In addition, the Minister appoints inspectors who attend meetings of the Stock Exchange Council and brokers' meetings, act as chairmen of the Listing Committee, and generally supervise business on the Stock Exchange floor.

Apart from appointing inspectors, the Minister of the Treasury has further powerful rights, for example, to fix the number of brokers, and suspend them if necessary, ratify Chamber of Commerce decisions, fix commission rates, opening hours and the calendar, and arrange for the quotation of foreign government bonds. With the establishment of CONSOB in 1974, however, the latter has taken over many of the specific powers of the Minister, leaving him with supervisory powers of a more general nature.

The Commissione Nazionale per la Società e la Borsa is dealt with more fully later. It is worth noting here though that CONSOB has taken over the powers previously exercised by the Listing Committee.

Types of markets

There are 'spot' markets for equities and bonds, 'forward' markets for equities, and a market for 'options'. In addition there is a 'mercato ristretto' (regulated OTC market) where separately listed securities are traded. There is also a market for trading in foreign currency. The first three markets are straightforward and self-explanatory.

The mercato ristretto (mercantino) was completely unrestricted in terms of control by the Chamber of Commerce and Treasury until Law No.49 of February 1977. From this time, a legal framework was established, setting out rules of trading to which the market must conform. It is now under the authority of CONSOB, the Chamber of Commerce, and the Association of Brokers. Dealings are subject to the 'grida' system, i.e. they must take place through a broker. CONSOB can seek information on the administration of securities. The mercato ristretto may be obliged to transform into a 'mercato di acclimatazione' i.e. it should aim at adopting as many rules and procedures as exist on the official Exchange. There are several other rules tightening up the ristretto, e.g. a 'Comitato de Mercato Ristretto' has been established, whose members are nominated by CONSOB, credit institutions and the Chamber of Commerce. This Committee has assumed certain responsibilities, e.g. for publication of the List, regulating meetings, and overseeing admission of securities. A prospectus must be published, and a minimum of owners' capital must be invested in any security admitted. In short, the mercato ristretto is now much more like the Official Exchange and its procedures more rigorously established. Prices must be published, e.g. in '24 Ore' as 'Prezzi Informativi a Milano di Titolo Non Quotati Ufficialmente in Borsa o al Ristretto' (prices published in Milan of unlisted securities in the Stock Exchange or unofficial market), and 'Prezzi Informativi Rilevati fuori Borsa a Milano di alcune obbligazione Non-Quotate Ufficialmente' (prices published relative to Milan of any unofficially quoted bond).

Types of securities

Bonds

1. State bonds: (a) consolidated (dividend paid on paid-up capital); (b) Prestiti redimibile (loans with second maturities, and some with medium term maturities, e.g. short term Treasury bonds, Treasury certificates of credit, etc.).

2. State-guaranteed bonds: (a) bonds issued by autonomous agencies; (b) 'Cartelle fondiare' (continuously issued paper by mutual funds, carrying pre-determined maturities).

3. Corporate bonds: many different types, e.g. convertible, ordinary, nominal sample and dividend sample, etc. Bonds are always in bearer form.

Equities

Ordinary and preference, and savings equities, cumulative preference. Savings equities attract tax concessions similar to bonds. Equities of all varieties must be registered, by law.

Trading procedures: orders, price determination, delivery and settlement

Orders may be 'ordine al meglio' (at best) and are carried out in the current session if it is possible. 'L'ordine curando' (at discretion) and 'ordine limitato' (limited order) are carried out by the broker in the current session as he believes most appropriate. A variant on the 'ordine limitato' is 'debordant'. In this case, the broker may depart from the strict limit on price if circumstances suggest it is preferable; it is an 'uncovered order'. Further variations on purchases and sales at limited price are 'circa' (execution of order at price indicated, plus or minus commission); 'piccolo circa' and 'largo circa' and 'il doppio' are, as their names imply, instructions to vary by small or large amounts or double the 'circa' tolerance. As far as guarantees to clients are concerned, these may be 'simplice' (simple) or 'scarto a mantenersi' (refuse to keep) — in which case the broker can liquidate the client's position.

With regard to the way prices are determined, for bonds there is one price fixing per day, for equities mostly two, but sometimes several. Prices are fixed in an auction manner, and brokers call out bids or offers within their 'ring' or 'gride', as a 'commissionario' calls out each security in turn. Bonds are dealt for cash, equities for an account day. Option deals are common and are available for periods of up to three months. Bonds are dealt in nominal amounts with a per cent quotation. Equities are quoted 'tel quel' (i.e. coupon attached).

On delivery and settlement, the Stock Exchange has arranged a calendar, which is uniform throughout the Italian stock markets for the settlement of future contracts. Briefly, the order is as follows: (i) 'Risposta premi' (first reply), (ii) 'Riporto' (contango), (iii) 'Compensi' (last day to settle after which compensation is due), (iv) 'Spunta' (account checking), (v) 'Consegua foli' (delivery of financial balance), (vi) 'Correzione degli errori' (verification of title etc. by the 'Stanza di Compensazione' (clearing house), (vii) 'Consegua titoli' (delivery of notes to the Stanza by vendor), (viii) 'Liquidazione' (settlement — balances paid).[5]

Listing and transactions expenses

All issues of securities must be authorised, either by the Banca d'Italia, or by the Treasury when the amount exceeds a certain minimum. Securities are usually offered to the public by selling to groups consisting of credit institutions or banks, which have prior authorisation. State securities are handled by a banking syndicate managed by the Banca d'Italia. Barriers to listing securities are psychological rather than financial. A company seeking listing must pass certain documents on its financial position to CONSOB (but the degree of disclosure is not onerous), and the company must have a minimum size of capital (L1,000 million) and reserves (L500 million). Its net assets must total at least L50,000. Listing fees are generally small, and the enrolment fee is variable according to the size of company, i.e. proportional to capital.

Expenses are made up of brokers' commission, stamp duty, VAT, and banks' commissions if banks are used as intermediaries. Brokers' commissions are currently (1981) as follows:

Cash transactions

    (a) Government securities: 0.15 per cent of nominal value.

    (b) Debentures and bonds: 0.30 per cent of nominal value.

        (minimum commission: Lire 2,000)

(c) Equities: only equities traded on the regulated over-the-counter market and foreign listed equities are transacted for cash. Commission is as for forward transactions.

Forward transactions
(a) Convertible bonds: 0.30 per cent of market or nominal value (whichever is the greater).
(b) Equities (average of): 0.7 per cent of market value (minimum commission L2,000).

Contangoes
The commission fee, which is 1 per cent is added to the interest rate established by the banks. Both rates are variable.

Options
Half of the normal equity commission fee is charged for put and call options.

Commission sharing
Banks, commission agents, investment and nominee companies and mutual funds are granted reduced commission fees. In principle, foreign stockbrokers may also be conceded a share of the commission fee charged up to a maximum of 50 per cent of the amount. But foreign banks usually receive no concession.

Stamp duty on officially listed Italian security transactions is as follows: Government notes L2.5, bonds L5/L7.5, equities L12.50/L18.75, carry-overs L10/20/30. These rates apply to every L100,000 (or fraction) of market value of transactions. The two rates for bonds and equities refer to cash and future terms. VAT on consultancy etc. is 14 per cent.[6] Fees on the 'Mercantino' are very low.

Clearing
Clearing is effected through a clearing agent or house (Stanza di Compensazione) to which each broker reports his position. In addition, the Milan Exchange maintains a computer centre for all stock market bookkeeping of the members of the Genoa, Milan, Rome and Turin Exchanges. The computer centre does not handle the transfer of bonds, however. There are in fact ten clearing houses in Italy for the respective Exchanges, the Milanese one being located in the Banca d'Italia. A new system is in the process of being set up, the 'Monte Titoli', but although it is programmed to begin in late 1981, it will not handle all equities or all bonds. In fact, the current situation is that most transactions in securities are still settled in cash, and cleared at the end of each month.

Supervision

The Commissione Nazionale per la Societa e La Borsa (CONSOB) has been mentioned briefly already. With the decision to establish it in law in 1974, the Stock Exchanges in Italy were placed, for the first time, under the control of a professional single supervisory organisation with (theoretically) far-ranging powers. It has responsibility primarily for the protection of security holders (by the supervision of listed companies) and for management of the Stock Exchanges and control of the dealers themselves. In these respects, CONSOB has acquired many of the supervisory powers previously exercised by such bodies as the local Chambers of Commerce, the erstwhile Listing Committees, Stock Exchange Councils, brokers, and the Treasury. However, CONSOB itself has the power to delegate some of its responsibilities as it deems appropriate, and in fact it has done this. It can request its own officers to be seconded to Stock Exchanges as 'Stock Exchange inspectors', where they have tended to take over the roles previously exercised by the Treasury inspectors.

One of CONSOB's most practical day-to-day powers is that of formally calling for brokers' books and inspecting them, as well as relevant documents and accounts of credit institutions and public bodies, with the prior consent of the Banca d'Italia. Generally, if CONSOB detects irregularities in documents or practice in the Stock Exchanges, it will report it to the relevant public body concerned with sanction, e.g. the Banca d'Italia for credit institutions, or the Ministry of State Participations. But in addition to surveillance proper, CONSOB has administrative responsibilities, e.g. for determining the conditions for listing securities, such as the disclosure of information necessary, or the minimum financial requirements for listing companies.

In many respects, however, CONSOB has weaker practical powers than its counterparts in other member states of the Community. It cannot insist on such full disclosure of company information. Accounting and auditing rules are weaker, there are no rules on prospectuses issued to the general public, and it has little or no powers over security transactions outside the Stock Exchanges proper. Rules on take-overs and mergers exist, but they are not very productive. CONSOB has discussed insider trading, but in the Italian context this is very difficult to detect or prevent, and there are no specific rules.

Evaluation

There are plainly many external factors hindering the development of the Italian Stock Exchanges, and of Milan in particular as the centre of operations. Not much can be done, from a Stock Exchange point of view, about widespread tax evasion, a high propensity for household savings which is almost completely risk-averse, companies' preference for bank borrowing, poor company profitability, large State controlled corporations existing on direct Government grants, excessive Government consumption spending to the detriment of investment, itself partly caused by the 'Scala Mobile', and so on. The Milan Stock Exchange does not function in an external commercial or political climate that favours its steady growth and the encouragement of savings and borrowing through the instrument of the equity on an official stock market. Only a small proportion even of large companies has their securities listed on the Exchange, and there is a far more marked absence of small and medium sized companies. The level of annual new issues of company securities is low. On the lending side, much is institutional, but much more bypasses the Stock Exchange altogether.

However, the present structure and practice of the Stock Exchange in Milan could be improved in several areas without undue difficulty. Some of the large scale problems were identified by the Italian Senate Inquiry of 1978, and reforms suggested. These are discussed later. But mere comparison with the experience of contemporary Stock Exchanges in other Community countries suggests improvements in technical efficiency which could be made within the Exchange framework itself. Since the list is rather extensive, detailed treatment will be left to a later section, and here a catalogue is drawn up of some of the weaknesses leading to under-performance.

Supervision of Stock Exchange trading is inadequate and fragmented. Although with the creation of CONSOB a certain amount of centralisation of surveillance has taken place, its powers still overlap with other bodies, its own legal powers are limited, e.g. on sanctions, and its actual performance in the first seven years has been disappointing. The area of transfer of control of companies is poorly covered by the regulations. The fact that CONSOB's offices are in Rome, and the major Stock Exchange in Milan, is illustrative.

The Stock Exchanges outside Milan do nothing to encourage savers and borrowers to come to the securities markets. They are all far too small to be of interest.

Brokers are not allowed to make prices on their own account. It reduces the liquidity of the market, although at the present time Italian brokers do not have sufficient owned-funds to take up such positions anyway. In practice, some brokers do act as 'jobbers' if they are backed by banks, but it is illegal. There is too much emphasis on account trading and too little on cash. Trading for account should also be speeded up. The position of the banks in security dealing is ambiguous. They are not permitted to trade on the floor, but being large lenders and borrowers, and powerful institutions in the flow of funds, particularly in term lending to companies, they tend to trade blocks of securities off the Exchange anyway.

Although the modified auction system of trading is well thought of elsewhere, it does not work well in Milan. Non-continuous pricing does not clear bids and offers well, and in fact the level of noise on the trading floor on a busy lunch-time is disruptive. Ordering techniques are over-elaborate, delivery of notes and settlement slow. Clearing is improved by computer handling, but this is only voluntary.

Disclosure of information at time of listing is inadequate for analysis by prospective equity holders, and accounting and auditing standards variable. Listing and transacting costs are modest, but stamp duty is heavy, and small margins on commissions lower the quality of broker-age services. Research and analysis by the Statistics Department of the Comitato Direttivo degli Agenti di Cambio is outstanding, but the data are weak. Bonds and equities are not treated equally on fiscal grounds, and the Government issues stock in a jerky fashion, upsetting prices and crowding out equities. The 'Mercantino' is livelier, but the present policy of partially clipping its wings has increased expenses without increasing efficiency. Far too little information on companies' financial positions is made available, and much of this is based on doubtful accounting.

These are some of the weaknesses in current structure, practice and organisation, and it is sad that the list is so long. However, the 1980/81 bull market was not entirely speculative, and contained seeds of genuine investor 'buy and hold' interest. There is reason to hope that the Milan Stock Exchange may organise itself more effectively in the near future. Some of the proposed reforms are discussed later.

Performance and efficiency of the Milan Stock Exchange

Although in late 1980 and early 1981 the Milan General Index of Equity Prices (Base 1979) showed a dramatic rise and then fall, a longer view of the Stock Exchange shows a picture that is generally inactive.

The equity market

Table 4.8 shows the change in the number of equities listed on the Milan Stock Exchange, and the nominal value of capital from 1960 to 1979 (1960 = 100).

Over a period of nineteen years, the number of equities listed increased by only twenty-six, and in fact delistings exceeded new listings from 1977 onwards. In May 1981, listings totalled 162. The growth in capitalisation of equity in the Exchange was also slow, rising from L2,496 million in 1960 to L7,838 in 1979, only just over three times.

Table 4.8
Equities in the official list of the Milan Stock Exchange, 1960–79

End of year figures	Equities	
	Number of equities listed (index 1960 = 100)	Total par value in thousand million Lire
1960	145 (100)	2,496 (100)
1965	138 (95.2)	3,324 (133.2)
1970	144 (99.3)	4,012 (160.7)
1975	171 (117.9) (a)	4,650 (186.3) (*)
1976	173 (119.3) (b)	4,559 (182.7) (*)
1977	178 (122.8) (c)	4,544 (182.1) (*)
1978	174 (120.0) (d)	7,360 (294.9) (*)
1979	171 (117.9) (e)	7,838 (314.0) (*)

Source: Comitato Direttivo degli Agenti di Cambio, *Rapporto Annuale*, 1979.

(a)   Including 2 suspended equities.
(b)   Including 4 suspended equities.
(c)   Including 10 suspended equities.
(d)   Including 9 suspended equities.
(e)   Including 7 suspended equities.
(*)   Excluding the par value of suspended equities.

By comparison over the same period, the number of listed fixed interest securities rose by 556, and total par value by L81,659 million. The years 1978 and 1979 were better for equities — average capitalisation per company on listed equities nearly doubled — and 1980 was a further year of growth.

Further analysis of listings of equities shows that from end-year 1963 to end-year 1979, although the number of listings increased by 21, from 150 to 171, net variations among 15 major sectors of industry showed 22 delistings by electrical companies, and 8 by textiles. Each other sector of industry showed small positive movement.

The big rise in equity capital in 1978 and 1979, measured either by par value or market value, and despite the reducing number of companies listed, was because firms connected with the issuing companies underwrote listed companies' equities, paying the cost of the premium at which they stood above market quotation. That is, rising equity prices were probably not the reason for the total increase in equity capital. This is substantiated by the figures in Table 4.9, which show a long term rise in the proportion of equities held in company portfolios, and a decline in that held by the general public.

There was an uninterrupted increase in the proportion of equities

Table 4.9
Equity capital by class of investor
(amounts at end year, percentage breakdown, total in billions of Lire)

Investor	Yearly average 1965–75	1976	1977	1978	1979
The public	30.1	25.0	25.6	21.1	16.9
Companies	48.4	56.4	57.5	63.1	68.9
Foreign sector	18.0	12.9	11.9	10.8	9.2
Banking system	1.7	3.4	2.9	3.0	3.3
Other financial intermediaries	1.8	2.3	2.1	2.0	1.7
Total	100.0	100.0	100.0	100.0	100.0
Listed	32.2	23.4	25.1	26.5	20.4
Unlisted	67.8	76.6	74.9	73.5	79.6
Total equity capital at market value	20,774	37,298	35,723	52,019	68,074

Source: Banca d'Italia, *Annual Report*, 1980.

held in companies' total assets, at the expense of the general public. Between 1976 and 1979 the swing amounted to a rise of 12.5 and a fall of 13.2 per cent respectively. The other trend was for unlisted State controlled companies to make more new issues, in contrast with listed smaller companies over the period.

More recent figures for equity turnover show the considerable rise in 1978 and 1979 mirrored by figures for capitalisation. Table 4.10 shows turnover by volume and value to mid-1980.

Table 4.10
Listed Italian equities: total trading volume and value

Period	Number of equities traded	Value of turnover (million Lire)
1978	2,219,010,505	1,583,410
1979	3,712,140,526	2,871,144
1980 (Jan.–June)	1,817,412,489	1,990,191

Source: Mediobanca, *Indici e Dati Relativi ad Investimenti in Titoli Quotati Nelle Borse Italiane*, 1980.

The table shows the beginning of the bull market in 1980, following on strong growth in 1978 and 1979. Whereas in 1979 the market value of equities traded ranged between L107.4 billion and L429.8 billion per calendar month, the value of trading in late 1980 shot up to between L40 billion and L50 billion *a day*.

In terms of the index of equity prices on the Milan Stock Exchange, and corresponding yields, the long run Milan general index for equities shows a depressing picture for all but the very recent past (see Table 4.11).

Table 4.11
Price index and net yield on equities

	1958	1972	1973	1974	1975	1976	1977	1978	1979	1980 (July)
(Mean) Index (1958 = 100)	100	126.5	163.4	149.5	111.0	91.5	73.7	75.2	92.2	105.2
Yield (%)	5.24	3.40	2.50	2.95	4.89	4.15	4.58	4.91	3.18	2.73

Source: Adapted from Banca d'Italia, *Bolletino*, June/July 1980.

But there are well known statistical problems in long series of prices. Re-based at 1975 and including 1981 as well (to May) an equity price index behaved as shown in Table 4.12.

Table 4.12
Price index on equities (1975 = 1000)

	1978	1979	1980	1981
Index at February each year	700	900	1220	3100

Source: Comitato Direttivo degli Agenti di Cambio (CDAC Index).

The rapid rise in early 1981 is apparent, most of it occurring from June 1980 onwards. Using another index, that of the Banca Commerciale Italiana (1972 = 100), Milan equity prices rose 56 per cent between January and end-April 1981, compared with a 107 per cent rise in 1980. From 6 January 1980 to 30 April 1981, the BCI index recorded a massive rise from 82 points to 271. The Milan Stock Exchange was a bull market for equities until June 1981, when a drastic fall occurred.

However, this more recent performance has both negative and positive elements. On the minus side, the 1981 bull market started from a low base, and was preceded by several years of stagnation. The equity market benefited from a reduction in competition from comparable investment outlets at a time when annual inflation in 1981 ran at 24 per cent. Also, the tight credit squeeze directed bank money towards the Stock Exchange. At the beginning of 1981, the Interbank (one month) rate was 17 per cent, banks were paying deposit rates of around 11 per cent, Government stock was yielding 17.5 per cent, and average equity yields were around 1.4 per cent. The last figure reflects the general unwillingness of Italian companies to remunerate minority equity holders properly through dividend pay-outs. But many equities shot up in price from June 1980 onwards. Bank equity prices nearly doubled in the first three months of 1981. In one month, from mid-January to mid-February, the Banca di Roma equity stock recorded a 29 per cent rise in price, Banca Commerciale Italiana 24 per cent, and Credito Italiano 21 per cent. Industrial equity prices moved up fast too. In the month mentioned, Montedison (chemicals) rose by 21 per cent, and even Finsider (steel) by 13 per cent. But it must be recalled that only a small part of the total of Italian companies are listed on the Exchange, and of those which are, many are dormant. In 1981, twenty companies' equity provided 70 per cent of the value of turnover. To some extent, buying was concentrated on a small number of equities, and thereby fuelled rapid price rises.

The positive aspects of recent performance are that more and more companies are reporting increased earnings and sales, despite the general move of the Italian economy deeper into recession. The corporate sector is benefiting from restructuring its financial position. For example, Rinascente, Italy's leading stores group, returned a profit of L15 billion for 1980, the first profit returned since 1974, with inflation-adjusted sales up 3 per cent, and the store is planning a capital increase. Pirelli, the very large private tyre and cables group, employing 30,000 people, made a profit for the first time in ten years in 1980. A major factor was its financial restructuring programme, which took its equity capital from L65 billion to L173 billion, partly by self-financing and selling off assets, converting short term bank loans into medium term, and increasing bank borrowing from a syndicate. It is also launching a L50 billion new equity issue through rights, and L50 billion in convertible bonds on the Milan Stock Exchange.

The bond market

It has already been pointed out that the Government is a strong presence in the Stock Exchange, with its requirements to fund PSBR.

Table 4.13 shows the growth of bonds in the official list of the Milan Stock Exchange.

Table 4.13

Bonds in the official list of the Milan Stock Exchange

End of year	Number of bonds (index, 1960 = 100)	Total par value in thousand million Lire (index, 1960 = 100)
1960	283 (100)	4,943 (100)
1965	359 (126.9)	9,645 (195.1)
1970	467 (165)	32,277 (653)
1975	638 (225.4)	44,884 (908)
1976	690 (243.8)	52,924 (1,070.7)
1977	731 (258.3)	59,178 (1,197.2)
1978	782 (276.3)	77,401 (1,565.9)
1979	839 (296.5)	86,602 (1,752.0)

Source: Comitato Direttivo degli Agenti di Cambio, *Rapporto Annuele*, 1979.

The fast growth of bond issues and increases in capitalisation are readily apparent. In 1979, although gross capitalisation of bonds increased, net issues of Government stock fell over the year (from L25.634 billion to L14.517 billion). The main reason was greater company borrowing from banks, and a decline in the PSBR. The year 1979 saw the continuation of an earlier trend: a switch by households to Treasury bills and Treasury credit certificates, i.e. toward Government stock with shorter maturities. In 1979 these notes accounted for 82 per cent of total net issues and 73 per cent of total net investment of the public and banks, compared with 49 and 53 per cent in 1978.[7]

Table 4.14 shows the composition of new Government stock issues in comparison with that of equities.

Several trends are apparent; the dramatic fall, almost to zero, in corporate bonds, the rapid rise in State and Treasury notes (particularly bills and certificates), and greatly increasing ratio of bond/equities — from 1.5:1 in 1970 to 9.1:1 in 1979. All these trends continued into 1980 and 1981. If State bonds are considered in isolation, i.e. not the enlarged public sector, the switch from long matury holdings to short maturity holdings is clear (see Table 4.15).

There has been a steady rise in certificates of credit and, in 1979, in Treasury bills, and a corresponding fall, in 1979, in longer dated

Table 4.14
New issues of bonds (percentage composition)

Year	BOT*	State and Treasury	Credit Institutions	Public bodies	Private companies	Total	Total bonds	Equities	Bonds/equities
1950	43.5	35.2	10.3	2.8	8.2	100.0	1.9	1.5	1.23
1962	20.1	28.8	38.8	8.1	9.6	100.0	10.0	18.9	0.5
1970	7.1	35.5	39.2	14.3	3.9	100.0	30.9	20.3	1.5
1974	18.4	32.3	37.8	9.8	1.7	100.0	71.2	25.5	2.8
1975	21.6	31.9	36.0	9.1	1.4	100.0	92.8	21.0	4.4
1976	25.2	30.1	34.9	8.5	1.3	100.0	111.0	21.0	5.4
1977	23.6	36.2	31.5	7.6	1.1	100.0	140.2	18.6	7.5
1978	22.1	41.1	28.7	6.8	1.3	100.0	173.5	19.1	9.1
1979	24.3	40.7	27.8	6.3	0.9	100.0	198.1	21.5	9.2

Source: Sarcinelli, Mario, 'Il Fabbisogno di Finanziamento degli Utilizzatori Finale dei Fondi Tendenze Recenti', *Bancaria*, April 1980.

*Treasury bills.

Table 4.15
Types of State bonds outstanding (by percentage of value)

	Dec. 1977	Dec. 1978	Dec. 1979
Short term Treasury bills	40.2	35.9	38.2
Certificates of credit (variable interest)	6.8	14.2	20.1
Long term Treasury bonds	9.4	16.0	14.9
Other long term bonds	26.9	21.8	17.1
Treasury fixed term bonds	16.7	12.1	9.7

Source: Sarcinelli, Mario, 'Il Fabbisogno di Finanziamento degli Utilizzatori Finale dei Fondi Tendenze Recenti', *Bancaria*, April 1980.

Table 4.16
Average maturity yields on fixed interest bonds (percentage)

Assets	April 1977	December 1978	June 1979	March 1980
Government securities	15.37	13.04	12.83	14.82
Consolidated	6.43	7.20	7.48	8.06
Redeemable (shorts)	15.49	14.14	13.87	16.16
Treasury bonds (longs)	15.42	12.92	12.75	14.74
Other bonds				
Credit institutions (ENEL-ENI-IRI etc.)	14.94	13.54	13.65	15.16

Source: Banca d'Italia, *Report for the Year 1979*, 1980.

Treasury bonds and other long-term bonds. Between 1976 and 1979, there have been large swings in net purchase of bonds between the four major categories of holders of fixed interest debt: Banca d'Italia down from 26 to -19 per cent, banks up from 71 to 82 per cent, companies and households up from 2 to 25 per cent, and 'other financial intermediaries' up from 1 to 12 per cent (figures rounded). Average maturity yields on fixed interest bonds from 1977 have behaved as shown in Table 4.16.

By January 1981 secondary market bill yields had reached a record 16.5 per cent compared with the Interbank rate mentioned earlier, of 17 per cent. Consequently, tax-free yields on Treasury bills vied with price rises on the equity market. In 1980, non-bank investors bought around 50 per cent of Treasury bills on offer.

By virtue of attractive interest rates, and the Italian Government's consistent borrowing in the domestic market, there is no doubt that the bond market is a thriving form of investment.

Efficiency

This section considers the efficiency of the Milan Stock Exchange from the viewpoint of its success and speed in processing information into market prices. Other, equally important, criteria for the efficiency of the market, e.g. providing new finance for industry, are considered elsewhere.

Surprisingly, the Milan Stock Exchange has attracted quite a lot of attention among Italian analysts. It has much to do with a strong school of statisticians at the University of Bergamo, and the impressive research unit at the Exchange itself, together with the attentions of Banca d'Italia economists. A selection is presented here.

Apart from the Solnik study of European equity prices mentioned in other chapters, there are several more studies. Giovanni Cristini,[8] of the Banca d'Italia, tested market data on equity yields. On the basis of the values of autocorrelation coefficients found between expected yields and yields in the preceding period, only weak-form efficiency could be supported. In a further test of how the market reacted to firms' announcements about the distribution of dividends, Cristini found both the timing and the market's anticipating action to be slow and erratic. Similarly, the market's response to privileged information was weak (the Fiat Libyan deal). Finally, Cristini undertook efficiency testing on the basis of institutional investors' planned portfolios. 'Good' risk-yield portfolios beat randomly chosen ones. The Milan Stock Exchange could not be said to be more than 'weak-form efficient'.

Silvia Biffignandi and Silvana Stefani[9] investigated equity price behaviour on Italian Stock Exchanges by applying tests of randomness on Italian financial time-series through autocorrelation analysis. Daily price observations on the Stock Exchanges did not show random walk behaviour, but weekly and monthly observations did.

Giovanni Zambruno[10] studied a particular type of bond on the Italian bond market, termed the 'sinking-fund random-drawing Bond', which is repaid by annual instalments instead of once-only redemption. This bond is characterised by a fall in price as its drawing date approaches (speculators hope to earn ex-post returns). Zambruno tested the price of the security for correlation with the Banca d'Italia's 'General Bond Index'. There was no apparent correlation — the efficient market hypothesis did not hold.

Zambruno also studied, with Anna Torriero,[11] rates of return on Italian bonds, to determine the extent to which they could be used as predictors of future inflation rates. Regression coefficients for returns to bonds in three different holding periods showed that no relationship existed with inflation in the next month. It was completely independent of the preceding rates of return. Inflation therefore was considered to be only one among many factors used by the market in determining prices, and the link was barely discernible. This does not increase confidence in the efficiency of the Italian bond market.

Finally, Bottazi[12] studied a sample of quarterly equity returns, from 1968 to 1977 for thirty equities listed on the Milan Stock Exchange, for the value of 'beta' (relation of equity returns to the general market index). He found that approximately 50 per cent of the variability of returns to equities was caused by unsystematic variations unconnected with the general market performance, i.e. that could not be explained by the general equity index.

New legislation and Stock Exchange reform

The only major innovation to affect the Italian stock markets has been the Law of 1974[13] concerning their regulation, and the tax treatment of equities. Primarily, this Law established the Commissione Nazionale per la Società e la Borsa. Since the initial Law, there has been a number of subsequent amending decrees, in 1975, 1977 and 1978, modifying the powers of CONSOB.

CONSOB's powers are both general and specific. It has general responsibility for the protection of equity holders, and for the correct observation of Stock Exchange rules and regulations. For many of its more general responsibilities, it took over functions previously exercised by such public bodies as the Chambers of Commerce, the Stock Exchange Councils, and even the Ministry of the Treasury. In the course of time, however, some of these responsibilities have been delegated back again. In 1974, it was given specific powers to (a) approve new listings, (b) determine the Bourse calendar, (c) determine brokers' commissions, (d) receive notification of AGMs, (e) require notice of transfers of control of companies by equity purchasers (with penalties for non-compliance), (f) scrutinise profit and loss accounts of listed companies, (g) pay special attention to issues of convertible bonds and options, and 'savings equities'.

The March 1975 decree extended CONSOB's powers of scrutiny of profit and loss accounts to credit and financial institutions, and its inspection powers over credit institutions and State participations, as well as more specific powers over the admission of securities. Transfers of responsibilities from other bodies were made clearer, and CONSOB was given powers to appoint 'Commissari di Borsi' (inspectors). Also in 1975, rules were set up controlling capital increases and mergers — mostly regarding notice of intent.

The 1977 decree modified rules on dividends, profits and capital increases, minimum capital of listed companies, and certain tax arrangements. The 1978 decree introduced rules for private insurance against damages arising from Stock Exchange errors.

These powers are apparently extensive, but there are notable gaps between legislation and practice. The disclosure of information from companies is compulsory only on admission of securities to the Stock Exchange, and even then the extent of disclosure required is modest.

Although the Milan Stock Exchange grew up autonomously, and is to some extent self-regulatory, any changes in constitution or practice must be subject to legislation. This is a cumbrous business, and the current position on control and supervision is still somewhat unclear, with at least six bodies having legal powers of supervision. There are bound to be questions of ranking and overlapping. CONSOB and the Stock Exchange Council are appointed by decree. The Comitato Direttivo degli Agenti di Cambio and the Consiglio Nazionale are professional, elected bodies. On top of this the Minister of Finance has ultimate control over all these bodies, but in practice his role has been rather passive.

Italian Stock Exchange rules are legally based. The sanctions are legal, and CONSOB's sanctions as a public body are mostly by recourse to the Civil Code. In theory, CONSOB's directives can overrule any opinions by the Stock Exchange management bodies, since these directives have the force of law. At least in one respect, CONSOB has supplanted powers completely — those of the local Chambers of Commerce.

These legal powers extend to the activities of brokers, who are appointed and can be dismissed by ministerial decree. On finding irregularities, CONSOB can refer a broker or brokers to the Minister of the Treasury for legal sanction. However, in CONSOB's own case, no Government inspector or commissioner specifically supervises the Commissione on behalf of the Minister of the Treasury. CONSOB has some degree of autonomy. The Treasury inspector can, in theory, dismiss all members of the brokers' association and effectively dissolve the Stock Exchange, but the effect would be catastrophic. Brokers regard the fact that they are ministerial officers as an obstacle to any form of association or partnership. They must be sole dealers.[14] The Guarantee Fund for brokers has been mentioned earlier. As for control of the brokers' activities, CONSOB does not have permanent powers of scrutiny over their documents etc., but exercises its authority in a more *ad hoc* way. Sanctions against brokers (which are rare) are mainly the prerogative of the Minister of the Treasury or his inspector.

CONSOB has the right to approve listings, but this is a contentious right when the Stock Exchange Council may be thought closer to the market and better informed. Approval is usually based on the status of the security in question rather than (say) any general benefit to be derived by the stock market as a whole. In the Italian case, there are no rigid or predetermined rules on disclosure of information. CONSOB is given a good deal of discretion, but against the background of inadequate Italian accounting this cannot be said to safeguard high standards. In general, admission of a company to the Milan Stock Exchange will give it what Wymeersch calls 'stock exchange status' — and obliges it to greater public openness and accountability. It becomes subject to rules concerning take-overs and mergers, although in the case of CONSOB there is confusion or weakness in the implementation of its powers. In 1978 and 1979, CONSOB was faced with several 'Offerte Pubbliche di Acquisito' (take-over bids), e.g. the American company, Quaker Oats, for Chiari and Forti. An original bid for 27 per cent of the equity ended up with an 80 per cent bid and Quaker Oats issued no prospectus regarding its future operations in Europe. But the take-over was not disapproved. CONSOB can call for additional information, but cannot disapprove the bid.

CONSOB requires half-yearly accounts, although the content is not specifically set out, and no cases of sanction are known. There are no legally enforceable, detailed guidelines.

Neither is there any legal requirement to bring securities to the Stock Exchange for execution. Thus banks can deal in securities, often in blocks, outside the Exchange, by matching.

On insider trading and variations of it, rules are set out in the ministerial decrees, but they do not apply to banks, and in any case such practices are hard to detect.

Finally, CONSOB has been given powers to regulate the 'mercato ristretto', but as it applies rules at least as rigorous as those on the Official Exchange, this otherwise lively market is inhibited. In most countries the 'third market' or 'unlisted market' is normally regarded as a 'nursery' for the official market. When companies trading in the mercato ristretto were first subject to demands for prospectuses by CONSOB, it prompted the following statement by the President of the Comitato Mercato Ristretto: 'Queste pagine — nella loro offerta di dati, grafici, comparazioni, nouche esplicazioni concettuali varie — danno una relazione sul Mercato Ristretto Milanese 1978-1979 . . . ' (These pages, with their offers of figures, graphs and comparisons as well as much qualitative reasoning, diminish relationships on the Restricted Market . . .').

A lot of space has been devoted to CONSOB and its activities because, although its establishment was seen as an important event — by virtue of its supervisory powers, raising standards in the Stock Exchanges — it has been disappointing. In March 1981, a new director of CONSOB was appointed, Professor Guido Rossi, who was quoted as saying, 'We have an imperfect and crude securities market . . . one gambles and speculates, but does not invest'.

These weaknesses and others were the subject of an Italian Senate Commission of Inquiry into the functioning of the Italian Stock Exchange, which set to work in October 1976, and had its report approved by the Senate Commission for Finance and the Treasury in October 1977.[15] In fact this Commission took up the work of an identical Commission of the Sixth Legislation, which was prevented from reporting by political elections.

The preceding Commission made the following recommendations:

1 No listed securities should be traded outside the Stock Exchange.

2 All deals to be on cash and carry-over terms, and forward plus options deals abolished.

3 Reduction in the number of Stock Exchanges and the introduction of computer handling.

4 CONSOB to be more strict in its control of the stock markets.

5 Rationalisation of the law on the Stock Exchanges.

6 Non-discriminatory tax treatment of equities and bonds.

The Commission of the 7th Senate Legislation recognised the external constraints on the Italian stock markets — low company self-financing, high household savings directed to short term bank deposits, excessive Government fixed term debt, etc. Leaving the solution of these more macroeconomic problems to Government action, the Commission recommended legislation on certain specific aspects of Stock Exchange activity, in contrast to the wider reforms suggested by its predecessor:

1 Strict control of transfers of controlling blocks of securities and take-over bids, to ensure fair treatment for minority holders of equity.

2 Reform of CONSOB to give it more clearly defined and stronger powers.

3 Tighter regulations on admission of securities to listing.

4 Concentration on the Stock Exchange of all trading in listed securities.

5 Establishment of a central depository for security certificates.

6 Establishment of a self-regulating Stock Exchange with a rationalised structure of management.

7 Reform of the procedures for examining and appointing Agenti di Cambio.

8 Encouragement of stockbroking partnerships.

9 Strict rules on insider trading.

10 Establishment of a sub-stock market in short term Government notes, bank acceptances, and similar debt.

11 An improvement in the Official List by requiring more complete company disclosure of information both before and after official listing.

These recommendations have seen nothing like wholesale implementation. In fact, legislation has been confined to modifications of the Law of 1974, but some of the legislation, and some practice in the Milan Stock Exchange, as well as a set of new elections to CONSOB, have meant the *ad hoc* introduction of some small improvements, and higher hopes than before for the future.

In 1979, the Comitato Direttivo degli Agenti di Cambio (CDAC) pursued a much firmer and more persuasive policy towards the production of company balance sheets and six-monthly financial reports. Until this year, the flow of listed company information was erratic. The response was very good, and nearly all listed companies are now depositing their balance sheets with the Stock Exchange in Milan on a regular basis, and the number of six-monthly financial reports being received has trebled. These reports are being filed and integrated in the Stock Exchange Reference Library. As a result of the greater amount of information available, the Comitato is in the process of producing a new publication containing up-to-date figures on listed manufacturing enterprises. In addition the Research and Statistics Department of the Exchange is providing a new layout and content of listed company information files, in order to acquaint prospective and existing equity holders with the greater amount of information that is now available. In its monthly report, the Comitato has introduced company 'identi-kits', identifying major items of company financial information, ratios and measures of performance.

In August 1979, new regulations of CONSOB were published, including the calendar for the gradual introduction of compulsory company audits. There are two parts to the new company accounts regulations. The first established a Register (Albo Speciale) of twenty CONSOB approved auditors. The task of the auditors is to certify the balance sheets of all companies listed on the Stock Exchanges in Italy (162 at the last count, disregarding subsidiaries). On their own initiative, these auditing companies set up their own professional association, Assirevi, which will be able to represent them with companies and public authorities, etc. The calendar for presentation of audited accounts is as follows:[16]

		Last date for commencement of audit	*First audited accounts*
1	Financial institutions and companies which at 31 December 1974 had capital > L50 billion (excluding manufacturing companies and credit institutions	April 1981	1983
2	Companies having at 31 December 1974 a capital > L10 billion and < L50 billion (excluding manufacturing companies and credit institutions)	April 1982	1984
3	Other companies on the Official List (excluding manufacturing companies and credit institutions)	April 1983	1985
4	Manufacturing companies and credit institutions who have the required amount of capital (to be determined).	April 1984	1986

The register will be kept by CONSOB. CDAC has advised companies and auditors of the need to use the interim period to ensure the presentation of balance sheets is upgraded. There is a serious shortage of qualified auditors in Italy and company accountants are not experienced at drawing up detailed accounts to the standards of the 1979 EEC draft directive.

In 1979, three take-over bids were successfully concluded (Quaker Oats for Chiari and Forti, the Berec Group for Superpila, and the Beni Immobili Italia for Subalpina Investimenti). CDAC has established a Code of Behaviour for such bids — to compensate for the lack of legislation — and its 1979 Annual Report announced with pleasure that the bids had respected this Code of Behaviour. It also recorded that there had been no more than three similar bids over the last eight years on the Milan Stock Exchange. These take-over bids achieved total control of the companies under offer. On the other hand, during the same year, eight listed companies purchased their own equities directly on the Exchange. CDAC noted that these and earlier self-purchases were seriously lacking in the degree of disclosure of information required by the relevant EEC directives. The Italian Government is hoping to improve this situation by Bill No. 250, which will require disclosure of the objectives, duration, value and procedure of all such transactions.

In the field of EDP, the Milan Stock Exchange increased the service provided by its EDP Centre by substituting more powerful computers, thus doubling the memory capacity and enabling the centre nearly to treble the speed of its operations.

In early 1981 CONSOB had elections to five of its six strong membership, and the new Chairman, Professor Guido Rossi, has undertaken to rejuvenate the present practice of CONSOB and strengthen its powers. In particular, he would like more active companies to be listed on the Exchange, with those which are dormant, if necessary, removed. CONSOB will back up the new auditing and balance sheet disclosure laws with as much pressure as possible to disclose information to equity holders. CONSOB is especially keen for AGMs to be open to outsiders, and not least to journalists. The use of large blocks of votes by equity holders representing outside interests is a particular *bête noir*, and Professor Rossi wants their transactions and motives to be more widely known and explained to minority holders of equity. Two more improvements are high on Rossi's list: an attempt by companies to keep a minimum number of equities in circulation each year, and clear and effective legislation to prevent the worst abuses of insider trading. Much of what the new CONSOB intends to do under its dynamic new chairman depends on political will and tactics, since

CONSOB had always had practically sufficient legal powers to prevent the worst abuses on the Exchanges, and to raise standards.

Other prescriptions for Stock Exchange reform

Many of the more important and obvious improvements that could be made to the Milan Stock Exchange have been set out in the Report of the Senate Commission for Finance (1977). However, there are some specially urgent areas which would benefit from attention.

The failure to internationalise the Exchange has decreased interest among Italian and overseas investors. Many overseas investors would like the option of both investing in lire, with the prospect of currency gain, and of buying stock of multinational companies, with all their advantages. Similarly, Italians are blocked from exporting lire for equity investment, and if foreign stocks were listed on the Milan Exchange, they are effectively cut off by the onerous 50 per cent non-interest bearing deposit rule. The official list is even smaller than at first appears, since many companies' ordinary and preference equities are listed separately. The Italian investor would have more opportunity to diversify his investment if the 20 per cent rule were rigorously applied, i.e. that 20 per cent of a company's equity should be available for trading. But both families and institutions hold their equities tighter than this, and frequently only 5 per cent is available. If the 50 per cent rule were abolished, foreign companies would undoubtedly be interested in having a Milan listing in view of the liquid state of the market.

A determined effort should be made to concentrate dealings on the Milan Stock Exchange to give the market a longer and more active trading list, and to increase turnover on the secondary market. At the present time only 20–25 equities are continually traded, and one company alone, Assicurazione Generali, accounts for up to 13 per cent of market turnover, and 12 per cent of market capitalisation. The restricted market (mercato ristretto) is a special case. It is almost entirely composed of banks, particularly regional and savings banks and finance companies, who prefer to transact once a week, and usually in blocks. The mercantino is now in a difficult position, since recently it has become increasingly subject to official regulations such as are current on the official market, although costs are much lower and information required smaller. Since trading on the mercantino is of the order of 2.5 times that on the official list, and in securities of high cash-flow banks, it is quite wrong that the public should be deprived of the same investment opportunity as it enjoys in official trading times on the Milan floor. Apart from the official market and the mercantino, there is a thriving market between banks in the matching of blocks of securities, undertaken by telephone. Since prices here are not reported to the stock market, it is clearly difficult for the investor to make anything like a correct analysis of future equity price movements, or of true value of a company's equity. In short, the total stock market is fragmented — it is made up of the Milan Stock Exchange and small regional exchanges, the mercato ristretto, bank-to-bank market and in-house trading. Thus, stock market prices can fluctuate for reasons not apparent from information available on the official market alone.

There is fiscal discrimination against equities. At the present time, stamp duty on equities traded on the 'account' market is seven times that on long dated Government stock. Dividends are taxed at 10 per cent, bonds at 20 per cent, Treasury Bills are tax free. The disincentive to equity purchase could easily be removed, although this would, of course, reduce demand for Government issues in the market. In view of the revenue brought in, the tax is out of proportion, but it must be admitted that the boom in equity returns on the current market weakens this argument somewhat.

The Government, which has a large volume of debt in the market, especially Treasury Bills, could regulate both the amounts and timing of its issues better. With the fiscal advantage and high interest rates giving rise to a large reverse yield gap, there is an element of 'overskill' in Government fixed interest borrowing. It is too easy, and probably too expensive. The Government bond and corporate equity market could be much better integrated and made less unfairly uncompetitive by a better planning calendar of issues, and by less concentration on domestic borrowing.

The past performance of CONSOB has been criticised earlier in this chapter. It has also been the subject of constant review and criticism by the relevant Italian authorities, even though its constitution and powers, as set out in ministerial rules, are quite formidable. It has not used its powers properly, and it is to be hoped that, with the elections in 1981 of a new set of less academically inclined Commission members, there should be an improvement. But in fairness it must be said that the overlapping supervisory powers and attitudes of the many organisations on the scene have not helped CONSOB to maintain standards. A perusal of its annual reports (Raccolta Delibere CONSOB) reveals much discussion of events — transfers of company control by mergers and take-overs, insider information, matters of admission to listings — but little or no presentation of criteria for unfair trading, or pressure for better information on which to take decisions. The contrast with such bodies as the Commission des Opérations de Bourse in Paris or the Council of the Stock Exchange in the UK is marked.

CONSOB, for example, has suspended companies from the official Stock Exchanges in Italy, but always for provision of information inadequate for their valuation, or a turnover that has contracted to nearly zero. In other words, suspensions have not been for malpractices in trading. These suspensions are usually temporary. CONSOB has not interfered with mergers, and has done little more than discuss the prevention of the abuse of privileged information.

The position of the 'agenti' needs modification. Legally they are not permitted to deal for their own accounts, though in fact they do, but the brokers have too little in the way of funds to be really effective. So there is no effective market-making. The banks, which are powerful, respected and currently liquid, are not permitted to trade as brokers, and therefore cannot use their substantial assets to make an effective secondary market by self-trading. Instead, they are forced into the undesirable practice of trading off-market with other banks, or matching deals in-house. This is to the detriment of the official stock market.

The system of admitting securities by public contract 'alla grida' of the Stock Exchange has given rise to criticism. This system does not make for neutrality and objectivity in fixing prices, and consequently, since they are not equilibrium prices, they tend to be unstable. There are clearly other superior ways of quoting to be learned from the experience of stock markets in the other Community countries.

The number of listed companies purchasing their own equities directly on the stock market has increased steeply in Italy recently. In 1979, eight such transactions took place. Although these purchases conformed with Article 2357 of the Civil Code, the amount of information disclosed was seriously deficient, nowhere near the standards required by EEC Directives 2 and 4. A Bill before the Italian Parliament (No. 250) should rectify this; in the case of the eight companies mentioned, total purchases of equities to the value of L100 billion took place in an atmosphere of near ignorance by the remainder of the investing public. Quite clearly, this type of hidden manoeuvre is not good practice, and ranks with insider dealing and transfers of control of companies as another important aspect of trading that is improperly regulated and about which too little information is forthcoming.

It is not intended here to catalogue the improvements and reforms to the Milan Exchange that have been suggested by Senate Commissions of Inquiry or the Comitato degli Agenti de Cambio itself, but instead to discuss the central weakness of the Exchange as a whole — inadequate financial and commercial information. The many elements all add up to a picture of poor and even misleading information available to Italian and foreign individual and institutional investors.

Prospectuses are slight, the accounts submitted subsequently are late and thin on detail, some companies do not submit audited accounts to the Exchange at all, and periodic financial reports are not yet compulsory. Prospectuses shown in the mercato ristretto list are all different; some less than a page in length — and as most are bank prospectuses, this is a remarkable situation. Often the information disclosed on admittance of a company to the official list is erroneous and misleading, and gives an incorrect view of company performance. Clearly, companies' attitudes on tax affect their attitude to complete balance and profit and loss account sheets. It may be that an improved system of tax structure, liability and collection is a prerequisite to giving company treasurers enough confidence to draw up official accounting statements to a higher standard.

Fiscal and investment/savings incentives

Although in 1981 a greater proportion of household savings has turned to equity investment, in view of the high level of these savings in Italy, the amount is still small. In 1979, equity investment as a percentage share of household savings was only 1.5 (see also Table 4.4), virtually unchanged since 1970. But, by taking another measure, the proportion of equities in the stock of assets of households, this portion of assets has been falling sharply since 1969. In that year, it stood at 11.4 per cent; at the end of 1979, 4.2 per cent. In fact, despite this small figure, there has been an upturn in 1981. Earlier in this chapter the trend towards greater securities investment was noted as including a big swing to Treasury bills by households as well.

Regarding external financing of companies in Italy, it was also pointed out earlier that the proportion taken by equity financing, whilst having fallen over the last fifteen years, was still reasonably high compared with other Community members, and had even shown an upturn in 1981. At the end of 1979, for example, it was 13.2 per cent compared with 16.5 per cent at the end of 1969 (see also Table 4.3).

Clearly, both households and companies have a good deal of capacity for greater equity investment, and any incentives to either companies or savers would have a proportionately large effect.

Considering first corporation tax, Italy has a full imputation system introduced in 1977, applicable to resident equity holders. There are both national and local taxes. Apart from national individual income tax (imposta sul reddito delle persone fisiche) there is a national corporate income tax (1973) (imposta sul reddito delle persone giuridiche, 'IRPEG'). The general rate of corporate income tax is 25 per cent. In addition, there is a local tax on individuals and companies (imposta locale sin redditi 'ILOR'), established in 1973. This is a complicated tax, and a number of exemptions and reliefs are available. The uniform rate is 15 per cent. For individuals, it is deductible from national income tax, and for corporations, up to one-quarter of it can be set off against the basis of assessment of corporation tax. The actual overall rate comes to 36.25 per cent.

The Italian Government, like several others, has introduced a tax credit system. This establishes a rate of tax credit at 33 per cent of the gross dividend, and at 100 per cent of the tax on distributed profits. In Italy, the imputation extends to only one of the two taxes levied on income, the IRPEG (tax on the income of legal persons), the other, ILOR (local income tax) being final and not deductible. The withholding tax on dividends is 10 per cent for residents and 30 per cent for non-residents. Treasury bills, currently yielding 20 per cent in Italy, are tax free. There are also some exemptions relating to equity dividends. Securities purchased within the framework of a long term savings account are exempt from all income tax. The exemption takes the form of final taxation at a lower rate (15 per cent for 'savings shares', 'azioni di risparmio', and 10 per cent for units in co-operatives).

Italy also has a scheme whereby capital invested in equities can be deducted from taxable income. It is limited to consortia set up to rationalise enterprises.

Capital gains are treated as follows: they are totally exempt for individuals if they are made 'non-speculatively', but they are not exempt for companies. Unlike some countries, there are no exemptions from tax on the equivalent value of equities distributed by a company to members of staff.

As in other countries, Italy uses taxation as an incentive in the field of corporate profits. In Italy it has been particularly directed to the south (Mezzogiorno). For example, there is accelerated depreciation in the Mezzogiorno and many regional incentives: a ten-year exemption from ordinary income tax for profits invested in the area, subsidies on interest payments, credits for expansion of small and medium sized companies, subsidies 'à fonds perdu', grants and cheap medium term loans for enterprises, Banco di Napoli and Banco di Sicilia credits, and reduction of social security charges. Regional policy has been the main influence on Italy's system of investment incentives, though less dominant since the 1974 tax reforms. These basically simplified investment incentives, with something of a shift to credit and low rate loans. Nevertheless, tax incentives remain important, including the accelerated deduction of research costs, and concessionary rates of tax for banks operating medium and long term credits.

Early in July 1980, the Government introduced a 'detaxation' policy which included a sizeable cut in the tax rate for the social security charges of manufacturing industry. About one-fifth of the social security burden on employers was lifted, amounting to L1.8 billion of relief in 1980 and L3.7 billion in 1981. This tax rate was 38.6 per cent of the wage bill in 1979 as against a 24 per cent average in other countries of the EEC. The level in Italy fell to about 32 per cent, though even at that level it was still the highest in the Community. Table 4.17 shows the beneficial effect of this recent amelioration of tax on Italian industry.

Table 4.17
The effects of the 1980 detaxation reforms on Italian industry

Description		1979	1980			1981 (est.)
			I	II	Total	
A	Total labour costs in manufacturing (bn. lire)	55.4	29.5	37.5	67.0	77.6
B	Social security charges					
	(a) Billion lire	15.4	8.2	10.5	18.7	21.6
	(b) As percentage of labour costs	27.8	27.8	27.8	27.8	27.8
C	Wages (A –B (bn. lire)	40.0	21.3	27.0	48.3	56.0
D	Detaxation					
	(a) Billion lire	–	–	1.8	1.8	3.7
	(b) Percentage of labour costs	–	–	4.8	2.7	4.7
	(c) As percentage of security costs	–	–	17.1	9.6	16.9
E	Increase in labour costs (percentage over previous period)					
	(a) Gross of detaxation	–	–	13.8	20.9	15.8
	(b) Net of detaxation	–	–	8.3	17.7	10.4
	(c) Difference (a –b)	–	–	5.5	3.2	5.4

Source: *Italian Trends*, vol.XXI, no.8, August 1980.

Summary

The Italian economy has been the last in the Community to move into general recession. Always bedevilled by internal problems such as tax avoidance, risk-averse household savings, and unprofitable State owned industry, the Government's main problems now are inflation, unemployment, and a rapidly rising PSBR. Yet some companies, particularly in the financial sector, are returning better profits, and the Milan Stock Exchange out-performed the other Community Exchanges between mid-1980 and mid-1981, until the crash in prices in June.

As the decade of the 1970s ended, most Italian companies were experiencing a rise in gearing ratios together with a fall in self-financing and investment. Household savings were swinging strongly to Treasury bills (and to a smaller extent company equities). By 1980 and 1981 however, more desirable trends became apparent. The banks were squeezed by credit restrictions and rising Treasury bill rates and equity prices caused them to increase the size of their portfolios. Households too were more interested in stocks. Following the relatively low PSBR in 1979, it has subsequently soared, and in 1981 the Government took firm steps to bring down the level. There is little doubt that 'crowding out' is a problem for equities that will increase in the future.

The Milan Stock Exchange, which accounts for the bulk of Italian stock trading, is a complex market, composed of an elaborate supervisory structure, and a great variety of trading instruments, types of orders and price determinants. Regrettably, the Exchange suffers many organisational and functional weaknesses, ranging from fragmented and inadequate supervision to the lack of a Stock Exchange monopoly of trading and insufficient and often misleading company information.

Nonetheless, from mid-1980 to mid-1981, the Milan Stock Exchange was the Community's star performer in terms of rising equity prices and turnover. Further analysis showed this to be based on a very small number of securities, combined with a lack of alternative outlets for investors' burgeoning liquidity. But there were positive aspects; many companies restructuring financially and returning better cash flow, and taking advantage of a strong equity bull market to make an increasing number of new issues. The Government bond market is currently strong, encouraged by very high interest rates and tax advantages, as well as a flood of issues.

There have been several statistical studies of the efficiency of the Milan stock market by variants on the efficient market hypothesis. All of them show slow response of prices to information changes on the market, and Milan can be deemed to be no more than 'weak-form efficient', i.e. investment analysis can beat any simple 'buy-and-hold' strategy.

Official stock market reform rests on the 1974 Law whose main objective was to establish CONSOB (Commissione Nazionale per la Società e la Borsa) — the official supervisory body for stock market trading and regulation. Its powers, although extensive, have been inadequately used, and it is to be hoped that the 1981 re-elections to the Commission will give it a tougher disposition. Other official reforms were suggested by a major inquiry of the Senate Commission for Finance in 1977; these amount to a long catalogue, ranging from establishing a Stock Exchange monopoly of trading in securities to correcting the tax bias between bonds and equities. Whilst most of these reforms are yet to be implemented, the Comitato degli Agenti di Cambio is quietly improving affairs in such fields as EDP book-keeping, and pressing for company financial reports. This chapter suggests other areas ripe for reform including the encouragement of new listings, the abolition of the 50 per cent foreign equity deposit requirement, and a more regulated Government calendar of bill and bond issues.

Savings and investment incentives in Italy are briefly treated, and it is concluded that the Italian Government has followed a generally supportive role in these respects.

Notes and references

1   *Italian Trends*, September—October 1975, 'The Deteriorating Financial Structure of Italian Corporations'.
2   Banca d'Italia, *Bollettino*, no.2—3, September 1978.
3   Deaglio, Mario, 'How Italy Works', *The Banker*, May 1979.
4   *Economic Survey of Italy*, OECD, Paris, March 1980 (annex C).
5   Tagi Giorgio, *Manuale di Borsa, Aspetti Economici e Operativi*, Istituto Editoriale Internazionale, Milan 1977.
6   Information from Fédération Internationale des Bourses de Valeurs, *Fees on F.I.B.V. Member Stock Exchanges*.
7   Banca d'Italia, *Report for the Year 1979*, 1980.
8   Cristini, Giovanni, 'I Rendimenti delle Azioni e l'Efficienza della Borsa', *Contributi alla Ricerca Economica*, 1978.
9   Biffignandi, Silvia and Stefani, Silvana, 'Modelli Stocastici per l'Analisi dei Prezzi e dei Volumi Azioneri' (Stochastic analysis of share prices in Italy), unpublished paper in Italian and English, University of Bergamo.
10   Zambruno, Giovanni, 'The Pricing of Italian Bonds', unpublished paper, University of Bergamo.
11   Zambruno, Giovanni and Torriero, Anna, 'Inflation and Rates of Return in the Bond Market in Italy', unpublished paper, University of Bergamo.
12   Bottazi, Giovanni, *Variabilità dei Rendimenti Azionari — Analasi Empiriche in Tema di Selezione del Portafoglio* (The variability of equity returns — an empirical analysis regarding portfolio selection), Borsa Valori di Milano, Comitato Direttivo degli Agenti di Cambio, Quaderno n.14.
13   Legge 7 giugno 1974, n.216, *Gazzetta Ufficiale*, n.149, dell'8 giugno, 1974.

14   Wymeersch, E., *Control of Securities Markets in the European Economic Community*, Collection Studies, Competition — Approximation of Legislation Series no.31, Brussels, December 1977.

15   *Funzionamento delle Borse Valori in Italia*, Indagine Conoscitiva della 6ª Commissione Permanente (Finanze e Tesoro), Raccolta di Atti e Documenti, Tome I e II, Commissione Parliamentari, Senato della Repubblica, VII Legislatura, Servizio delle Commissione Parliamentari, 1978.

16   Private communication, Banca d'Italia, Rome, 'Ogetto: Revisione e Certificazione dei Bilancia' (mimeo), October 1979.

5 Netherlands

Company financing

In a study by Algemene Bank Nederland (ABN),[1] the 1970s were found to be generally an unfavourable period for listed Dutch companies' balance sheet ratios. Three categories of companies were selected for study — manufacturing industry, distribution, and multinational companies. After 1975, for these three categories of companies, financial structure weakened. It is pointed out that in the 1960s and up to 1973, companies attempted to increase the rate of return on equity by borrowing cheaply and obtaining tax advantages. After 1973, inflation and weak economic growth kept the solvency ratio (equity/total capital invested) low. After 1975, in all three categories of listed companies, short term debt increased as a source of capital (long term loans were expensive). Eventually, both short and long term borrowing increased at the expense of equity.

After 1975, distribution companies, and to some extent manufacturing concerns and the multinationals, suffered low rates of return on equity and on total capital employed, and low rates of cash flow to total debt. Curiously, the balance sheet structures of small companies (< F1.100m.) in industry and distribution were stronger than those of large companies (> F1.500m.). The industrial group also recorded a rate of profitability lower than the other Stock Exchange categories. A further study by ABN divided manufacturing industry into eight major lines, and found considerable differences in their financial positions. For example, in 1978, in transport, the solvency ratio was the lowest of all eight categories, and borrowing was concentrated on the short term. Profitability was very low. Construction, on the other hand, with low equity total capital and high short term debt, enjoyed high profitability. Textiles, paper and metal industries showed relatively favourable financial balance sheet ratios, but low profitability. Although 1978 saw a fairly general recovery in profitability for listed manufacturing companies, the picture was mixed between different sectors, and was exceptional for Dutch industry, much of which is unlisted.

The latest figures from the Dutch Central Bureau of Statistics were published in 1980, but refer to 1978 as the latest date for compiled statistics. However, the survey of listed companies is very comprehensive, and Table 5.1 shows main components of financing.

The small part played by the Stock Exchange in external financing is noticeable − of the order of 6 per cent. Naturally, there is great variability between companies. In 1979, Ceteco NV had 29 per cent equity in its balance sheet total, Borsumijwehry 25 per cent and Internatio-Müller 28 per cent (all international trading houses). But in fact, this borrowing was up on 1977, when the percentage was 4.4 per cent (domestic corporate bond borrowing is negligible). The really astonishing figure is short term outside borrowing for all categories of companies. This is to be expected of multinational companies, but shows great dependency by domestic Dutch companies on external borrowing from the banks, life assurance and pension funds. The relatively low rate of retained earnings (a reflection of low profits) is also noticeable for Dutch companies (multinationals excluded) in comparison with companies in other member States of the Community. In 1978, net profitability (net income, after deduction of tax and interest payments, as percentage of equity) was 8 per cent for all manufacturing and distribution companies listed on the Amsterdam Stock Exchange.[1]

Table 5.2 gives the sources and uses of funds for all listed Dutch companies, in percentages. It shows up the dependency of Dutch listed companies on short term external borrowing. In 1978, it amounted to 35 per cent of total external financing.

Table 5.3 shows the changes which have occurred between 1973 and 1978 in the components of company finance as per cent of total financing.

During most of the 1970s, several trends were apparent, which are still continuing. Long term capital borrowing (including equities and long term debt) was irregular, but generally declining. Short term borrowing increased at the expense of retained earnings. Sinking funds for depreciation fluctuated, but were generally at high levels. As for

Table 5.1
Origin and uses of finances, Dutch listed companies, 1978 (Fl. million)

	Multi-national companies	Trade, industry and misc.			Ship and air transport	Total
		Total	Trade	Industry		
	(a)	(b)=(c)+(d) + misc.	(c)	(d)	(e)	(=(a)+(b) +(e))
Number of companies	5	137	38	85	6	148
Origin of finances:	(Fl. million)					
1 *External financing*						
Equity capital (real value	16	218	25	187	146	379
Minority third party holdings	581	–17	1	–18	0	563
Loans and long term debt	0	424	–13	449	18	441
Outside short term liabilities (banks, insurance companies etc.)	1529	3182	606	2897	57	4767
Total external financing	2125	3805	617	3514	220	6150
2 *Internal financing*						
Retained earnings	1758	469	78	376	60	2287
Provisions	668	286	53	231	82	1036
Depreciation	4507	1631	226	1325	612	6750
Revaluations	–2450	27	–7	48	–44	–2469
Total internal financing	4481	2414	349	1980	708	7603
Total financing	6606	6219	966	5494	928	13754
Uses of funds:						
1 *Long term permanent assets*						
Permanent assets	6619	2549	377	2193	912	10080
Long term advances	75	210	1	165	14	299
Participations	83	11	19	2	25	118
Total long term permanent assets	6776	2770	397	2361	951	10497
2 *Short term permanent assets*						
Stocks and debts owing	–45	3421	494	3206	–42	3333
Liquid assets (cash)	–123	28	75	–72	21	–75
Total short term assets	–169	3449	570	3134	–22	3257
Total uses	6606	6219	966	5494	928	13754

Source: Central Bureau voor de Statistiek, Statistiek van Balans en Resultatenrekeningbeurs — n.v's, 1978, s'Gravenhage, 1980.

Note: Figures are rounded.

Table 5.2
Sources and uses of funds, all Dutch listed companies (percentage), 1978

	Multi-national companies	Trade, industry and misc.			Ship and air transport	Total
		Total	Trade	Industry		
Number of companies	5	137	38	85	6	148
Origin of finance						
1 *External financing*						
Long-term capital finance	9	10	1	11	18	10
Short term capital finance	23	51	63	53	6	35
2 *Internal financing*						
Retained earnings and provisions	37	12	13	11	15	24
Depreciation and revaluations	31	27	23	25	61	31
Uses of funds						
Long term permanent assets	103	45	41	43	102	76
Short term permanent assets	-2	55	59	57	-1	24

Source: Central Bureau voor de Statistiek, Statistiek van Balans en Resultatenrekeningbeurs — n.v's, 1978, s'Gravenhage, 1980.

Note: Figures are rounded.

Table 5.3
Financing components as per cent of total financing

| | Total number of companies | Origin of funds | | | | Total of origin and uses of funds (Fl. mill.) | Uses of funds | |
| | | External financing | | Internal financing | | | | |
		Long term capital formation	Short term capital formation	Retained earnings and provisions	Depreciation and revaluation		Permanent long term assets	Permanent short term assets
All listed companies								
1973	190	–3	34	41	28	13,018	42	58
1974	177	8	47	28	17	25,438	34	66
1975	172	35	–3	24	44	12,502	83	17
1976	168	4	28	52	16	6,826	61	39
1977	157	12	27	22	39	17,858	78	22
1978	147	9	37	24	30	14,272	73	27

Source: Central Bureau voor de Statistiek, Statistiek van Balans en Resultatenrekeningbeurs – n.v.'s, 1978, s'Gravenhage, 1980. (1978 figures revised).

Note: Figures are rounded.

assets, there was a large build up of long term investments over the period, and a corresponding fall in short term ones. It would seem that Dutch companies were classically borrowing short, and investing long, which does not seem an optimum strategy.

The role of the banks and other credit institutions (insurance companies and pension funds) is important in the financing of Dutch companies.[2] Life assurance companies and pension funds are 'catchment areas' for the savings of private householders, taking over 60 per cent of these in the second quarter of 1980. Savings banks held the remainder. Liquid savings were very small. The swing from long to short term borrowing by companies has taken place over a long period. The 'Handelsbanken' (universal commercial banks) are a growing force in medium and long term finance for industry. Other credit institutions are the agricultural co-operatives and savings banks. Although there is a number of specialised credit institutions, the most important group is the mortgage banks, which lend on long term by the issue of mortgage bonds for individual building projects, or on the basis of borrowers' notes.

A particular Dutch characteristic in the capital market is the sub-market for 'private loans' ('onderhandse' market). In effect, it is a domestic bond market for institutional investors. With pension funds and life assurance companies able to make long term loans on the basis of contractual household savings received, they lend money on a regular basis outside the issues market. The savings banks also lend a small amount this way. Commercial banks act as brokers, and borrowers include business enterprises as well as central and local government. It is, in fact, a wholesale market, with loans on fixed term with long maturity. In 1979, the market accounted for one-third of total demand and supply on the capital market, but will probably decline in the future under pressure from low company profitability.

The Government provides loans to industry (e.g. through the Nationale Investerings Bank) as well as investment incentives which were, until recently, mainly intended to encourage regional restructuring. More recently, the Government has increased its assistance to industry (dealt with in a later section).

Government and local authority financing

The central government funds its budget deficit from three main sources: by monetary financing — the issue of Treasury bills (which tends to have a directly inflationary effect through the banking system, and so limits of good management are soon reached), by recourse to the civil servants' pension fund which is placed with it, and by borrowing on the domestic (or foreign) capital market(s). The Netherlands Government has had a budget deficit for a number of years, but it was not until the post-1973/74 depression that this began to climb. The Government's first issue of loans in the private loans market, which became an annual event on a big scale, was in 1976. In the same year it began borrowing abroad. Although private borrowing on the capital market is also large (believed to match Government borrowing in 1981), the steep upward trend in Government borrowing is a matter of concern for the economy and the capital market. Table 5.4 sets out on an abbreviated basis the changes since 1975.

Table 5.4
Central government finance, on a cash basis (Fl. billion)

Item	1975	1976	1977	1978	1979	1980 1st Qtr	2nd Qtr
Tax receipts	57.5	65.7	73.5	80.5	85.5	21.1	18.9
Other receipts	9.4	11.2	13.6	19.3	20.3	3.2	7.1
Expenditure (–)	–73.0	–85.6	–95.0	–110.3	–119.4	–27.9	–32.8
Financial deficit (–)	–6.3	–8.4	–8.1	–9.3	–13.1	–4.3	–8.5
Borrowing in capital market:							
(a) Issues	1.9	2.7	2.6	3.2	3.9	1.2	2.4
(b) Changes in presubscription a/c	3.3	3.6	3.9	3.9	4.3	1.0	1.4
(c) Private loans	–	1.4	2.1	2.9	3.3	0.8	1.0
(d) Repayments (–) of Funded debt	–0.9	–1.4	–1.8	–2.3	–2.7	–1.0	–0.7
Net borrowing	4.3	6.3	6.8	7.7	8.9	2.1	4.1

Source: De Nederlandsche Bank NV Report for the Year 1979, and De Nederlandsche Bank Quarterly Statistics, September 1980.

Figures are rounded.

Note: Financial deficit is not covered by net borrowing. The difference is the 'liquidity deficit' including such items as floating debt and IMF position.

As the table shows, the Government's financial deficit began accelerating in 1978 until the first two quarters of 1980 were nearly equal in size to the whole of 1979. The 1980 annual figure is estimated high, and 1981 much higher still. On the capital market, borrowing also accelerated in all sectors from 1978, so that, again, total borrowing in the first half of 1980 nearly equalled in size the amount borrowed in the whole of 1979. New issues of Government bonds increased especially fast, and refunding slowed down in 1980.

The remainder of the public sector (local authorities) must also be counted in since it has a net borrowing impact on the capital market (Table 5.5).

Table 5.5
Local authority finance, on a cash basis (Fl. billion)

Item	1975	1976	1977	1978	1979	1980 1st Qtr	2nd Qtr
Financial deficit (–)	–3.6	–2.3	–1.4	–2.0	–1.9	–2.4	–1.1
Net borrowing in the domestic capital market:							
(a) *Gross borrowing:*							
(i) By provinces and municipalities	1.0	1.5	0.9	0.4	0.9	0.3	0.3
(ii) By Bank for Netherlands municipalities (BNM) and Netherlands Polder Boards Bank (NPBB)	4.7	3.6	4.1	3.9	4.7	1.7	1.0
(b) *Repayments* (–)	–2.0	–2.5	–2.6	–2.8	–3.0	–1.0	–0.7
(c) *Net lending by BNM and NPBB*	–	–0.4	–0.5	–1.2	–1.1	–0.4	–0.3
Net borrowing	3.7	2.2	1.9	0.3	1.5	0.5	0.2

Source: De Nederlandsche Bank NV Report for the Year 1979, and De Nederlandsche Bank Quarterly Statistics, September 1980.

Figures are rounded.

The local authority sector financial deficit has not fluctuated wildly, except in 1980 with a steep rise beginning. Even so, as far as the capital market was concerned, net borrowing was kept to quite low levels over the period because of sizeable repayments.

Table 5.4 does not show that transfer payments (social security payments to households) increased tremendously in the period 1970–80, and these are the main reason for the high growth of the general Government financial deficit.[3] The 'crowding out' of the capital market (of equities by Government bonds) is a question taken up later; there is evidence that this has occurred to some degree. The size of the net national debt is another worry for the Government: from Fl. 39.5 million in 1975 to Fl. 80.1 in 1979 is an enormous jump.

Structure and practice of the Amsterdam Stock Exchange

Organisation

The Amsterdam Stock Exchange was trading in securities in the seventeenth century, and therefore must rank among the oldest established exchanges in the world. The Vereeniging voor de Effectenhandel (Association for Trading in Securities) was founded in 1876.[4]

The Vereeniging is a private corporation, subject to the civil law, and is effectively the management committee of the Exchange. It owns the Stock Exchange building (in Amsterdam known as 'Beursplein 5') and is responsible for operating the Exchange and organising security dealings within it. Amsterdam is the only official Stock Exchange operating in the Netherlands, the two provincial ones — at The Hague and Rotterdam — having closed some years ago, although some unofficial dealings in securities occur there.

Perhaps owing to its early dealings in securities of the Dutch East India Company, and the West India Company, Amsterdam had a strong foreign list very early on. American securities were traded from the eighteenth century, and Amsterdam financed the Russian railway network before World War I.

Since the Amsterdam Stock Exchange is a privately owned organisation, it makes its own rules and regulations. There is some governmental supervision of the market, but nowhere near so extensive as in countries (like the USA) where the Exchange is public property. There are two Parliamentary Acts relating to the Stock Exchange. One is the Stock Exchange Act of 1914, which places the Exchange under the general supervision of the Minister of Finance. His major responsibilities relate to the approval of the admission of securities to the official list. This itself is in the nature of a formality since his approval usually follows a recommendation by the Vereeniging. He also decides on which days the Exchange shall be closed. More recently the Minister has also assumed supervision of the Netherlands Securities Giro. The second Act is the Decree for Stock Exchange Operations (1947), which was basically a war-time measure. But two prescriptions have remained: (i) the Minister of Finance can exempt dealers from going through a Stock Exchange broker, although this will be regarded as exceptional, (ii) securities must be bought for cash, not by loan.

The 1914 Stock Exchange Act (Beurswet) was followed by an implementing decree setting up the Stock Exchange Regulations (Beursvoorschriften, 1919). But all other rules are established by the Vereeniging, and are not subject to any other administrative supervision. In practice, the Vereeniging governs the whole securities business. Its principal rules concern the following: (i) trade in securities,

(ii) admission of securities to quotation, (iii) quotation methods, (iv) commission rates, (vi) authorised and non-authorised clerks.

The Governing Board of the Amsterdam Stock Exchange, which establishes the broad lines of Exchange policy, is elected from and by the members of the Vereeniging. The Chairman and three members of the Board form the Board of Delegates which has a number of permanent sub-committees.

Membership

Conditions for admission of members are laid down by the Vereeniging. They are divided into stockbrokers and banks' representatives, and 'hoeklieden' (close to the American 'specialist'). The former are the brokers proper acting between investors and savers. The hoeklieden specialise in securities of certain types, e.g. AKZO, Philips, Royal Dutch Shell, shipping. They act as go-betweens and also on their own account.

Other professional dealers are admitted as trading members to the floor, e.g. 'Commissionairs in Effecten', who are intermediaries between the banks and hoeklieden, and also trade on behalf of third parties. In addition, there are arbitrageurs dealing in securities which are also listed on other European Exchanges and in New York. Professional floor dealers buy and sell for their own account, and earn their living by buying and selling within price fluctuations. They often act as counterpart to the arbitrageurs. On the European Options Exchange (which is a post on the floor of the Amsterdam Stock Exchange), there are three types of 'Premie Makeler' (option specialists): floor brokers, executing orders for others and on their own account on instructions from other members of the Options Exchange; market makers, who act only on their own account with a certain number of option shares assigned to them; and order book officials, taking orders from the public, who have preference in this respect.

Types of companies, securities and quotations

The most common type of company listed on the Exchange is the Naamloze Vennootschap (NV), very similar to the Anglo-Saxon limited liability joint stock company. There are also private companies and partnership companies of the usual Continental type. Securities fall mainly into the following types: equities, bonds (ordinary, convertible, subordinated and subordinated convertible), private placings, e.g. industrial equities, mortgage bank bonds, shares in banks, then there is government, local authority and foreign paper, and Euroguilder notes. There are also some unusual bonds: (a) variable interest rates, (b) indexed interest rates, (c) profit sharing bonds, (d) local authority lottery loans.

All securities admitted to official quotation are in bearer form except for some direct trading in American securities, and dealings in registered equities can be carried out only on the unofficial (unlisted) market. Most securities are traded on the basis of one price fixed at the end of the first or/and second round of dealing, on 'closed' pitches on the floor. However, there are some more 'active' securities which are traded at continuous prices, in 'open' pitches. But the distinction between closed and open pitches is not rigid. Bonds are quoted in per cent of nominal value, whether in guilders or foreign currencies, and all other securities, whether domestic or foreign, are quoted in guilders. All trading is on a cash basis. Official business trading hours are 1130 hours to 1315 hours, but the Vereeniging has recently introduced a permitted increase in the number of securities that can be dealt in before and after official hours. This reform is discussed in more detail later.

Listing and issuing costs

The handling fee for a new issue is Fl.1,000. For subsequent parts it is Fl.100. Admission fees charged by the Stock Exchange on domestic funds and foreign funds issued and placed in the Netherlands are 0.05 per cent of the nominal amount of bonds and depository receipts issued, and 0.05 per cent of the market value of all other securities. For foreign funds or depositary receipts issued and placed abroad, the fees are: (i) for bonds 0.05 per cent on the first Fl.25 million admitted, 0.025 per cent on the tranche Fl.25—50 million, 0.01 per cent between Fl.50—100 million and 0.001 per cent on the tranche > Fl.100 million, with a minimum of Fl.12,500; (ii) for equities Fl.25,000 increased by 0.001 per cent of the market value of admitted equities, with a minimum for both amounts together of Fl.50,000; (iii) for depositary receipts representing registered equities, Fl.20,000. Also, the admission fee is increased by 0.1 per cent of the market value of securities, with a special rate for depositary receipts under certain conditions.

Annual listing fees are 5 per cent of the admission fee. If this exceeds Fl.100,000, the listing fee is increased by 1 per cent. The annual listing fee must total at least Fl.10. For foreign-placed funds, the fee is Fl.2,500 plus 0.0001 per cent of the market value of the listed notes, with a minimum of both amounts together of Fl.5,000. For foreign-placed equities, the fee is Fl.2,000.[5]

Transaction costs and taxes

New regulations came into force in April 1980, part of them dealing with new commission rates for the purchase and sale of securities. Fees are now as follows:

	Equities %	Bonds %
Up to Fl.5,000	1.25	1.25
Fl.5,000—Fl.20,000	1.0	1.0
Fl.20,000—Fl.100,000	0.7	0.7
Fl.100,000—Fl.500,000	0.7	0.4
Fl.500,000—Fl.1 million	0.7	0.25
> Fl.1 million on the whole amount	0.7	0.36

Increased by Fl.3 for each transaction in any individual security.[6]

A stamp duty of 0.12 per cent is charged, and for bonds the market value includes accrued interest. No value added tax is paid on the amount of commission. There is no withholding tax on any fixed interest securities, nor any interest payment on private loan issues. Private resident investors pay income tax (at the general progressive rate) on all interest revenues, but there is no special capital gains tax, although a 25 per cent tax is levied on equity dividends (subject to relief according to double tax agreements with individual countries).[7]

Supervision

The Vereeniging voor de Effectenhandel has high standards of supervision and control of information and practices in the Stock Exchange. But in the field of take-overs and mergers it does not seem to have quite the same grip. A Decree of 1945 forbids the unauthorised transfer to non-residents of securities issued by Dutch residents. The 1946 Act, which makes it a general rule that securities must go only through stockbrokers, also applies to take-over bids. The 1975 Public Bids and Mergers Code ('Fosiegedragsregelscade'), approved by the Economic and Social Council representing employers' and employees' organisations, set up a Mergers Commission and required copies of all documents relating to take-overs to be filed with the Board of Governors of the Stock Exchange, but there is no penal sanction. The Mergers Code ignores transfers of blocks of securities.

Within the Stock Exchange, there is a Disciplinary Committee and an Appeals Committee. A Control Bureau supervises conduct of members and looks after the interests of investors. The Mergers Commission (comprising nine members appointed by the Economic and Social Council) applies merger rules and reports any proposed merger to the Board of Governors and Minister of Finance. The Board of Governors scrutinises merger information, and can stop an offer going through if it finds breach of contract. The Nederlandsche Bank and Chamber of Assessors have exclusive control over transfer of holdings in banks and insurance companies. The Mergers Code is applied by the Board, but it does not have the force of law, and is deficient in several respects, e.g. omitting to provide equal treatment for all equity holders in a company. The Vereeniging attempts to deal with insider trading by ensuring that prices or terms of an offer do not diverge from those in information supplied to the Board. In addition, the Board may suspend a company on rumour of a merger, and once a firm offer has been made, insist that the offer price must not be exceeded for three years.

Types of markets and trading procedures

The Amsterdam Stock Exchange is unusually elaborate. It has a reputation for adaptability and innovation, and for accommodating foreign investors and borrowers. Seven major sub-markets may be distinguished: (i) the company market for equities, (ii) the company and public sector bond market, (iii) the private placement market, (iv) the bank loan market, (v) the options market for securities and gold, (vi) the unofficial (unlisted) market, (vii) the market for Euroguilder notes (not listed). For the purposes of this analysis, mortgage and real estate loans may be omitted as a separate market category.

1   *The equity market*   Most of the technical features of the Amsterdam equity market have been covered with the exception of trading procedures. Orders may be 'at best', 'at a specified limit', or permitting a fluctuation, usually about ½ per cent. The proviso 'without forcing' may be added. Limit orders may be executed at the day's median price. There are stop-loss orders. The Stock Exchange has published new rules for dealing in securities, and those concerning order procedures are dealt with in the section on reforms. Clearing of equities is also dealt with in a separate section. It is worth remembering that, although of late the bond market has been livelier and faster growing than equities, the equity market still accounts for a large part of the total capital market, and some major domestic and international companies have their equities listed. For example, at June 1980 the nominal value of Dutch equities was Fl.14.9 billion and market value Fl.56.4 billion. The nominal value of Dutch bonds at the end of 1980 was Fl.74.3 billion. But new listings of equities are generally lower: e.g. January/June 1980 Fl.915,076 for equities (market value), Fl.1,494,762 for bonds (nominal value). At June 1980 there were 557 listed equities against 1,533 listed bonds. Finally, in 1979 the annual turnover of bonds was Fl.20,036 million compared with Fl.18,521 million for equities.

2   *The bond market*   The main classes of borrowers in the bond market are the central government, local authorities, and the private sector. At June 1980, out of a nominal value of listed guilder bonds outstanding of Fl.74.3 billion, the central government accounted for 36 per cent, local authorities 16 per cent and the private sector 48 per cent; 1,533 lines of bonds were listed. The main holders of listed guilder bonds are the central bank, commercial banks, specialist banks, the savings banks, insurance companies, pension funds (the largest holders) and the social security funds.

The largest single borrower is the central government. It also guarantees capital and interest of other loans like the State-owned Netherlands Railways, and the Netherlands Investment Bank for Developing Countries. The second largest single borrower is the State-owned Bank voor Nederlandsche Gemeenten (Bank for Netherlands municipalities). The Bank relends funds to other public bodies. Other smaller issuers are semi-government financial institutions like the national Investment Bank, commercial and mortgage banks, and trade and industry organisations including the multinational companies. Foreign bonds, which originate from international organisations or national governments are on a small scale (seventy-nine listed loans) but are an important trading group. The marketability of central government bonds is high.

The most common form of new issues of bonds is by public offer for sale at a fixed price, although the State usually offers for tender. Non-State bonds are allotted to a managing syndicate, stockbrokers and underwriters, and then distributed to customers. Dealing is strictly supervised by the Board of Governors of the Stock Exchange. The Central Bank must approve large issues (> Fl.16 million), and the bank applies an issue calendar for its own and other large issues. The Bank also controls the frequency of foreign bond issues and the proceeds of loans.

The secondary market for listed bonds is uncontrolled, and prices are determined by ordinary supply and demand, although the Government can affect it indirectly by its monetary policy.

3   The private placement market (the 'Onderhandse' market)   The long term private placement market is the largest single sub-market of the Dutch stock market. It is a peculiarly Dutch phenomenon, which accounted for an average 43 per cent of net supply and demand for securities in 1979. It has never accounted for less than one-third of the market since 1970. In the Dutch capital market, a private placement is a fixed interest loan with a maturity up to 20 years, offered by institutional investors like savings banks and pension funds. This market is sustained by the high level of institutional savings in the Netherlands. Pension funds, for example, are large suppliers of funds to the market. Since Dutch pensions are based on the capitalisation principle, pension funds and insurance companies can lend on very long maturities. The commercial banks act as brokers between borrowers and the lending institutions. Private loan placements are cheap and easily arranged. The only documentation is a loan agreement. Interest rates are usually slightly above bond rates because the secondary market for private placements is thin. But generally, this is a highly efficient wholesale market, where institutional investors can make advance placements of funds.

4 The bank loan market This is a domestic medium and long term market which has been growing fast, although strictly it may not be deemed part of the stock market. At the end of 1978, the Dutch banks' external guilder claims amounted to Fl.8.8 billion. A medium term fixed rate guilder bank loan is a very simple debt instrument to arrange, large loans can be syndicated and redemptions negotiated.

5 The options market Options and traded options offer useful investment instruments which can be used to hedge risks on the stock market. Although the concept of issuing options to buy or sell equities ahead at predetermined prices is not new, 'premium' options have been used for a long time. But the new 'European Options Exchange', opened in 1978 in Amsterdam, offers the opportunity to trade options under standardised prices and expiry dates, on an official, regulated market. The EOE is modelled on the Chicago Board Options Exchange, and is recognised as a Stock Exchange under Dutch Law, operating under a Supervisory Committee appointed by the Minister of Finance. Members are firms and individuals worldwide. The terms of options contracts traded are guaranteed by the European Options Clearing Corporation, by taking one side of each option traded. Trade settlement procedures are fully computerised, and swift. Although growth has not been over rapid, the volume of contracts reached nearly 2,900 a day during 1980 with Royal Dutch Shell accounting for nearly half the total. The Commission system is complicated, but generally considered lower than on straight equities. In April 1981 the EOE decided to graft on a gold options market to the existing one, hoping to improve contracts by about 1,000 a day within a year of start-up. The trading unit of the gold option is ten troy ounces of fine gold, and options will be for a fixed expiry date. One major advantage is that premiums will be paid. But like the securities options market, the gold option market needs wide appeal to be successful.

6 The 'unlisted' market ('incourant' market) Many issuers do not apply for listing, and their securities are traded off the Exchange by telephone deals. It has been estimated that there are probably some 1,000 unlisted bonds and equities with around 70 being dealt in regularly, like Holland Sea Search. Two member firms of 'incourante kantoren' handle domestic unlisted securities, Brockman's Commissiebank and D.W. Brand. The Nederlandse Credietbank is another participant; but certain information and guarantees are still required by these dealers. Commission charges are higher than on the official Exchange, and the two specialised firms publish their turnover weekly.

7   *Eurobonds*   Most Eurosecurities bought on the Amsterdam Stock Exchange are guilder notes. A Euroguilder note issue is a medium term financing instrument, for which the maximum amount allowed for issue is Fl.75 million. Maturities range from five to seven years; no underwriting is necessary, and the notes may not even be listed or marketed with a prospectus. As far as issuing technique is concerned, the placements are semi-private. Documentation is simple and cheap, and interest rates compare favourable with other types of borrowing. Growth is limited by the Nederlandsche Bank's ceiling of Fl. 900 million on annual total issues. Between 1969 and 1978 there were 68 domestic issues at Fl.14,180 million and 85 foreign issues at Fl.5,300 million.[8]

Clearing

The Stock Exchange maintains a Securities Clearing Organisation ('Effectenclearing BV'). In principle, securities must be delivered the fourth day following the day on which the transaction has been effected. But delivery and receipt without physical transfer of the certificates can be undertaken through the Effectenclearing. In 1979, the Effectenclearing handled 1,211,000 transactions, but this figure had fallen consistently since 1977. Recently, legislation was passed to set up a Securities Giro in the Netherlands. In this system, the holder of securities is no longer the individual owner of specific units, but instead is a joint owner of a proportionate part of combined blocks of securities of the same type, kept in a collective depository, the Effectenclearing. The system is managed on behalf of member institutions (banks, etc.) by the Nederlands Centraal Instituut voor Giral Effectenverkeer BV which, in turn, is supervised by the Minister of Finance. It does not replace any other clearing arrangements. It transacts only in listed securities.

Evaluation

The Amsterdam Stock Exchange operates under high, self-regulating standards, and maintains a growing bond market as well as a variety of borrowing instruments. The trading environment is liberal, and the Exchange has always had a policy of welcoming foreign savers and borrowers. It has a large foreign listing for its size, and is the home of several large Dutch multinationals.

The number and type of markets and of professional dealers is impressive, although there is quite a large parallel market in unlisted securities. Fees are not excessive, and the corollary to this is a tendency for direct trading and off-hours trading to grow. The tax burden on investment is also moderate.

However, several criticisms can be made of techniques and practices within the Exchange, ranging from the short official trading hours to lack of futures trading and the ban on trading in registered securities on the official Exchange. Certainly, small companies have not been encouraged to be active on the Exchange, which is dominated by the five Dutch multinationals and the Robeco Funds group. These and other points will be taken up in the later section on reform. Supervision is less developed than in many contemporary Exchanges. Perhaps because Amsterdam is a private bourse and largely self-regulating, its supervisory committees (like the Merger Commission), although carrying much weight, have neither the force of law nor compelling sanctions. Less information is disclosed on companies' operations than would be desirable for purposes of investigating insider trading, and all the various practices (like 'warehousing') akin to it. This will also be taken up later.

Performance and efficiency of the Amsterdam stock market

1 The equity market

Although the Amsterdam stock market is regarded as efficient in the management of equity savings and borrowing, it must be admitted that since about 1970 the equity market has lacked lustre. The relative unattractiveness of equity investment and savings has been partly due to the same reasons that have caused flatness on stock markets in the rest of the Community. With prices low, companies have been loath to raise equity capital, and savers have found other higher returning outlets for their funds.

Table 5.6 indicates the divergent trends in listing of bonds and equities in Amsterdam since 1972. Listed Dutch and foreign equities have fallen in number by 25 per cent between 1972 and June 1980, but Dutch and foreign bonds increased in number by 6 per cent. If the figures for bond listings are disaggregated, they show that Dutch bonds listings rose by 12 per cent, and (a smaller number of) listings for foreign bonds fell by 51 per cent.

In terms of value, the nominal value of Dutch equities rose 3.6 per cent and their market value by 11 per cent. But in contrast, the

Table 5.6
Listed securities on the Amsterdam Stock Exchange

	1972	1973	1974	1975	1976	1977	1978	1979	June 1980
Dutch bonds	1,251	1,272	1,289	1,310	1,334	1,359	1,379	1,412	1,410
Foreign bonds	191	187	170	168	150	135	136	126	123
Equities in Dutch investment trusts	36	33	34	34	32	31	30	30	30
Equities in foreign investment trusts	47	44	43	38	38	36	32	32	30
Dutch equities (certificates)	326	307	295	275	256	249	237	229	224
Foreign equities (depositary receipts)	289	292	303	295	290	292	288	274	273
Total	2,140	2,135	2,134	2,120	2,100	2,102	2,102	2,103	2,090

Source: Amsterdam Stock Exchange, half-yearly review, 30 June 1980.

nominal value of total listed Dutch bonds rose by more than 50 per cent over the same period. By 1979, bonds accounted for 52 per cent of the total value of turnover. And this does not include the lively unlisted market for bonds, for which figures are not available.

However, the general sluggishness of Dutch equities is not typical of all sectors of economic activity. Since 1970, the overall performance has been good in banking and insurance equities, and worst in domestic manufacturing. The multinationals have also fared rather poorly. Table 5.7 shows the behaviour of equity prices over the period, for major sectors.

The table (5.7) clearly shows a steadily falling general index of all-share equity prices, with multinationals and manufacturing doing poorly. Unfortunately, the weighting of these two groups is heavy in the all-share index (weighting by market capitalisation). Together they account for 87 per cent of the movement of the all-share index. Royal Dutch Shell itself accounts for 20–40 per cent of turnover. By contrast, banks' and insurance companies' weighting is 0.06 combined and, although the prices of their shares rose strongly over the period, they had little impact on the general index. Shipping and trade were cyclical, but ended the period with small gains.

Table 5.7
Equity prices on the Amsterdam Stock Exchange

Period	Multi-national companies	Domestic	(of which) Manufacturing	Ship and air transport	Banks	Insurance	Trade etc.	All-share index	All-share index per cent change on previous period
(weights)	0.48	0.52	0.39	0.04	0.05	0.01	0.03	1.00	
1970	100	100	100	100	100	100	100	100	-8
1971	91	98	95	110	119	76	99	94	-6
1972	96	121	114	132	164	88	127	109	16
1973	97	133	126	148	188	97	135	116	6
1974	73	104	97	120	145	90	105	89	-23
1975	72	107	97	116	183	101	107	90	1
1976	84	105	92	118	196	106	103	95	6
1977	81	99	83	105	213	118	108	90	-5
1978	77	104	83	102	254	148	120	91	1
1979	79	100	75	102	272	165	113	90	-1

Source: De Nederlandsche Bank NV, Quarterly Statistics, no.2, September 1980.

Turnover on the Stock Exchange improved for all major categories of equities, but the performance of each group differed. Table 5.8 shows this performance, and compares it with that of bonds.

Table 5.8
Security turnover

Period	Amounts actually paid in billions of guilders					
	Equities (ordinary and preferred)				Bonds, incl. mortgage bank bonds	Total
	Multinationals*	Domestic	Investment companies	Foreign		
1970	4.4	4.8	1.2	0.6	4.3	15.5
1971	4.4	4.4	1.3	0.8	6.0	17.0
1972	6.1	10.1	2.8	1.2	8.1	28.4
1973	5.6	9.4	2.9	1.1	6.5	25.6
1974	3.2	4.9	1.8	0.5	5.9	16.3
1975	4.3	6.8	1.6	1.1	10.7	24.5
1976	5.4	6.4	2.5	1.6	12.9	28.8
1977	5.9	7.1	4.5	0.8	17.9	36.3
1978	4.9	9.3	5.0	0.9	22.2	42.3
1979	5.8	6.8	5.1	0.8	20.0	38.6

Source: De Nederlandsche Bank NV, Quarterly Statistics, no.2, September 1980.

*AKZO, Hoogovens, Royal Dutch, Philips, and Unilever.

Figures are rounded.

In terms of inflation-adjusted prices, multinationals have not done well, neither have foreign equities. The turnover of domestic equities has done a little better, partly aided by steady (unadjusted) prices, and investment companies as a group and bonds have done very well, accounting for most of the rise in the total market turnover over the period.

As far as yields are concerned, whilst for domestic and foreign equities between 1970 and 1980 (July) they have improved to a small degree, they have consistently been below bond yields, with the exception of the 3.25 per cent Netherlands 1948 (9.8 years) loan. Table 5.9 gives an indication.

Table 5.9
Capital market yields, 1970 to 1980 (July)

Item	Dec. 1970	1971	1972	1973	1974	1975	1976	1977	1978	1979	July 1980
				(monthly averages)							
Latest 3 long term central government loans (12.1 years)	8.01	7.98	7.63	9.64	9.55	8.52	8.22	8.13	8.48	9.91	9.67
International equities	5.0	6.1	5.0	6.6	10.0	7.0	7.0	7.1	7.8	7.9	7.6
Domestic equities	4.7	4.7	3.3	4.3	5.3	4.8	5.1	5.6	5.5	6.7	7.0

Source: De Nederlandsche Bank NV, Quarterly Statistics, no.2, September 1980.

With Government yields consistently higher, and with lower risk, there has clearly been little incentive for savers to invest in equities in general, unless they could pick special groups (like banking and insurance) or particular stocks. But even this option was narrowed down in 1977, when the Central Bank placed restrictions on direct credit. In comparison with mortgage loans, for instance, there continually has been a differential of 4.5 to 5 per cent in yield over the period.

There are several reasons for the generally disappointing performance of equities on the Dutch Stock Exchange. The economy is low growth, inflation (although not excessive) rose to 6.5 per cent in 1980, the balance of payments is in deficit on visibles and invisibles account. And the Government has generated a large, continuing budget deficit, financed 70 per cent (1979) on long term through the capital market, causing some crowding out of private sector demand for capital.

In the capital market, contractual savings have been deposited with institutional investors (e.g. savings banks) rather than used to buy securities. The institutional investors themselves have tended to increase their lending on fixed term, long maturity, outside the issues market. The share of the personal and business sector in supplying funds to the market fell from 8 to -1.0 per cent in 1979.[9] On the demand side, this sector takes 55—60 per cent of net demand in the capital market, but it is mainly made up of mortgage loans to households, and medium term bank loans to companies. The banks, in making these loans, have turned to the institutional investors to refinance their credit operations. Two more factors have been in operation, both very important.

First, Government spending and borrowing has greatly increased in the 1970s for reasons explained earlier. There has been 'crowding out' of equities in the sense that, as companies' profits fell, institutional investors were less interested in lending to them. Second, the companies then turned to the banks for medium term loans, but this source is now drying up.

2   The bond market

The strength of this has already been seen in comparison with the weak performance of the equity market in Amsterdam since 1970. Yields, turnover and number of listings were all higher than the equity category counterpart in most of the seventies. The growth of the various parts of this market is shown in Table 5.10.

Table 5.10
The Dutch guilder bond and loan market and its sub-sectors
(gross amounts in Dutch guilders, billions)

	1969	1971	1973	1975	1976	1977	1978
Public issue market	2.6	3.6	2.2	5.6	4.8	6.6	6.7
(of which issues by non-residents)	(—)	(0.2)	(—)	(0.4)	(0.4)	(0.3)	(0.5)
Private placement market	5.2	7.8	10.5	15.8	16.8	20.9	22.1
(of which placements by non-residents)	(—)	(—)	(—)	(0.1)	(1.4)	(0.6)	(0.5)
Medium term bank loan market	no reliable estimate available						
(of which loans to non-residents)							3.6 (est.)
Euroguilder notes market	0.1	1.0	0.6	1.5	1.1	0.8	0.8
(of which by non-residents)	(—)	(0.5)	(0.2)	(1.0)	(0.8)	(0.6)	(0.6)

Source: Nagtzaam, R., 'The Dutch Capital Market: a Special Case', *Netherlands Banking Digest*, no.7, December 1979.

The public issue market (central government and local authorities and guaranteed banks) has grown apace, and accelerated since 1978. New issues in the domestic bond market amounted to Fl.7.5 billion in 1979 compared with Fl.2.6 million ten years before. The main reasons for this huge increase have been (i) growing budget deficits of the central government, (ii) banks borrowing on long term on an increasing scale, especially under present Government credit policies, (iii) savers' preference for Government paper, (iv) companies' low level of fixed investment and therefore lower demand for long term loans. In 1979 the market grew again by 13 per cent over 1978. The strength of central government borrowing can be seen in its rise in 1980, by Fl.2.4 billion in the first three months, compared with Fl.4 billion for the whole of 1979. In the middle of 1980, long term central government debt amounted to 21 per cent of net national income, and short term debt to 6 per cent.

The private placement market, whose importance was described earlier (over 40 per cent of net demand/supply of securities) quadrupled in value 1969—78 (see Table 5.10), although credit restrictions in 1977 forced the banks into longer term lending.

Although not part of the issue market, the domestic medium and long term bank loan market has grown very rapidly since the sixties, especially lending to foreigners. It is estimated that the market nearly doubled in value between 1975 (Fl.4.7 billion) and 1978 (Fl.8.8 billion).

The Euroguilder note market is very small by international standards, but has built up a good base in Amsterdam. From the time of the first issue, in 1969, 153 issues totalling Fl.9.5 billion have been successfully placed in Amsterdam. About one-half were made by foreign borrowers. The market is not likely to grow a good deal more, since as mentioned before, De Nederlandsche Bank places a limit on the total.

The unlisted market in Amsterdam is not very well documented. Although about 1,000 equities and bonds are listed in the annual market guide produced by the brokers in the market, only some 70 or 80 are traded actively. Among these are Verkade Fabrieken, a biscuit manufacturer, Zuid Pacific Koper, a company with mining investments, and Holland Sea Search.

A number of Indonesian plantations are also listed, whose assets are post-nationalisation claims for compensation. Water boards make issues on this market, and secondary trading is active and perfectly respectable. Although no figures are published on the size of the market, the daily turnover is believed to be in the region of Fl.1—8 million. But, since many companies see this market as a stepping stone to official listing, there is a steady drain of companies moving to the official Exchange.

Finally, the options market, which began trading in calls in April 1978, has been rather slow to develop. In the second quarter of 1978 a daily average of 750 contracts was reached; in the third quarter of 1979 2,100 contracts a day. Break-even point was originally thought to be 7,000 contracts a day, but the introduction of put options in March 1979 reduced that point to 5,000 a day. By July 1980, average daily turnover was 3,000 contracts, and it is noted that break-even will have been reached by the end of 1981. The biggest lack is of foreign securities. Royal Dutch Shell dominates trading. As a result the Exchange showed a loss of Fl.4 million in 1979. However, these are early days, and the addition of gold options should help turnover. The European Options Exchange hopes to start trading options on fixed interest securities during 1982.

Efficiency

In addition to the paper by Solnik[10] which tested a number of European securities, including 24 Dutch securities, for their conformity to the random walk hypothesis (and found market inefficiencies) the author is aware of studies by Tombros, Ballendux, Kolk and Schoorl, and Wierez (on the European Options Exchange).

Tombros[11] (Erasmus University) asks the question, in the context of the Netherlands stock market, whether prices of equities are affected by changes in the supply of money? This question has its roots in the monetary portfolio model developed by Friedman and Schwartz (1963), and Patinkin (1972). Others, e.g. Hamburger and Kochin (1972) supported the model with actual research. More statistical studies on the basis of the efficient market hypothesis (EMH) by such authors as Pesando (1974) and Vinso and Rogalski (1977) refute these earlier findings. In particular, a practical study of the Netherlands by Spaans (1980)[12] has shown that changes in the money supply do not affect Dutch equity prices. Tombros used data for a longer period than Spaans, and tested the proposition that money supply affects stock prices with a lag. He concluded that seasonally-adjusted changes in the M1 money supply did not influence returns on Dutch equities (using the ANP/CBS general index) either with a lag of time, which would contradict the EMH, or immediately, when it would not. But the weak efficiency test of EMH could not be rejected for the Amsterdam Stock Exchange because the average of stock prices every third month appeared to move randomly.

Ballendux[13] (Erasmus University), studied the efficiency of perpetual Dutch consols to see if interest rates on them approximately followed a martingale sequence (i.e. whether long run interest rates can be expressed as a function of expected future short term rates). This happens in an efficient market when all information is known by everyone. By using correlation techniques, Ballendux concludes that, in general, market efficiency for the Dutch long term bond market seems a 'very reasonable approximation of reality'. This is confirmed by the order of magnitude of observed autocorrelation of changes in the consol yield prewar.

Kolk and Schoorl[14] (University of Amsterdam) considered data for the Amsterdam market from the points of view of the capital asset pricing model and the efficient market model. They found the distribution of yields of equities in the market to be leptokurtic (i.e. a high concentration around the mean). It was more normally distributed over a longer period. Much of the variation in equity yields was the result of the use of specific information on equities. The authors could not reject the weak-form test of the EMH.

Finally, Jacques Wierez[15] has looked at the European Options Exchange in Amsterdam and tested for efficiency, using the model devised by Black and Scholes (1973). For options, the model indicated that undervalued options should be purchased, and overvalued options sold, where 'under' and 'over' were values calculated by reference to the real value of the option, and where short maturity options were undervalued, and long term options overvalued. No positive correlation between theoretical values and maturities was found. The EOE could not be considered 'efficient' in this sense.

New legislation and Stock Exchange reform

The Amsterdam Stock Exchange Board of Governors has been innovative and imaginative in reviewing its procedures and practices over the past few years but, perhaps because it is a private organisation, there has been no official large scale Commission of Enquiry. The Board has moved in a piecemeal manner, both introducing EEC directives as smoothly and quickly as possible, and attempting to revitalise what is clearly a sluggish equity market.

On 1 April 1980, as a result of a long inquiry, the Board of Governors introduced new commission charges on securities. These were detailed earlier in this chapter. The differences between the new rates and the old are a higher rate on small lots of equities and bonds (up to Fl.5,000) (to discourage fragmentation of bargains), and over Fl.500,000 a discriminatory rate in favour of bonds, until at the highest size of bargains the rate of commission on equities is twice what it is on bonds. Previously, equities and bonds were subject to the same rates.

At the same time as it introduced the new commission rates, the Board established new Regulations for Dealing in Securities.[16] The motive behind these changes was to provide regulation of those dealings that took place before and after the official trading hours of 1130 to 1315 hours. It is hoped that dealings will be concentrated within the wider hours of 1000 hours to 1630 hours, that turnover will be increased on the Exchange, and prices established that reflect more nearly the normal workings of supply and demand as better information on after-hours bids and offers becomes known.

But the number of securities that can be dealt in after official hours has been limited at present to a further twenty-seven listed securities of large companies like AMRO Bank and Heineken NV. This number was added to the securities of multinational companies like AKZO and Unilever that have been traded out of official hours for many years. This limitation to large companies was designed to ensure a large daily turnover, and therefore a reasonable price.

The criterion for admitting equities to dealing before and after official hours is a minimum effective turnover for three years.

Dealing before and after official hours is now also possible in bonds issued by the Netherlands Government and the Bank voor Nederlandsche Gemeenten (Bank for Municipalities), plus some types of mortgage bonds.

Under the new system, an order which a client wishes executed before or after official hours has to be stated as 'valid for all Exchanges'.

The conditions which may be imposed by a client on an order to buy or sell a security are also now more explicitly defined under the April 1980 Regulations. These conditions concern price and time.

Where *price* is concerned, there are five possible conditions:

(i) a limited order — no purchase above price stated or sale below, but a client may be obliged to accept a partial execution of an order

(ii) order 'at best price' — on execution, the principal obtains full settlement at the next dealt price

(iii) 'no forcing' order — the broker or banker has the right to determine the moment of settlement and mode (instalments) if the price is largely unaffected

(iv) stop-loss order — at the lower price limit stated

(v) yield order — executed at a price at which a prearranged yield is obtained.

Where *time* is concerned, there are four possible conditions:

(i) standing order — valid until the time when the limit is cancelled

(ii) day order — valid only on the day when it is given

(iii) period order — valid only for the first or second period

(iv) exchange order — a security is exchanged for another on the same day and/or in the same period.

In September 1980, the Stock Exchange began direct trading in American equities during the new extended trading hours. The system devised to handle the equities is called 'ASAS' (American Shares Amsterdam System or Amerikaanse Aandelen Amsterdamse Usance), and the American equities handled by the Bankers Trust of New York. Two subsidiary nominees of the Amsterdam Stock Exchange have been created, to hold and account for delivery respectively. These are the Nominee Amsterdam Stock Exchange NV, and ASAS Servicing Company NV, both located in Amsterdam. The Nominee Company holds the American equities for the Amsterdam System, and the Service Company accounts for and delivers (by book transfer) securities held by the Nominee, five business days after the transaction date (which conforms with US practice).

For each 'ASAS' recorded in the Nominee Company's books, an actual equity is deposited in New York for the account of the Nominee. Trading in American equities takes place from 1000 hours to 1630 hours, and quotations and fractions are in American dollars. As with securities to be dealt in before and after official hours, an order for an American equity must be stated as 'ASAS', and otherwise the normal regulations of the Stock Exchange apply. A reasonable commission is charged by the broker for handling ASAS equities. From 15 September 1980, trading subject to ASAS procedures applies to twelve large American companies, e.g. Citicorp, General Motors and Sears Roebuck. Investors can also trade options on the EOE on these twelve American equities.[17]

The ASAS system is an improvement on the previous method of dealing in American equities. Then, Dutch investors and borrowers had to apply directly to Wall Street, and deal in bearer certificates. Bearer certificates of US equities are currently traded on the Amsterdam Stock Exchange, but with high costs and delays in settlement, and price distortions arising from arbitrage. It is hoped eventually to increase the number of listed US equities that can be traded ASAS and add to the volume of transactions taking place within the Exchange's new trading hours' limits.

Recent reforms or innovations which have been dealt with in some detail in earlier sections concern the opening of the European Options Exchange in 1978, and the gold options market in 1981, and the establishment of the Securities Giro, in which securities are delivered by Giro and a central depot is set up to hold paper in the names of members of the Stock Exchange. The Board of Governors of the Stock Exchange was also instrumental in persuading the Government to abolish double taxation of corporate dividends. Currently, a new Stock Exchange Act is under study, in which the role of the Minister of Finance will be redefined and adapted to changed economic and social conditions.

Although it is not an internal change in stock market functioning, there has recently been agreement at Government level on Dutch bank equity participation in industry, which should have the effect of stimulating equity turnover in the market. Anxiety has been expressed over the increasing gearing of listed companies, which reached 73 per cent on average in 1979. Until 1980, the Government restricted bank equity participation in non-banking activities to 5 per cent, unless exceptionally approved by De Nederlandsche Bank. Originally, the rule arose out of fears of the implications of bank mergers in the 1960s. Since more recently medium term bank lending to industry has increased, there would appear to be no reason why greater equity participation should not be allowed. The Ministry of Finance and De Nederlandsche Bank have now agreed to relax the 5 per cent rule permitting banks to increase their holdings subject to certain conditions, i.e. as long as the equity participation:

(i)   does not exceed a minority holding

(ii) does not exceed an (unspecified) percentage of equity and reserves of the banks involved

(iii) does not exceed Fl.2.5 million

(iv) is held in a single company for not more than five years (renewable by agreement with the Government).

Other prescriptions for stock market reform

Already it has been stated that the 1914 Stock Exchange Act (with amendments) is under review, with especial emphasis on the self-regulatory aspect of the Exchange. Whilst no criticism need be made of self-regulation *per se*, it does appear that the present role of the Ministry of Finance in relation to the Exchange is ambiguous. In comparison with the experience of other self-regulating Exchanges, there should be a move towards greater powers of sanction either by the Board of Governors, or by the Ministry of Finance. Insider dealing is one example of a gap which can exist through lack of specific controls. Also, in other countries, company law is tighter on aspects of company affairs, taking away some of the responsibility from the Stock Exchange or Government.

In a market for equities in which at present half the trading is dominated by the equities of a few large companies, and the turnover is not increasing fast, there would appear to be a plethora of professional dealers of different types in addition to the banks who have full membership. Trading costs are not high and, although the structure of commissions has changed, the level of the new charges of intermediaries is below the average for the Community bourses. But this does not mean efficiency is high. There is no published information about speed of transactions or (say) costs of commissionairs. It is known that the number of commissionairs has fallen steeply: in 1955 it was 235, in 1976 82, and they do not profit equally. In 1976, their average pretax earnings were of the order of Fl.34,000, apparently only 13 per cent of revenue received. Among the 53 hoekmen in 1976, earnings were four times as high. With the new commission charges from April 1980, which are generally lower than those they replaced (in percentage terms), the commissionairs and hoekmen will presumably need greater turnover of business to earn reasonable profits. The whole question of the profitability and efficiency of intermediaries requires close attention since it affects the total efficiency of the Exchange. Other Exchanges in the Community have the same problem.

Among smaller items, whilst the Exchange has made direct trading in registered American securities a reality, it would be desirable if the general position of registered securities were regularised on the Exchange. Although most Continental securities are in bearer form, easing restrictions on registered securities could make a difference to UK clients, especially with exchange controls now removed. The new listing charges seem quite high in comparison with other Exchanges, e.g. more than twice those in Belgium. The fee for foreign-placed securities is very high. This may operate against medium and smaller sized companies who currently place issues in the unlisted market, or avoid the Stock Exchange altogether as a vehicle for borrowing. Otherwise, the tax burden on companies has been made easier.

In Amsterdam, in addition to the rules of company law and the articles of association of companies, the Exchange has model regulations regarding the sort of information needed for issue approval. This is usually additional to what is required by law. For example, there are special rules for the certificates of investment companies. Naturally, there are rules on disclosure. The Amsterdam Bourse has generally high standards of scrutiny of the type just described, and Dutch companies seek 'Stock Exchange status' keenly. The transparency of the market is further increased by requirements for half-yearly or quarterly (unaudited) information.

But while the Stock Exchange can hardly be faulted on the information and conditions required for listing securities, it is less rigorous in its supervision of the transference of controls between companies listed on the Exchange. This may be a result of the private nature of the Vereeniging voor de Effectenhandel, and could be improved if the Stock Exchange Act is revised in any radical way. For example, one way of anticipating companies with dominant equity holdings is to require a breakdown of capital ownership in prospectuses drawn up in connection with listing. There are no specific requirements for this in the Netherlands.

The Decree of October 1945 forbids the unauthorised transfer to non-residents of securities issued by Dutch companies, but the weakness here is that the Stock Exchange authorities have no way to apply the law. However, another piece of legislation which helps prevent damaging transfers of securities is the one requiring Government authorisation for the purchase of large equity holdings by banks. Since the Stock Exchange has a monopoly, it has ruled that listed securities must be traded on the official floor (Ministerial Order of 1946), which means trading through an official intermediary. This Ministerial Order is also used against take-over bids; but, although copies of all documents relating to take-overs should be filed with the Vereeniging, there is no legal penalty for non-compliance. All the Vereeniging can do is reprimand or prohibit its members from dealing in the offer — which effectively blocks it.

The Merger Code in the Netherlands needs strengthening to cover the many different variations in take-overs. The Code, although recently amended to provide (for instance) equal treatment for all equity holders, does not have the force of law. Under the Code 'mergers' are not distinguished from 'take-overs', a point that could be clarified.

Fiscal, company and savings/investment incentives

As far as corporation tax is concerned, the Netherlands has a 'classical' system under which corporate profits are fully subject to corporation tax, and dividends fully subject to personal income tax. The rate of corporation tax on profits ('veunootschapsbelasting') at the end of December 1979 was 48 per cent with reduced rates for profits under Fl.50,000. There is no tax credit, and there is a withholding tax on equity dividends, but none on fixed interest securities. Double taxation agreements exist with many countries. Capital gains from business assets are exempt from tax.

From 1978, some measures of tax relief were introduced for individuals and companies to offset the effects of inflation. Domestic and foreign companies became eligible for 1.15 per cent relief on business income (and individuals 1.4 per cent). Later in 1978 there was a further allowance of 3 per cent on business income. In the same year, several investment incentives were introduced in some key industries, ranging from 23 per cent on new buildings to 7 per cent on plant.[18] These measures represented a change in the system of giving incentives. Instead of relating incentives to assessment, the new system sets off a fraction of the amount of new investment, in the form of basic and additional premiums, against the sum of tax, with any excess being refunded by the State. Thus loss-making companies qualify for State financial aid as well as profitable ones. Generally, the burden of corporation tax in the Netherlands is one of the highest in the Community (probably Luxembourg leads).

There are some restrictions on equity investments by institutions. The State Pension Fund is limited to investment solely in listed Dutch securities. If insurance companies hold foreign securities, they must also hold foreign assets to an amount equal to the liabilities.

In addition to the 1978 scheme, which introduced differentiated investment premia, another group of incentives was introduced in 1980. These encouraged environmental protection and energy saving investments by giving them an additional 10 per cent premium on top of the basic premium.

Since the Government's 1978 'Blueprint' plan to encourage investment by sectors, the policy has been rather muted in subsequent years. The 1980 initiative has been modified, with the new emphasis being placed on capacity restructuring at the sectoral rather than the company level, so that individual projects can gain Government financial aid only within the framework of a sectoral plan. Such a project can receive up to 20–25 per cent Government financial contribution, and subsidies of up to 40 per cent are awarded in sectors with a high share of small to medium sized companies.

Research and development investment is given special treatment, e.g. 5 per cent fixed interest development credits subsidising up to 70 per cent of R & D spending. In addition, a fund called 'Spearpoint' which has been in existence for three years, is a major governmental instrument for supporting technological investment. It had Fl.50 million available in 1977, and disbursed Fl.43.7 million on 15 projects.[19] There are two more, well established sources of equity capital for Dutch industry – the Industriel Garantie Fonds, which was given increased lending powers in 1977, and NV Noordelijke Ontwikkelings Maatschappij (NOM). NOM has a special responsibility for development lending to the north region of the Netherlands. Set up in 1974, and owned by the Economics Ministry, it operates independently and, in 1980, had equity holdings of between 11 and 100 per cent in twenty-seven companies making such varied products as bricks, printed carpets and industrial robots. The Province Limburg is also served by a local development agency, the Limburg Institute for Development and Financing, and the northern Netherlands also has OOM and GOM (Overijssel Development Company and the Gelderland Development Company).

Summary

The Netherlands ran into the same recessionary problems as its Community partners in 1979/80, with the worst problems being stagnant industrial production, weak profitability, rising unemployment, a current account balance of payments deficit, and burgeoning Government deficit financing. Government economic policy in 1981 was set fair for massive public spending cuts and deflation.

The story of Dutch company finance in the seventies is one of increasing gearing ratios associated with weak profits, with short term debt predominating: although some sectors of industry (banks, insurance companies) fared well. Stock market financing has been low, but is now increasing. Domestic corporate bond financing is negligible. But the 'private loan market' (onderhandse) is large and has grown strongly.

The central government has had a budget deficit for some years, and in 1981 it reached massive proportions, leading to criticisms of 'crowding out' equities in the stock market.

The privately owned Amsterdam Stock Exchange has a sophisticated structure — many types of intermediaries, many sub-markets (up to seven, according to definition) and an innovatory attitude. New commission rates are cheap, but listing is still dear. Supervision is largely self-controlled and not over-rigorous. Some of the sub-markets — options in securities and gold, Euroguilder notes, and the unlisted market — are particularly interesting. Clearing is well organised.

But the equity market has been sluggish since about 1970, with most indicators of performance down (listings, general index down, turnover barely rising, yields static). Several reasons, external and internal to the economy, are responsible. The bond market over the same period, by comparison, has been lively, especially the market for private placements. Such statistical tests of market efficiency as there are, by reference to the random walk hypothesis and the efficient market model, show the Amsterdam Stock Exchange and the European Options Exchange to be no better than 'weak-form efficient'.

The Stock Exchange has introduced several reforms: direct trading in American registered equities, new and attractive broker commission rates, extended trading hours to regulate the unlisted market better, a Securities Giro, and greater bank participation in equities.

It is suggested that a new Stock Exchange Act could clarify the role of the Ministry of Finance better, that the number and type of professional dealers could be examined, that registered securities might be admitted to trading, and that supervision of such management practices as take-overs and mergers could be better enforced.

Finally, a survey is made of the wide-ranging incentives (especially tax and subsidy) made to Dutch industry by the enlightened Dutch Government.

Notes and references

1   *ABN Economic Review*, I, December 1979 and *ABN Economic Review*, II, February 1980,'The Financial Position of Companies Listed on the Amsterdam Stock Exchange'.

2   Dealt with in some detail in Freundlieb, Konrad, 'The Role of the Banks in Financing Fixed Capital Formation in the Netherlands', *Euro-coöperation*, no.21, June 1979.

3   ABN Bank, *Economic Review*, no.83, December 1980.

4   Information on history of the Amsterdam Stock Exchange from Bleekroode, H., 'The Amsterdam Stock Exchange', Amro Bank conference paper, November 1979.

5   Vereeniging voor de Effectenhandel, *Fondsenreglement* (Rules concerning the inclusion of securities in the official list), August 1978.

6   Beursplein 5, *New Regulations for Dealings in Securities*.

7   De Nederlandsche Bank, *Dutch Bond Market* (undated paper).

8   Nagtzaam, R., 'The Dutch Capital Market: a Special Case', *Netherlands Banking Digest*, no.7, December 1979.

9   ABN Bank, op.cit. (see note 3).

10   Solnik, B.H., 'Note on the Validity of the Random Walk for European Stock Prices', *Journal of Finance*, vol.XXVIII, 1973.

11   Tombros, G., 'Money Supply and Stock Prices in the Netherlands', unpublished paper by courtesy of the author.

12   Spaans, F., 'Geldhoereelheid en aandelenkoersen: een causaliteitstoets', *De Nederlandsche Bank NV*, 1980 (cited in note 12).

13   Ballendux, F.J., 'Bond Market Efficiency and the Record of Dutch Government Consols, 1919–1978', unpublished paper by courtesy of the author.

14   Kolk, M.H., Schoorl, J.S., 'De Efficiënte Markttheorie en de Amsterdamse Effectenbeurs', *Research Memorandum no.8011*, University of Amsterdam, Department of Economics, 1980, unpublished paper by courtesy of the authors.

15   Wierez, Jacques, 'Le Nouveau Marché d'Options d'Amsterdam; Conditions de Fonctionnement et Efficience', thèse de l'Institute de l'École Supérieure de Lille.

16   Beursplein 5, *New Regulations for Dealings in Securities*.

17   Beursplein 5, *American Shares (ASAS)*.

18   Platt, C.J., *Tax Systems of Western Europe*, Gower Publishing Company, 1980.

19   Hamilton, R.T., Alma, N.M.G., Hugenholtz, J.B.Th., Tjon, A., Hen, A., *Risk Capital in the Netherlands*, Indivers Research, Amsterdam, private paper by courtesy of Mr Hamilton.

6 United Kingdom

Company financing

As early as 1976, a Midland Bank article[1] looked at the question whether the continuing low level of investment in the UK was a prime reason for Britain's relatively low average rate of growth, both in manufacturing and industrial output and in the whole economy. The conclusions were, briefly, that the levels of investment that were attained represented some success, and there were no great problems in raising money. The problem has been to achieve a corresponding increase in output and real returns. This bears out the conclusions of the 1975 National Economic Development Organisation's study,[2] that there was virtually no constraint on the availability or cost of finance for companies, at least until 1973. With the 1973/74 slump, a temporary shortage did appear, but even at that time the degree of capital utilisation and confidence were more important determinants of investment. In 1973/74, NEDO believed equity borrowing was 'crowded out' in the stock market by government gilts which attracted tax concessions. These findings were confirmed in June 1980 by the report of the Committee to Review the Functioning of Financial Institutions (the 'Wilson Committee') which concluded that real investment had not been held back by shortages in the supply of external finance. But the Committee deplored the associated burden — high and fluctuating inflation. Its central finding was that '. . . it is the price of finance in relation to expected profitability which is the major financial constraint on real investment at present. The perceived real cost of capital is now almost certainly higher than the average real profitability of industrial and commercial companies'.[3]

The following tables show the long term financing pattern and uses of funds by listed industrial and commercial companies, up to the period when the UK entered the 1979 recession.

Table 6.1

Sources of funds of UK listed industrial and commercial companies
(£ billion)

	Internal funds*	Bank borrowing	Other loans and mortgages	UK capital issues**	Overseas†	Import and other credits
1963–66	2.5	0.5	0.1	0.4	0.2	–0.1
1967–70	3.0	0.7	0.1	0.3	0.3	0.0
1971–74	4.8	3.1	0.3	0.3	0.8	0.0
1975	5.0	0.5	0.5	1.2	1.2	–0.1
1976	7.1	2.4	0.5	0.8	1.4	–0.5
1977	10.3	3.0	0.1	0.7	1.5	0.0
1978	12.9	2.9	0.3	0.8	1.3	–0.4
1979	13.1	4.9	0.6	0.9	0.5	–0.1

Source: Bank of England *Quarterly Bulletin*, June 1980 (adapted).

* Undistributed income (net of stock appreciation), capital transfers (net receipts), increases in tax balances.

** Equity and company bond issues.

† Overseas capital issues, etc.

Table 6.2

Composition of UK issues (£ billion, average annual rate)

	1963–67	1968–72	1973–75	1976–79
Equities	0.1	0.2	0.4	0.8
Company bonds	0.3	0.2	0.1	–

Source: Bank of England *Quarterly Bulletin*, June 1980 (adapted).

Table 6.3
Uses of funds, industrial and commercial companies
(£ billions, annual averages)

	1963–66	1967–70	1971–74	1975–79
Fixed assets	2.3	2.8	4.6	9.5
Acquisitions	0.3	0.3	0.6	0.8
Stocks	0.6	0.9	2.8	5.2
Other (mortgages, etc.)	0.8	1.2	3.6	4.0
Total (A)	4.0	5.2	11.6	19.5
Amount required to maintain:				
Stocks (= stock appreciation)	0.2	0.5	2.2	4.6
Fixed assets (= depreciation at replacement cost)	1.1	1.5	2.5	6.2
Total (B)	1.3	2.0	4.7	10.8
A/B percentage	33	38	41	55

Source: Bank of England *Quarterly Bulletin*, September 1980.

The structure of financing has changed over the long term. In the early 1960s, internal funding was nearly 70 per cent of total funding; it then fell steadily to a nadir of 52 per cent in 1974, rising erratically to 66 per cent in 1979. The item is mainly a function of profits. Bank borrowing has increased strongly, although again erratically, reaching 24 per cent in 1979 after a higher position in the early 1970s. There is a long term tendency for bank borrowing to be more important in new external financing of secondary industry as a whole, and the emphasis is increasingly on term lending rather than overdraft. The other significant change has been in the structure of industrial borrowing on the Stock Exchange. As Table 6.2 shows, equity issues have risen consistently over the period, in absolute and relative terms, and company fixed interest borrowing virtually disappeared after 1975.

The larger firms have increased their equity borrowing, usually by rights issues, in conditions of reasonable market liquidity and in 1979 equities provided about one-sixth of external funds. British industry is still low geared in comparison with most of EC industry. The decline in the company bond market is linked to increasing interest rates and increasing inflation.

Companies also borrow from Finance for Industry (owned by the Clearing Banks and the Bank of England) and its subsidiary, the Industrial and Commercial Finance Corporation. The latter specialises in lending to smaller enterprises. The non-bank market for loans and credits includes the pension funds, insurance companies and various finance houses, inter-company lending, Department of Industry loans and grants in assisted areas, and a strongly growing leasing business by banks and specialised companies.

But financing is in a vacuum unless related to use. Table 6.3 sets out categories and derives a 'net necessary borrowing requirement'. Total (B) in the table represents finance required to maintain a 'steady state' compared with expansion. This proportion of total funding has steadily increased over sixteen years. In the seventies, however, for many sectors of industry and individual companies, post-tax returns have not been adequate to cover this necessary minimum.

With the steep decline into recession in 1979, the financial position of industrial companies, in particular, changed radically. Many of them disappeared. In 1980 and the first part of 1981, the rate of liquidations continually rose. In the first quarter of 1981, Dun and Bradstreet, the business information company, reported a record rise of 86 per cent compared with the same period in 1980. In April 1981, liquidations were occurring at the rate of 174 a week.

The fall in manufacturing production in 1980 caused financial havoc. For the first nine months of the year, the financial deficit of the total company sector amounted to £1.7 billion. Gross trading profits fell 15 per cent in the first nine months of 1980, and stock values and retained earnings fell, the latter by 50 per cent. Distributed dividends were cut in the manufacturing sector, although they continued at reasonable levels in oils, mining, financials and overseas trading. Price cutting and falling output caused financial crises in all sectors of manufacturing industry. In chemicals, for instance, cash flow was reduced by £1.6 billion. The strength of sterling and high rate of inflation put British chemical product prices on average 37 per cent above those of West Germany. Manufacturing companies reacted to the drop in cash flow by cutting stocks, investment and output.

Another response to the recession was a swift rise in bank borrowing. From April to September 1980, industry and commerce borrowed 60 per cent more than in the same months of the previous year. Payments of interest on bank loans naturally went up, along with tax payments. Overall, the sector produced a six-months' deficit of £2,000 million. As the end of 1980 approached, net bank borrowing declined from this high level as the level of stocks fell. For the whole year, industrial and commercial companies' profitability reflected the poor trading conditions. In durable consumer goods, they fell by 27 per cent, in non-durables by 8 per cent, and the entire capital goods sector rose by a mere 3.5 per cent. Earnings shifted from capital goods to resources and finance. Oils, for instance, accounted for 33 per cent of total listed company profits, yet the companies make up only one-sixth of capitalisation in the *Financial Times* All-Share Index.

As the recession deepened in 1980, it began to weed out the weaker companies in industry. One quarter of all industrial and commercial profits in the year (excluding oil profits) were made by the eight largest companies; compared with just under 22 per cent the year before.[4] For the bulk of companies, experiencing lower profit, gearing rose to 45 per cent of liabilities in September and liquidity remained very low throughout the year.

The 1981 Bank of England study written by N.P. Williams[5] demonstrates clearly the decline in real profitability of British industry from the early 1960s to the late 1970s. This is incontrovertible whichever way profitability is measured — pre- or post-tax, as a rate of return on trading assets or equity, or as share of profits in income, and whether the data is taken from national accounts or companies' published accounts. Williams' paper analyses several measures of real profitability for seventeen sectors of manufacturing industry and five sectors of distribution and services over the period 1961–77. His conclusions are that 'a downward trend in post-tax real returns . . . has been common to most sectors, with many sustaining losses in recent years'. He believes major factors in this trend to be the acceleration of cost inflation in the seventies, and inappropriate pricing policies which have ignored current costs.

Central government and local authority financing

The gilt-edged bond market in Britain is large and active, and the current state of central government and public sector borrowing has an important influence on stock market financial flows as a whole. Table 6.4 indicates the size and trend of public sector borrowing.

PSBR is large in absolute terms, although in relation to GDP it was only 6 per cent in the financial year 1980/81. It has fallen from around 10 per cent in the mid-seventies following the 1973/74 recession. The March 1980 Budget forecast a £12.7 billion central government borrow-

Table 6.4

Public sector borrowing and contributions to the public sector borrowing requirement (PSBR) (£ million)

| | Central government | | | Local authorities | | | | General government | | Public corporations | | | | Public sector |
| | Borrowing requirement | | Direct borrowing from cent.govt. | Borrowing from other sources | Transactions in other public sector debt | | Borrowing requirement | Borrowing requirement | Direct borrowing from cent.govt. | Borrowing from other sources | Transactions in other public sector debt | | Borrowing requirement | Borrowing requirement |
	Total	of which own a/c			Cent. govt.	Pub. corps					Cent. govt.	Local authorities		
	1	2	3	4	5	6	7	8	9	10	11	12	13	14
1975	8,345	5,017	1,189	1,622	-2	-5	2,818	9,974	2,139	505	-34	33	2,645	10,480
1976	6,786	4,695	512	1,074	4	-33	1,615	7,889	1,579	1,692	160	293	2,818	9,128
1977	4,469	2,607	1,409	156	2	-29	1,592	4,652	453	1,152	20	-211	1,796	5,995
1978	8,371	6,171	362	639	5	-25	1,021	9,030	1,838	-325	175	199	1,139	8,331
1979	10,430	6,594	555	1,768	8	-27	2,342	12,217	3,281	27	-178	-174	3,660	12,596

Source: Central Statistical Office, *Financial Statistics*, January 1981.

Note: Relationship between columns: 1=2+3+9, 7=3+4-5-6, 13=9+10-11-12; Contributions to PSBR: Central government: 1, General government: 8=1+4-5-6=1-3+7, Local authorities: 4-5-6, Public corporations: 10-11-12, PSBR: 14=1+4-5-6+10-11-12 = 1-3+7-9+13 = 2+7+13.

213

ing requirement, which turned out to be £13 billion, mainly because of a Civil Service wage dispute. The dispute had an effect in constraining CGBR and PSBR in 1981/82 by causing a backlog of tax revenue. But the advantages could be lost through increased public spending. From 1981/82 onwards, PSBR will be influenced by the recession, rising 'real' costs and prices, higher debt interest payments (increases in PSBR), North Sea oil taxes and VAT, and EEC rebates (decreases). The 1981 Budget introduced a non-marketable certificate linked to North Sea oil returns, and made a second issue of index-linked national savings certificates more widely available. Also, the Government introduced the first issue of an index-linked gilt-edged security: £1,000m. nominal at 2 per cent interest.

In 1979, 92 per cent of PSBR was financed by the non-bank private sector, of which 75 per cent (£8,805m.) was raised by British Government securities. This proportion has fluctuated since 1975, but the average of 1975—79 was 70 per cent of PSBR. The Government regards the gilt-edged bond market as its major source of financing, and is assisted in this by the fact that investors have received no real return from gilts for a long time (index-linking may alter that). The FT 2.5 per cent Consols Index, based on January 1971 = 100, never reached more than 83 over the period, and in early 1981 stood at 65. Over two-thirds of net issues of government securities mature in fifteen years or longer, and this proportion has been quite steady since 1975, although turnover of gilts up to five years and of more than five years' maturity is about equal.

Clearly the impact of this borrowing on the Stock Exchange is that, although the UK equity market is relatively large in the European Community, it is still dominated by gilts. In 1980, 85 per cent of Stock Exchange turnover by value was in gilts. In the same year, total net cash issues amounted to £11,244m., fourteen times as much as net company (equity and loan) issues. Although erratic, gilts have tended to grow faster than corporate securities since 1976.

Structure and practice of the UK Stock Exchange

Size and status

The Stock Exchange of Great Britain and Ireland is by far the largest exchange in Europe in most respects, and is considered to be the most sophisticated in organisation, procedures and supervision, and to have high standards of trading. The Exchange accounted for over 52 per cent by number of securities listed in the entire European Community in 1979. It accounted for approximately 60 per cent of domestic listed securities (2,814), and 30 per cent of foreign listed securities (1,254). (The nearest exchange in size by this criterion was Paris, with about one-tenth of the UK total of both domestic and foreign securities.) It also had the highest equity turnover, around 38 per cent of the Community total.

The UK Exchange also scores first in the Community on number of new company listings: in 1979, 80 per cent of domestic, 39 per cent of foreign and 64 per cent of total new listings. UK Exchange listings have doubled over the last five years, in contrast to falls in nearly every other EC Exchange.

In the same year, capitalisation of listed domestic equities totalled £67.7 billion, 43 per cent of total Community equities, and double that of the next largest, the Associated German Exchanges.

The UK leads the Community in the size of its public sector fixed interest stock (total of par value) — 34 per cent in 1979 but not in the total of corporate or foreign bonds. Four other exchanges have larger capitalisation of private corporate bonds. The UK fixed interest market is undoubtedly the liveliest in the Community, having about three-quarters of total Community turnover in 1979.

Finally, the capitalisation of the UK Exchange (excluding foreign equities) was 35 per cent of UK GNP in 1979, and equity turnover 6.3 per cent of GNP. Both were the leading positions in the Community.[6] London is also a major centre for Eurobonds.

It is against this leading position in Europe that the structure and practice of the UK Stock Exchange is examined. In view of the complexity of the Exchange, major features only are evaluated to emphasise local characteristics and highlight differences from its Community counterparts.

Organisation

In 1980, the UK Stock Exchange consisted of 4,067 members. Of these, there were 240 firms with 2,104 partners and 1,433 associate members. There were 19 firms of stock jobbers with 203 partners and 281 associate members. Both brokers and jobbers employ a large number of authorised and unauthorised clerks, and the central administration of the Stock Exchange is also a large employer. The UK Stock Exchange is an amalgamation of London, Dublin and a number of UK regional centres. There is no limit prescribed on number of members or their freedom to establish new broking or jobbing firms, although total numbers of both have in fact been falling over recent years, in the latter case drastically.

No specific legislation governs the Stock Exchange. It is a private organisation which is self-regulating and was not created by statute.

However, statute law does recognise the existence of the Exchange, and to all intents and purposes the UK Stock Exchange, centred on London, is the 'official' and the largest organised market in the UK and Republic of Ireland. There are other securities markets in London, some a segment of the Stock Exchange itself, like the Unlisted Market, and others, like ARIEL (Automated Real-Time Investments Exchange Ltd), separated. But all these exceptions are small in comparison with the Stock Exchange.

The Exchange has detailed rules and regulations, whose authority is derived from the users of the Exchange themselves. They cover most areas of activity, from listing to commissions, dealing procedures, and codes of ethical conduct. In recent years, the regulations have been changed frequently to incorporate new practices and introduce new standards of behaviour. The ultimate sanction of this non-statutory type of regulation is the threat of being 'hammered', i.e. restrained from trading.

However, many of the activities of the Stock Exchange are also the concern of the Department of Trade. Through the Companies Act, the Department has legal control over such matters as prospectus requirements, capital structure, and responsibilities of directors. Also, the Prevention of Fraud (Investments) Act of 1958 has particular concern for the accurate content of dealers' circulars. The sanction for fraudulent information is cancellation of a dealer's licence. The Law of fraud and other statutory provisions can result in the intervention of the Director of Public Prosecutions, but this is rare. Supervision and management of the Exchange lie primarily with the Stock Exchange Council, and this has necessitated frequent changes in the rules. The Council, which is elected from its own members, is assisted in its non-statutory regulation by the Bank of England, which has a particular interest in the gilt market, the Panel on Take-Overs and Mergers (1973), and several specialised City Committees — EEC, Company Law, Capital Markets, Liaison, and the recently-established Council for the Securities Industries. The Exchange also take advice from several City organisations like the Accepting Houses Committee and Issuing Houses Association.[7] One consequence of the Stock Exchange's being a private organisation, is that it needs to take a commercial attitude towards its own balance sheets, and in this respect has a market-orientated business policy.

The corporate market: types of securities

Corporate capital divides simply into loan and equity capital, although in practice companies have issued very few bonds in recent years in London. Loan capital may be debentures (fixed interest and capital paid on certain dates, secured by charge on company assets), perpetual and irredeemable debentures, mortgage and unsecured debentures, unsecured short term bonds, loan stocks secured by outside guarantee, unsecured loans convertible to equities, and variable interest loans. At the present time, loan stock enjoys additional investor protection in respect of the income and capital structure of companies.

Equity capital consists of preference or ordinary. Non-voting preference equities carry fixed dividends and enjoy priority over ordinary equities in insolvency situations. Varieties of the former include cumulative, redeemable, participating, and convertible to ordinary. Ordinary equities are venture capital proper, and may be voting or non-voting, deferred, 'A' (non-voting), and 'B' (entitling holders to fully paid equities in lieu of dividends).

Warrants are more fashionable now in London. Strictly, they are contracts rather than securities, specifically a quoted, long term option to buy equities at a fixed price. In February 1981 there were eleven equities listed which included warrants. They are comparable to traded options, but the option is much longer, and they are not included in company balance sheets until issued. Traded options proper have been in existence for a long time, but from 1978 the right to sell as well as buy an option on an equity was introduced. Options are also contracts traded in units of 1,000 equities.

Like ICFC, clearing banks are now offering venture capital to small and medium sized business, sometimes in the form of medium term subordinated loans with equity options, or loans paying royalties based on the borrowers' sales. Most investment trusts are listed on the Stock Exchange. Their units are not securities, but investors purchase equity holdings in the trusts, which are closed-ended funds, and the market value of their holdings is related to the investment performance of their diversified units. Most equities are in registered form.

Markets

The 'official' listed stock market may be divided into two broad sections relating to settlement periods, although to some extent the division is artificial — this is between the 'cash' and 'for account' settlement dates. The cash market concerns the purchase or sale of all bonds, and new equity issues in the form of scrip (an allotment letter), as well as renounceable allotment letters sent to holders of rights issues. In all these cases, settlement must be made on the day following the day of purchase or sale. The market where settlement is 'by account' requires settlement on equities after periods of up to two weeks. There are 25 fortnightly account periods in the year, giving room for dealing within the account. Essentially bargains under this system are for forward account. Buying and selling for 'new time', on Thursday or Friday of an old account, it is possible to stretch the forward settlement to 12 business days instead of 10, since new account dates are normally Mondays.

There is also an after-hours market, dealing before 0930 and after 1530 (for equities). Any deals concluded are published as 'early bargains' the next morning, but not every mark is published.

Other sub-divisions of the equity market are as follows. The Exchange permits 'contango' dealing, i.e. paying a rate of interest to a broker to carry over a bought or sold position at the end of one account to the succeeding one, and reopen it. The operation depends on 'matching' bought and sold bargains. Last date for contangos is the afternoon of the last day of an account period.

The traded options market has developed modestly in London. Although one-way options on equities had been dealt in for a long time, two-way trading (buy and sell) was permitted in 1978, and business increased. Until then, contracts in options were not marketable, but numerous investors have since used the technique to vary their portfolio risks. Because options can be bought or sold on an equity several times over before expiry date (three months), they are clearly a flexible instrument. At the present time, only brokers and jobbers may trade on the floor in options (cf. Chicago), and the market has five jobbers and one broker acting as market makers. There were 60 industrial options, 7 properties, 8 oils and 4 mines listed on 1 June 1981, but only about 14 are active. Unit trusts are permitted to trade in (buy) options, as long as they are covered. In early 1981 contracts were running at the rather low level of 1,200 a day which is probably uneconomic. A Clearing Corporation has been established, option prices are displayed on the Stock Exchange 'TOPIC' service, 'put' options were introduced in 1981, and capital gains tax relaxed slightly on buying back options. Commissions are based on a fixed rate per bargain plus a variable percentage on the option money.

More important has been the opening of a properly regulated unlisted market for equities in November 1980. An unlisted market has existed for a long time, under Rule 163(2) of the Stock Exchange; in 1980 it involved 800 companies turning over some £45 million annually. But Stock Exchange control of the market was loose. The new market should attract the small and local investor more readily. The dealing floor is regulated but cheap (companies are charged a flat £1,000 annually). Brokers may act as market makers where companies are very small, and the 1980 Finance Act provided a useful tax concession, for capital losses on new equities in unlisted companies to be set off against income tax. Problems of the fledgling market include limited marketability, the low minimum set on companies' release of equity (10 per cent), possible loss of general availability through equity placements, and most important, lack of strict entry requirements for companies — for example, no complete prospectus is required, and companies need have been trading for only three years. Minimum commissions are the same as for listed securities, and EXTEL provides an information service. Main types of issues are by introduction, placement, or offer for sale.

There is a very small market in 'over-the-counter' equities operated by one company, M.J.H. Nightingale and Co., which matches buyers and sellers of securities in some unlisted companies on a 'best efforts' basis. Another small market is the one operated by the accepting houses — ARIEL — in which institutional investors may deal directly with each other without the intervention of a broker. But it has not been successful. In contrast, the London Eurobond market is massive for new issues. It is certainly the largest in Europe; but although most issues are officially listed, the market is a telephone one between market makers (mostly banks) and does not involve the Stock Exchange.

Intermediaries

A feature of UK Stock Exchange dealing is the jobbing system, sometimes called 'single capacity'. The nearest counterpart is the New York Stock Exchange 'specialist', but it is less well known on the European continent. Since jobbers act only for brokers, and trade actively, the Stock Exchange argues[8] that a greater degree of liquidity is given to the system. The separation of principal (jobber) and agent (broker) is a protection for the client. Execution of orders is assisted because brokers do not have to find matching orders, and they can also deal in odd lots of equities. Jobbers make their income by minimum price spreads between bid and offer prices. Brokers charge minimum commissions.

The jobbing system has been criticised as being expensive and manipulative, and the Office of Fair Trading is currently investigating the position. While no answer can be given in a few lines in comparison with an investigation whose cost may approach £1 million, some facts are readily apparent. The jobbing market is open to competition, yet the number of jobbing firms has fallen dramatically over the years. Admittedly those that remain are larger. Of the nineteen remaining firms, many are inactive; only two in fact are very active, and they concentrate on dealing in gilts. The jobbing system is probably short of capital to handle the increasingly large institution-held equity sums. It may fail because of low profitability.[9] Early in 1980 jobbers were permitted access to overseas markets, to deal with market makers only, including banks. They may also deal in Eurocurrency bonds with a non-member, given prior authorisation of the Council.

In common with most major Stock Exchanges (with the exception of the United States) the UK operates a system of minimum commissions for brokers. (In the USA they are negotiated.) In practice, brokers charge at the minimum rate, unless deals are uneconomically small. Commissions are charged under Rule 200, and were last amended in August 1977. The actual scales are described in Appendix 39 and are divided into commissions which may and may not be shared according to Rule 212(2). For example, commissions may be shared with members of the Bankers' Clearing House, and other banks in the City of London whose names are kept on a register in the Stock Exchange. In view of the elaborate nature of the commission scales, a selection only is given in Table 6.5.

There is a stamp duty of 2 per cent on equities and options, none on bonds or government stock. There is a variable contract stamp duty payable, and VAT on market deals and consultancy, etc. (which does not apply to non-residents). Withholding tax is 30 per cent basic.

Trading procedures, clearing, listing

Briefly, the system is designed so that transactions in listed securities should all take place on the floors of the UK Stock Exchanges, subject to the supervision of the Stock Exchange Council (Rule 163). There are, however, sub-sections of Rule 163 regarding unlisted securities which can still be traded, e.g. US, Canadian and South African securities, oil mining companies. The prices of these securities are marked and published. Although small, off-floor trading is multi-faceted, e.g. merchant banks trade in some specialist securities, licensed dealers maintain markets, auctions take place; and ARIEL is entirely off-floor. In June 1981, the Department of Trade was considering tightening up the operating rules for licensed dealers, following collapses of some investment management groups.

Although brokers have much discretion when acting for clients, orders may be limited: (a) firm for a day or some specified period, (b) refer back to client, (c) discretionary, (d) contingent (on sale and purchase of different securities, sometimes called 'switching'). Limits on orders are usually on prices.

The broker/jobber dealing system is central to the stock market. Unlike the auction systems commonly found on the Continent, the UK system consists of brokers seeking bargains with jobbers on particular trading 'pitches'. Jobbers quote two prices, the difference between their 'spread'. They deal between themselves and arbitrage with members of foreign stock exchanges. Brokers may make

Table 6.5
Examples of the scale of brokers' commissions*

1 *British and Irish Government funds:*

  (a) Securities having no final redemption date within 10 years:

      0.625 per cent on the first £2,000
      0.25 per cent on the next £12,000
      0.125 per cent on the next £986,000
      0.1 per cent on the next £3 million
      0.05 per cent on the next £6 million
      0.03 per cent on the excess

  (b) Securities have 10 years or less to redemption:

      0.625 per cent on the first £2,000
      0.125 per cent on the next £2,000
      0.0625 per cent on the next £996,000
      0.5 per cent on the next £3 million
      0.025 per cent on the next £6 million
      0.015 per cent on the excess

  (c) Securities having 5 years or less to final redemption and not in default:

      At discretion

2 *Equities (registered or bearer):*

      1.5 per cent on the first £7,000
      0.5 per cent on the next £93,000
      0.4 per cent on the next £150,000
      0.3 per cent on the next £500,000
      0.2 per cent on the next £1 million
      0.125 per cent on the excess

3 *Debentures, bonds, etc. (account transactions):*

  (a) Registered (including new scrip issues):

      0.75 per cent on the first £5,000
      0.375 per cent on the next £45,000
      0.325 per cent on the next £50,000
      0.3 per cent on the next £150,000
      0.25 per cent on the next £500,000
      0.2 per cent on the next £1 million
      0.125 per cent on the excess

  (b) Bearer:

      0.5 per cent on the first £5,000
      0.25 per cent on the excess

Source: Extracts from Rules and Regulations Relating to Commissions (containing amendments confirmed to 23 August 1977), *Commissions, Rule 200*, The Stock Exchange, London (adapted).

*Under review in early 1982, proposing an average 7.3 per cent increase in commissions.

'matching' orders, or 'put through' business with jobbers subject to rules. Thus two orders (buy and sell) may be executed simultaneously in the same security.

In April 1979, the Exchange introduced its new centralised settlement system, 'TALISMAN' ('Transfer Accounting, Lodgement for Investors, Stock Management for Jobbers'). The previous system for settlements had been partly computerised, but was not a pooling arrangement, and had been in operation, with minor changes, for over a century. In the sixties, with bull markets turning in very high daily trading volumes, it became clear that the system could not cope. With TALISMAN, all company securities are bought from and sold to a central pool. The central administration of the system has taken over the bulk of communications with registrars (the agencies which register the final ownership of securities), and also manages the identification of ownership of dividends, scrip issues, etc. Whereas sellers used to retain securities until the last possible moment in a transaction, TALISMAN predelivers securities from the seller via the jobber to SEPON, a nominee company which pools all jobbers' securities for later transfer. The advantages of the new system are: speed of settlement, cost savings, and greater capacity for dealing among members. It is capable of handling 45,000 transactions a day. Although the initial tariff structure tended to be rather heavily weighted towards the small and medium sized broking firms, once development costs are cleared, savings to all broking firms will begin to become apparent. The Exchange believes the development period for TALISMAN to be about seven years, i.e. to 1986.

Companies seeking listing on the Exchange approach the Quotations Department via the offices of a stockbroker. The timing of an issue for subscriptions of more than £3 million is controlled by the Bank of England through the Government Broker. The advantage of this arrangement is to give a good spread of timing for large subscriptions. New issues are underwritten by institutional investors by arrangement, which guarantees the success of an issue to the company raising money. Underwriters' commissions vary from 1.5 per cent upwards of the proceeds of the issue. For the Wilson Committee's Review, the Exchange estimated typical costs of issues raising £2m. in 1977 as follows:

Bringing a company to the market for the first time (35% of company's market capitalisation must be offered), the total cost of a new issue, prospectus or offer for sale would be 7.6% of proceeds of the new issue. Of the total cost of £152,900, four items make up 60%: capital duty at 1% = £20,000, advertising £25,000, accountancy fees £20,000 and underwriting commission at 1¼% = £25,000. Once the company is admitted, further costs are 2.6% of the issue proceeds for a Placement, and 4.0% for a Rights Issue. (The main difference in the costs of further issues is that no underwriting costs are required for a Placement.)[10]

The gilt-edged market

The large size of British public sector debt has already been mentioned. In December 1980, the nominal value of the 955 listed public sector bonds was £88,736m., and market value £76,613m. The equivalent values for company securities at the same date were £39,816m. and £275,963m. Turnover in 1980 was six times greater in gilts than all forms of company securities, and in 1979 and 1980 gilt-edged yields doubled, while ordinary dividends barely moved. This is the statistical background to a large and growing market.[11]

The market consists of British and Irish government funds, government guaranteed securities, local authority, public boards, and Commonwealth government bonds. Denomination is in sterling, and must be settled the day following purchase. British government bonds are short dated (up to 5 years' redemption), medium dated (5—15 years) and long dated (15 years +), or undated. The Government Broker (the senior partner of Mullens and Co.) conducts operations in gilts on instructions from the Bank of England. Issues are public and not underwritten. From March 1979, issues of government securities to the public have been made by tender, unsold stock being taken up by the Bank of England's Issue Department, and subsequently sold to jobbers specialising in gilts ('tap' sales). There is a variety of recent new instruments and issue methods.

Unlike some exchanges, particularly that in the USA, the gilt-edged market is part of the Stock Exchange. There is no 'over-the-counter' market in sterling gilts, although there is an after-hours telephone market in them. The single capacity system applies equally to gilts as to corporate securities. Also, in contrast with many other exchanges, short term papers (Treasury bills etc.) are traded in a money market (by the London discount houses) and the market for longer dated bonds is in the Stock Exchange. There are no banks involved directly in gilt orders; they can carry out an instruction only through a stockbroker.

The gilt-edged market is very popular. In recent years, the Treasury and Bank of England have lengthened the average maturity of the national debt, and therefore tended to encourage trade in long dated bonds. Not only does the gilt-edged market have depth (size) but also breadth (variety) — banks, discount houses, insurance companies, pension funds, building societies, savings banks, individuals, overseas holders, etc., all hold sizeable proportions of government debt. Insurance companies are particularly large holders: in 1979 they held 42 per cent of bond issues of over 15 years, and 23 per cent of 5—15 year bonds. The UK Exchange has market makers taking up 'positions' in bonds, and this is an efficient means of dealings. The marketability of gilts depends on the ability of jobbers to take positions: they do it in both the secondary 'tap' market and the primary 'tender' market. Jobbers may take very large positions by borrowing bonds. They normally quote prices for lots of £1m.; in this case a spread (between buying and selling price) of about 3/32 is quoted for a bond of < 5 years, and about 3/16 for a bond with > 5 years.[12] The British Government has never defaulted on payment of interest or capital on redemption, as many countries have in the past.

Non-residents do not pay tax on gilt-edged bond interest. Apart from the 'jobbers' spread', the other main dealing expense is brokers' commissions. Otherwise, domestic investors are subject to VAT (15 per cent) on commissions, but non-resident investors are exempt. Other fees are absent (transfer stamp duty) or very small (contract stamp duty, and the levy for the Council of Securities Industry). Thus dealing fees are small, especially for foreign investors. While most government bonds have a single redemption date, some are optional. The usual range is 2—3 years. For the financial year 1979/80, total cash stocks of government bonds by maturity were > 1 < 5 years + £2,333m., > 5 < 15 years + £2,905m., and > 15 years + undated + £6,940m., out of a total of + £8,977m., showing the heavy predominance of longer dated securities (77 per cent). There are also sinking funds (taxable), and variable rate bonds.

Government issues of gilts are designed to assist monetary policy, and to finance its budgetary requirements, current and capital, mainly by long dated bonds. Other aims of gilt-edged management are co-ordination with interest rates, and limiting dependence on bank borrowing. As mentioned above, settlement may be 'normal' (next day), 'same day' (exceptional) or 'delayed' (for various reasons including reinvestment of proceeds). Registered bonds are settled by transfer deeds. The Bank of England keeps the registers of ownership of gilts, and of transfers effected by separate deeds by jobbers. New issues by tender are settled by a 'letter of allotment' and a 'registration form' to be completed and deposited with the Bank of England. Issues may be partly or full paid on application.

Supervision

Regulation of the Exchange is a mixture of statutory and non-statutory provisions, with the latter predominating. Statutory rules are administered by the Department of Trade, and the major Acts of relevance are the Companies Acts and the Prevention of Fraud (Investments) Act,

1958. The Companies Acts concern such matters as duties of directors, capital structure, and inspection if necessary. The Prevention of Fraud (Investments) Act restricts dealing in securities to licensed dealers. The Department of Trade has been rigorous in its application of these laws. But in addition, there is comprehensive self-policing by the Exchange. The most important organisations involved here are the Council of the Stock Exchange itself, the City Panel on Take-overs and Mergers, and the more recently established Council for the Securities Industry (CSI).

The Council of the Stock Exchange has 47 elected members drawn from the membership of the Exchange. Including its sub-committees, like the City Liaison Committee and the City EEC Committee, total staff is around 1,000, with about three-quarters working on settlements. The remainder are concerned with regulation (quotations, membership, dealings, accounts and price statistics). A standing Disciplinary Committee, composed of members, and *ad hoc* Committees of Investigation look into infringements. Member firms are also obliged to maintain detailed audited accounts, and minimum solvency ratios. The Exchange maintains a compensation fund against default by member firms, as protection for investors, and firms must cover their staff by fidelity insurance. Infringement of the Council's Code of Dealing can lead to suspension or cessation of dealing for a member. Breaches of the listing agreement can lead to similar sanctions.

The Panel on Take-overs and Mergers, set up in 1968, exists to interpret and administer the City Code on take-overs and mergers. The 1960s were a period of intensive amalgamations, many based on weaknesses presented by historic cost accounting of assets combined with low returns. The panel is composed of fourteen representatives from different parts of the City's financial activities, and has an executive of eleven members with day-to-day responsibilities. The code itself is made up of a number of general principles and rules, and concerns offers made to all listed or unlisted public companies. For example, in 1980, the panel held two meetings to hear appeals by parties to take-over transactions against rulings by the executive, seven to hear three disciplinary cases, and four to consider cases referred. In 1980 there were 142 published take-over or merger proposals of which 99 eventually succeeded. The panel is guided by several objectives; in particular to ensure fairness between equity holders in a take-over bid, and to give them full information on which to judge an offer by directors. Its ultimate sanctions rest on public censure and professional associations.

The Council for the Securities Industry was established in 1978, also with wide representation from City financial organisations. Its brief is to maintain ethical standards, and review codes of conduct, forms of regulation, market practices, and procedures for investigating breaches of misconduct within the securities industry. It also has a more innovatory role — to consider improvements and the reform of existing practice and regulations. CSI has various sub-committees, e.g. a Markets Committee which reviews listing requirements, and an Appeals Committee. It is a voluntary body and, as part of the self-regulation of the Exchange, its authority rests on the commitment of organisations represented in it. In its first year's work it identified several areas of interest — insider dealing, dealing in unlisted securities, new issues, and investment advisers — as worthy of study. In its second year of operation, the Code of Conduct for dealers in securities was approved for publication, the question of responsibilities of sponsors of new issues resolved, and the Council agreed with the clauses of the 1980 Companies Act regulating insider dealing. The Markets Committee is continuing a revision of the City Take-over Code. The Council published 'Rules Governing Substantial Acquisition of Shares' (restrictions on 'market raids') in December 1980 and 'Guidelines for Personal Dealings by Fund Managers' in March 1981.

The final organisation involved is the Joint Review Body, established in 1977 with responsibility for a general oversight of Stock Exchange supervision. Its members are drawn from the Bank of England and the Department of Trade. There have been useful discussions, but the organisation fits uneasily in the existing framework of self-regulation.

Role of the institutions

The savings institutions have come to play a dominating role in the Stock Exchange, and their investment behaviour is a determining factor in all aspects of trading in securities. There is a number of reasons; firstly the increasing value of the average equity bargain, which is becoming too large for the individual to handle (1970: £2,150; 1980: £6,834). In addition, the individual has been squeezed out by taxation, high dealing costs, and a reverse yield gap on gilt-edged bonds. In 1980, the average value of a bargain in gilts was £93,568. Between 1975 and 1980, non-bank financial institutions' investment in the Exchange rose from £5,812 million to £7,559 million, an increase of 30 per cent.[13] In its submission to the Wilson Committee in 1977, the Stock Exchange Council showed that savings institutions had increased their share of UK listed equities between 1963 and 1977 from 26 to 52 per cent. (Individual equity holders, by contrast, had seen their total share fall from 55 to 32 per cent over the same period.) Table 6.6 demonstrates this rapid growth in more detail.

Institutional growth is clearly shown, except for the corporate bond market, which became increasingly weak in the later 1970s. Institutions gained an increased share of nearly 4 per cent in equities and 5.2 per

Table 6.6
UK major institutional holdings (percentages)

	Listed UK equities			Listed UK Co. bonds			UK govt securities		
	Holding as per cent of market value								
	1976	1977	1978	1976	1977	1978	1976	1977	1978
Insurance companies	16.3	17.3	18.0	39.1	39.9	37.8	20.0	21.6	23.5
Investment trusts	6.3	6.0	5.6	3.0	2.6	2.4	0.5	0.7	0.5
Unit trusts	4.1	4.3	4.3	1.4	1.4	1.9	0.1	0.1	0.1
Superannuation funds:									
− private sector	9.5	9.6	10.9	11.2	10.3	9.4	6.2	5.9	7.0
− local authorities	2.7	2.3	3.0	1.8	1.3	1.2	1.9	1.9	2.4
− other public sector	5.9	6.0	6.9	3.5	2.6	1.8	3.1	2.9	3.5
Total superannuation funds:	18.1	17.9	20.8	16.5	14.2	12.4	11.2	10.7	12.9
Total holdings:	44.8	45.5	48.7	60.0	58.1	54.5	31.8	33.1	37.0

Source: The Stock Exchange, *Fact Book*, March 1980, Appendix 4.

cent in gilts between 1976 and 1978. In contrast to the disadvantages faced by the individual investor in the 1960s and 1970s, the savings institutions enjoyed preferential tax treatment, increased premiums on insurance and pension schemes caused by inflation, and improved quality of pension benefits. The effect of this greater institutional involvement on the allocative efficiency of the Exchange is a matter of controversy, and will only be settled by detailed empirical work.

An evaluation of the current structure and practice of the UK Stock Exchange is best incorporated with the later discussion of new legislation and reforms, since in the last few years there has been a good deal of activity in this field.

Performance and efficiency of the Stock Exchange

The long term decline in post-tax real profitability of the bulk of UK industry, as a rate of return on equity (or an equivalent measure), has been described above, and is well documented in several Bank of

England studies. It accelerated from the end of 1979 onwards as British industry went deeply into recession. This experience is reflected in Stock Exchange indicators of corporate performance.

The number of company securities (equities and fixed interest) listed on the Exchange has fallen over a long period. Only overseas registered companies have shown a recent small, short term increase, but still a long term decline. On the other hand, the number of gilt-edged stocks listed has steadily increased. For UK and Irish registered securities, the number of fixed interest securities fell from 4,218 to 3,275 between March 1970 and March 1980, and that of equities from 3,074 to 2,332. The number of foreign registered bonds fell from 150 to 92 and equities rose from 378 to 381. By contrast, the number of British and Irish Government Funds rose from 66 to 150 over the period, and other public sector bonds from 1,185 to 1,371. In its submission to the Wilson Committee, the Council of the Stock Exchange explained the fall in gross new issues by companies by the pre-emptive effect of public sector borrowing, the fiscal advantage that gilts have had over company equities, and price and dividend controls keeping equity prices low and cost of new money high. While the 'pre-emption' explanation is arguable (there was, by and large, no liquidity problem in the seventies), the other points are more valid and contributed towards low profitability, sluggish investment, and a reluctance to 'go public'. The study by Williams[14] conclusively points to company pricing policies, as well as cost inflation, as reasons for the unattractiveness of investment in the seventies.

This disparity in attractiveness between equities and gilts is shown in Table 6.7.

Table 6.7
Yields on bonds and equities (per cent per annum)

Security Year	1974	1975	1976	1977	1978	1979	1980
British Government bonds:*							
5 years	12.51	11.48	12.06	10.08	11.32	12.64	13.80
10 years	14.21	13.18	13.61	12.02	12.12	12.93	13.90
15 years	14.77	14.39	14.43	12.73	12.47	12.99	13.78
Equities (750 classes)**	7.68	6.43	6.10	5.52	5.54	5.75	6.32
Debentures and loans (20 yrs)†	16.44	15.95	15.19	13.41	12.75	13.23	14.16

Source: Central Statistical Office, *Financial Statistics*, January 1981.

* Calculated gross redemption yields
** Dividend yield (gross)
† Redemption yield.

An earnings yield on equities is higher, of course, but although it is a net profit per share, it is also grossed up at the advance corporation tax rate, and full distribution of earnings is used.

The same contrast is apparent in turnover. Between 1975 and 1980, annual turnover in equities increased from £17,545m. to £30,801m. (75 per cent), and that in British Government securities from £67,246m. to £151,699m. (255 per cent). Although the number of bargains struck is much higher in equities, as one might expect, the rate of growth is different. In 1970, bargains in equities totalled 4,539,493; in 1979 they had fallen to 4,111,744. Annual bargains in gilts in 1970 totalled 426,203 and in 1979 had risen to 878,829, more than double. Corresponding average value per bargain of equities in 1970 was £2,150, and of public sector bonds £24,673. In 1979, the figures were £5,863 and £107,750 respectively; the rate of growth in value of public sector bonds being twice as great as that in equities over the period.

In terms of the size and activity of the domestic corporate market, out of total market capitalisation of £74,623m. in March 1980, the 100 largest UK registered companies accounted for £44,287m. or 59 per cent. But the five largest alone accounted for just under one-quarter (BP, Shell, ICI, GEC, Marks and Spencer). The foreign securities market is structured in a similar way. Out of total market capitalisation of £134,312m. the fifty largest companies accounted for £87,774m. or 65 per cent, and within this list of fifty, the five largest companies (IBM, General Motors, GEC, Royal Dutch Petroleum, and Schlumberger) took a 33 per cent share. Within the total company securities market, domestic and foreign registered, it is notable that the ten largest overseas registered companies accounted for 44 per cent of market capitalisation. Not only is the UK Stock Exchange a very international market in company securities, but a few overseas companies can have a determining effect on the price index if their prices move, by their sheer weighting.

Price performance in company equities has been surprisingly strong over a long period on the Exchange. Since the *Financial Times* Actuaries All-Share Price Index was started, based on 1962, there have been three bear markets, corresponding roughly with the years 1964–66, 1969–70 and 1972–74. Since 1974, there has been a vigorous upswing with a brief hiatus in 1976 when the sterling exchange rate temporarily plummeted. The pattern of the *FT* Actuaries Index is shown in Table 6.8.

Movement in these indices needs careful interpretation, since in 1981 the *FT* share index nearly reached 600 at a time when unemployment was above 2.5 million. Part of the reason is that this index (like others) is based on historical accounting information. The equity market

Table 6.8
Equity price indices (1962 = 100)

	1973	1974	1975	1976	1977	1978	1979	1980
Equities: all classes (750 equities):	184.61	106.75	133.11	153.04	191.91	216.68	245.52	271.32
Per cent movement								+ 47%
Financials (115 equities):	188.85	102.45	122.85	124.18	145.68	165.98	188.36	218.89
Per cent movement								+ 16%
Industrials (500 equities):	185.26	108.84	135.97	162.91	208.79	235.27	267.31	285.68
Per cent movement								+ 54%
Debentures and loan stocks (20 years):	65.48	45.31	46.25	48.68	55.58	58.32	56.27	52.42
Per cent movement								−25%

Source: Central Statistical Office, *Financial Statistics*, January 1981.

reflects the state of liquidity in the economy as much as the fundamental economic prospects of companies, and the 500 equity index is considered to be a good long term indicator. Classically, equity bull markets have momentum in a recession, peaking when recovery is clearly identifiable. But with UK exchange controls abolished (in 1979), the London equity market has been much more exposed to international currency movements than before, and more dependent on overseas economic trends. Table 6.8 shows strong gains in (non-adjusted) prices of the all-share index, and particularly industrials. As expected, prices of fixed interest equities have actually fallen. In 1980, 100 UK registered companies raised £1,054m. in rights issues of new capital, very similar to the previous year, but only a few companies accounted for the new capital raised. In fact, the total of money raised, inflation-adjusted, was much lower than in 1975 or 1976.[15] It cannot be said that the Exchange is the natural market to which all companies are turning in search of new money. Not only are the annual sums of new money recently raised on the Exchange small in relation to total company capitalisation (about 0.5 per cent), but they are raised by a few companies only. In recent years, new flotations of any size have been few. The true offer-for-sale and listing has become rare. In 1980 only one listing (Charterhouse Petroleum) was large (£26m.), and this was, in fact, a tender restricted to CP equity holders and staff. There were only four Rule 163 (listed) proper offers-for-sale, three of them by investment trusts for sums below £2m. Later in 1980 there was a movement to market under the cheaper, new unlisted securities market. Other forms of flotation, like reverse take-overs and reintroductions, do not strictly qualify in terms of raising new money. On the other hand, seven foreign companies were listed for the first time in 1980, with a market value of £6,000m.

A feature of a reasonably efficient securities market should be a certain stability of prices, notwithstanding external shocks. This is not particularly true of the London market, even over a short period. Between January 1979 and December 1980, the all-share index rose from 220 to 280, with troughs and peaks of some dimensions over short periods, e.g. from around 220 in March 1979 to 275 in May, to 240 in end June; and from 260 in September to 225 in November 1979. The all-share index would normally move slowly, being weighted by large industrial concerns, and less volatile than the 30 share index. Gilt-edged redemption yields have fluctuated similarly, rising from around 9.75 per cent at the beginning of 1979 to 13.75 per cent at the end of 1980, but reaching peaks of 15 and 14 per cent and troughs of 11 and 13 per cent in between with, for instance, an upward movement of 4 per cent in six months during 1979.

The UK Stock Exchange has high standards (compared with its EC partners) in the provision of information. Not only are accounting standards and audit requirements well developed, but scrutiny of listings is thorough, and the Exchange is active in seeking full disclosure of information when transfers of company control are involved. Provision and surveillance still probably do not reach American standards, but much control of trading standards is non-statutory and tends not to reach the stage of publicity. Dramatic scandals are unknown. But this does not mean that there is not room for improvement in the provision of information.

On the side of investors, there is probably less competition and price sensitivity than might be desirable in a highly efficient market. This is linked to the decline of individual investment and the strong growth in institutional penetration of holdings over recent years. CSO statistics [16] show that personal savings as a percentage of total personal disposable income have increased from 9.3 per cent in 1970 to 16.2 per cent in the third quarter of 1980. At the same time, personal savings in assurance and pension funds rose from £4,450m. in 1975 to £9,320m. in 1979. This was primarily at the expense of direct investment by individuals in the Exchange. As a result, superannuation funds held 49 per cent of the market value of all UK listed equities in 1978, and 37 per cent of British government securities. Between 1957 and 1978 the proportion of UK listed equities held by individuals fell from 60 to 32 per cent. The drawbacks of this are (a) less diffusion of ownership in risk capital, (b) institutional risk-averseness, (c) preference for investment in large companies rather than smaller ones and (d) tendency to over-deal in the secondary market, (e) the investment activities of pension funds, whilst on a large scale, are not rigorously controlled. They also tend to trade in second and third-line securities rather than leading securities, and in this area prices are more volatile and dealing spreads wider.

The range of investing instruments in the Exchange is wide. As well as voting and non-voting, scrip and accumulating equities, there are debentures (irredeemable, redeemable, convertible and sinking fund), loan stocks convertible and subordinated, preference shares redeemable, participating and convertible, and a whole range of gilts – corporation stocks and government stocks. The latter offer a wide choice of redemption dates, low dealing costs and no transfer duty or capital gains tax after one year. There is also a variety of Eurobonds on offer.

Although private corporation bonds have been mentioned, the market for them is now very small. At its peak (1966), 39 per cent of the listed capital issue market in the UK was for loans, but it virtually dried up from the early 1970s onwards. Between 1972 and 1980, net redemptions were positive in most years. The main reason for the market's decline has been uncertain prospects for inflation and interest rates, combined with the 'crowding-out' effect of gilt-edged stock more attractive to investors. Companies have turned instead to the banks, which since 1973 have financed around two-thirds of their requirements against one-half in the 1960s. The major advantage of bank loans over fixed interest notes is their flexibility.

There have been a number of studies of the cost of capital as a factor contributing to companies' increasing reluctance to raise new money through equities and bonds. But over the last twenty years the market valuation of equity interest has been high in relation to companies' current earnings,[17] and it would appear that decline in net income is a more important factor.

In the terms discussed so far, it appears that in some respects the Stock Exchange falls short of an 'efficient' market in raising new money for companies and ensuring the continuing marketability of equities. Gilt-edged stock has steadily taken a greater proportion of market liquidity, institutions have grown in importance as investors, at the expense of individual investment, listings and rights issues have dropped in number. Trading is dominated by a few large companies' securities. Equity prices have been volatile and yields low. Bank borrowing has become more attractive than stock market finance. Against this, one must set high standards and good circulation of information and surveillance, a wide range of investing instruments available, high and rising equity prices, a good secondary turnover in equities and gilts, a stable level of cost of capital, and a strong representation by foreign securities.

The Stock Exchange has been the subject of numerous tests for efficiency in the reaction of security prices to changes in information (the 'efficient market hypothesis') too numerous to be cited individually. The recent book by Richards[18] summarises clearly the results of such tests up to 1979. Generally, although not every informational change has been tested against prices, there is a good deal of evidence to support the 'weak' and 'semi-strong' forms of efficiency defined by Fama, i.e. that current security prices fully reflect all historical information available — mostly tested by randomness of price behaviour — and that security prices quickly reflect new information about the discounted economic worth of companies.

Richards holds that evidence of 'strong-form' efficiency, i.e. security prices adjust speedily to all available information, supersedes the necessity for 'lesser' efficiency tests. Thus, if 'inside' information on events affecting securities does not benefit the informed, or if no inside information exists, or is known by everyone concerned, the Exchange would be 'strong-form' efficient. Two points should be repeated here: one, that the notion of 'efficiency' is consistent with a wide range of (internal) market structures and imperfections;[19] the other, that 'information' itself can mean rumour, guess, high or low profitability diagnosis, misleading tactics, etc. The evidence for 'strong-form' efficiency of the UK Stock Exchange, even within the strict terms of the EMH, is not conclusive. For example, Samuels[20] related portfolio performance to skills of managers of unit trusts; the results showed unit trust portfolio performance barely different from the market's average performance. Richards[21] tested UK equity portfolios of pension funds over a recent seven-year period for the relationship between the 'market' rate of growth (proxy *FT* all-share index), and yields for a large number of funds. Some individual funds 'beat' the market, the average did not. This seems slightly more positive evidence of efficiency of the 'strong-form' definition.

New legislation and Stock Exchange reform

It has been pointed out above that the UK Stock Exchange is mostly self-regulatory. The bulk of the many recent improvements to practice and procedures has been introduced on a non-statutory or 'consensus' basis. At the same time, however, there is a statutory framework to the Stock Exchange's activities, and there have been changes here.

Statutory changes may be designed directly to affect the Exchange, or they may indirectly affect it. An example of the latter is the abolition of exchange control restrictions on sterling in 1979. Among the many results of this were the removal of the 'dollar premium' needed for direct investments abroad, lifting of the requirement to repatriate at least two-thirds of earnings from overseas subsidiaries, and closing of the investment currency 'pool' for outward portfolio investment. At first, foreign stock markets were weak, and little happened, but in 1981, with high US interest rates and a soaring dollar, British institutional funds went overseas in large quantity. A second example has been the Inland Revenue's decision in 1980 to permit sellers of traded options to set the cost of buying back an option against the proceeds of the previous sale before assessment of tax liability on capital gains. Options were consequently encouraged.

Some recent statutory changes directly affecting the Exchange have been incorporated in the 1981 Companies Act. Public and private companies are now allowed to repurchase their own securities without limit from profits or proceeds of new issues (articles permitting). All securities repurchased have to be cancelled. The most important result is that a company can be privatised, and family retention made easier.

In June 1980, insider dealing became a criminal offence, under the same Act. This piece of legislation followed many years of observation and investigation of the practice. Indictments are heavy, but there will clearly be difficulties in identifying such loosely defined concepts as 'unpublished price-sensitive information'.

The same Act incorporates clauses making 'concert parties' illegal, i.e. investors co-operating in building up ('warehousing') a large secret equity stake in a company without any individual holding the statutory disclosable 5 per cent. In addition, the law was amended to require an investor to disclose a one-fifth (previously one-third) holding in any public company. This aroused debate over who should supervise the control of 'warehousing', and the question has been under discussion for some time by the CSI. In this case, the CSI preferred the added weight of legislation.

Finally, resulting from the removal of exchange controls, the Bank of England issued revised guidelines regarding new issues in the UK capital market, in November 1980. The Bank has legal powers under the Control of Borrowing Order 1958 (as amended). New gilt-edged issues in sterling or sterling options by foreign entities in amounts over £3m. are now subject to timing consent; a queue has been created to apply to all new issues except sterling Eurobonds. The Bank issued its first ever index-linked Treasury bonds in March 1981, on sale to pension funds only. The bonds have a redemption value kept in line with movements in the UK general index of retail prices. This followed an official committee inquiry into the value of index-linked public sector pensions. Although they are clearly an addition to the Government's flexibility in funding its debt, there is anxiety about the deleterious effect they will have on equities, as well as on brokers' commissions.

Although these legal changes have important effects on the Exchange's practices and supervision, the major changes in the last few years have been introduced by the Exchange authorities themselves, under the umbrella of 'self-regulation'. The Council of the Stock Exchange has minor statutory powers, but its control of members and listed companies is based on its documents 'Rules and Regulations of the Stock Exchange', 'Code of Dealing' and 'Notes of Guidance', as well as other guidelines produced by associated supervisory committees. The CSE has a number of standing committees responsible for administering the market, such as the Membership and Firms Accounts Committees.

In the field of supervision, the Council for the Securities Industry was established in 1978, with wide ranging City representation, to co-ordinate self-regulation. The Panel on Take-overs and Mergers was brought within its area of responsibility as well. CSI's major policy committee is its Markets Committee, and since 1978, the latter has had some difficult problems to grapple with. In 1979, its first annual report made a statement on insider dealing, and subsequent discussions and comments were incorporated in the 1981 Companies Act. At the beginning of 1980, the practice of 'dawn raids' or 'market raids' became more widespread in the Stock Exchange. It amounts to the 'lightning' purchase of substantial blocks of equity in a company at a time in the market when investors are not closely watching events. As a result of a rash of these purchases, considered by the CSI to be unfair to small equity holders, the Council published new controls.[22] The two main provisions are (i) any investor holding more than 15 per cent of a company's voting capital, through the purchase of 5 per cent stakes from more than one party, must make a partial or complete tender offer to all equity holders; offers must give at least seven days' notice; (ii) substantial equity purchases by any other means, amounting to 15 per cent as in (i), must be notified to the company concerned and the Quotations Department of the Exchange by noon of the next dealing day. The first practical test of these new rules came in June 1981 with the attempt by Allianz Versicherung to add another 15 per cent of Eagle Star Insurance to an earlier 15 per cent. Allianz were obliged to put out a tender offer.

Another area investigated by CSI has been the lack of supervision of dealers in securities. Recent events added urgency to this question with several dealers going into financial crises. The Association of Licensed

Dealers in Securities produced a plan for controls in June 1981, and CSI produced guidelines in May 1980 and March 1981.[23] However, no steps were taken to amend the Prevention of Fraud (Investments) Act by the Department of Industry.

As well as strictly supervisory matters, the Council of the Stock Exchange has responded to changes in events on the Exchange, as well as independently introducing changes. In the first category, it announced new and complex rules for dealing in overseas securities in 1980, following the removal of sterling exchange controls. Under these rules, jobbers are put on a more equal footing with brokers in freedom to trade foreign securities overseas. Also, the whole concept of arbitrage was removed from the Rule Book. Now jobbers are able to deal directly with foreign brokers in foreign securities. At the same time, brokers have been given more freedom to bypass jobbers when dealing in foreign securities on the London Exchange.

Two new markets opened by the Stock Exchange have been described earlier — the (two-way) traded options market (1978), and the unlisted securities market (1980). Both are still in the developmental stage. In June 1981, a 'put' (sell) market was added to the options market, although since puts could be traded in only three companies, growth is likely to be slow. The unlisted market is also in a fluid state. The CSE published detailed procedures for it in October 1980,[24] but its growth in the future will probably require careful supervision, and amended rules.

For some time now, the Council of the Stock Exchange has been defending two practices before the Restrictive Practices Court — that of minimum brokers' commissions, and the question of 'single capacity', i.e. separation of function of jobbers and brokers. The pressure of this case, and the added pressure of large institutions in the market, has caused brokers to develop business unconnected with securities dealing — placing, research, or corporate finance for unlisted companies. The Exchange has made rules easier for jobbers to deal direct with foreign brokers; several have already developed direct access to new clients in such fields as gold shares. There is a tendency for brokers and jobbers to 'go upstairs', i.e. deal directly by telephone, and ignore the trading floor. On occasion, the Stock Exchange feels keenly the pressure of Government and the public on its 'in-house' regulatory practices. The Deputy Chairman made the point in 1980 that, 'The problems of the Stock Exchange . . . are compounded . . . (when) every time we wish to change our rules in order to adapt to new circumstances, or to take a new initiative, we have to consult our lawyers to see what impression the change will make on the Office of Fair Trading and the Court'.

The Stock Exchange's policy of self-regulation works well when members co-operate and companies adhere to the spirit of the Exchange's guidelines on transfers of control of companies. The Take-over Panel can control the relatively small group of City intermediaries well, but on occasion, a determined take-over bid which does not respect guidelines can expose the lack of legal censure behind the Exchange's controls. In 1980 a listed company, St Piran, was subject to a bid for the whole of its equity under terms considered unethical by the Take-over Panel. By April 1981, although the shares were suspended by the Exchange, and the Department of Trade's inspector had reported on the affairs of the company, no other sanctions had been taken. Clearly, the division of responsibility between the Exchange and the DoT can cause difficulties.

Other prescriptions for reform

It is not intended here to question the principle of self-regulation which, by and large, has served the practice of the Stock Exchange well over a long period, and of which there are examples elsewhere, like Amsterdam. But there is room for improvement in non-statutory and statutory supervision of the Exchange's activities, and its trading environment, as well as practical matters of day-to-day trading.

The demise of the company bond market is to be regretted. The statistical disappearance of significant bond issues was noted above. The reasons for its rundown are well known: high current prices and uncertainty about future inflation and interest rate trends, falling real profitability, and competition with gilt-edged bonds which have better yields because of tax concessions. Bank borrowing and leasing have filled the gap, but disadvantages include the weakening of the whole market for company securities, a more direct expansionary effect on the money supply, and further concentration of ownership of invest-ment capital in the personal sector.

In the gilt-edged market itself, the Bank of England, as issuer and dealer in gilts, has noted some improvements it believes would aid the smooth flow of funds.[25] Investor uncertainty about the future – in-flation, wage demands etc. – can mean periodic interruptions to buying strength. The Treasury has partly met this by introducing convertible bonds (1973) and partly-payable bonds (1977) as well as variable rate bonds. The Bank suggests further improvements could come from greater flexibility in pricing new issues, and directly placing bonds with financial institutions instead of using the mediation of the Bank. Bonds themselves might be shorter dated.

Despite the flow of information from the Stock Exchange, the publi-cation of markings and volumes traded could be faster. Prices offered

237

and bid do not get published, nor is every mark published as is the case in the United States. Investment analysis would be improved by fuller reporting. There is no pattern to the information supplied. It may be that, with the growth of institutional investment at the expense of individuals, the size of bargains increasing, and institutions dealing with each other on a continuous basis, they may have all the information they require. Some financial institutions listed on the UK Exchange have a tendency to regard their investments as static. As institutions continue to dominate the market in terms of holdings, and this static view of investment grows, the need for information decreases. This market structure is not responsive to technical treatment, it is a function of such factors as the high rate of personal savings in the UK, the personal sector's preference for liquid assets in investment, and fiscal encouragement to investment in institutions like pension funds.

At the present time, not only are individual equity holders a shrinking presence in the Exchange, but company staff have little part in company equity ownership. In June 1980, sections of the Companies Act became law which prohibited insider dealing, and exhorted company directors to pay some attention to employees' needs and interest, as well as those of equity holders, which are still placed first. There is little encouragement for employees to identify with company strategy in this new provision. Employee participation is stronger in individual companies. ICI, for instance, pays bonuses in the form of equities. Investment of this sort could be further encouraged by tax concessions, such as no capital tax.

Although the 'single capacity' system and minimum brokers' commissions are currently under scrutiny by the Office of Fair Trading, and the question is a complex one, it is most likely that movements in the economic base of the Exchange are more important in any evaluation than questions of unfair practices. This view is also contained in the Final Report of the Wilson Committee. The number of jobbers has fallen greatly in recent years; it is not clear if the remaining firms are more or less powerful. They are certainly larger. But their profitability is not high and most are seeking to diversify. The two really large jobbers remaining, Wedd Durlacher, and Ackroyd, require a big turnover to stay profitable. Nowadays, gilt-edged dealing is done in large blocks which a small gilts jobber finds hard to handle. The active jobbing function is undertaken on borrowed money. Jobbers should have a more substantial capital base to carry out two-way market making. The system will fail unless profitability increases, and trading would be thinner for its disappearance. It is also likely that minimum commissions are an emotive issue; the experience of the United States with negotiated rates was closures and disruptive competition in the early stages. Brokers are believed to be forced to supplement their commissions with cash services, e.g. investment advice. Any reforms of the single capacity system of dealing and commissions should bear in mind that there are still large sums of international money in search of investment. Stock markets must expand to cope with oil revenues, and this implies stability, close statutory or self-regulation, and some necessary restraints on unbridled competition.

The establishment of an unlisted securities market (USM) may prove to be a mistake. The market functioned quite well within the twilight market of Rule 163(2) when small public concerns like football clubs could have their shares traded. During the early discussions on the USM, the intention was to make it a 'nursery' on the way to full listing on the official Exchange. When the final rules were drawn up, conflicts of interest led to compromises which may prove unworkable. Entry qualifications for companies joining the USM are low; for example, they need offer only 10 per cent of their equity for sale, and do not need to produce full prospectuses. Yet they are regulated by the CSE in a manner hardly different from 'listed' companies. Being theoretically unquoted brings disadvantages, e.g. unit trusts may take up unlisted securities to only 5 per cent maximum of their portfolios. The danger is that investors may perceive the USM as higher risk and inferior. It would be logical either to increase entry standards or to ease up on supervision. The role of the jobber in the USM is not clear either: if, as it appears, brokers may match orders without going through a jobber, the single capacity principle is attacked. Fragmentation of the market has not proved beneficial in other countries.

A number of fiscal changes would assist the Stock Exchange in its business, especially in competition with the banks. Stamp duty at 2 per cent is too high. The EC recommended rate is 0.6 per cent. Contract stamps are expensive and should be abolished. The rationale behind these two Government levies is unclear. More favourable tax treatment on splitting partnerships could be introduced, and investors would be much encouraged by the abolition or reduction of capital gains tax on equities. Companies would also be encouraged to seek Stock Exchange funding if their issue costs were tax deductible.[26]

Taxation and savings/investment incentives

In comparative terms, UK direct tax is heavy, and until recently income tax rates were high at the top end of the scale. With the election of the Conservative Administration in 1979, the bulk of investment incentives to industry were continued, but some changes made.

In broad principle, the present Government continues to encourage manufacturing investment, and to support regions of the country with serious structural problems. But the new approach is more competitively orientated, with less emphasis on demand management and direct Government intervention than on financial engineering. The Government is attempting to reduce public spending, including general and regional public assistance to industry, in an effort to encourage private investment, particularly by small firms.

For companies, the main tax is corporation tax on profits, which for UK registered companies is 52 per cent. The rate is reduced to 40 per cent for smaller companies whose taxable profits do not exceed £80,000. Britain operates a partial-imputation tax system in which a tax credit is included (advance corporation tax, ACT). From 1973, companies paying a dividend have been able to pay ACT at 3/7 of the total dividend, which is then offset against their corporation tax liability. The actual amount of corporation tax paid is low in relation to other countries.

A capital gains tax, CGT, was introduced in 1965, whose burden is reduced if the proceeds of selling are reinvested or 'rolled-over'. Otherwise, the effective rate of tax of capital gains is 30 per cent. The tax has also been modified since introduction by abolishing separate treatment of short-term capital gains, and lifting exemption limits for small gains. Some relief of CGT is also available to UK groups of companies, e.g. as between subsidiaries, and some financial organisations like building societies, life assurance companies and superannuation funds are specially treated.

Increases in stock values due to inflation are tax deductible, and trading profits may be carried forward (unlimited time) or backwards (one year) to be offset against profit liabilities. Double taxation agreements are in force with a large number of countries, and subject to these withholding tax deducted from interest, royalty or rent payments is at a basic rate of 30 per cent.

For individuals, a UK resident's income from dividends includes a tax credit equivalent to ACT, and dividends and income are included in income for tax purposes.

The range of investment incentives is very wide in the UK in comparison with many countries, and to some extent is intended to offset high direct taxes. Briefly, they fall into three categories: incentives for capital spending (grants, loans and tax allowances), incentives for revenue spending (assistance towards relocation costs, training grants, employment subsidies, etc.) and domestic and international schemes to aid specific industries. Categorising another way, there is nationally available assistance, assistance depending on activity (small business, research, exporting), employment incentives; assistance depending on location (assisted areas), and local authority assistance. The 1981 Budget emphasised financial support of small businesses, and measures taken included higher limits for corporation tax, loan guarantees, a venture capital scheme and business start-up schemes.[27]

Finally, there are rules on investment in securities by financial institutions in the UK. These follow on from the fiscal concessions that many of them receive. They go some way to prevent crowding out of the private investor, as well as the accumulating of control in companies. In addition, the rules ensure liquidity safeguards and a certain amount of guaranteed investment in gilts. Insurance companies are limited in their investments in one company's securities. Local authorities are limited in their investments in fixed assets and foreign securities; their superannuation funds must be invested up to 25 per cent in gilts. All pension funds are limited to under 10 per cent of their holdings in unlisted equities, and unit trusts and investment trusts to under 15 per cent holdings on the unlisted market.

Summary

The UK, following a long term decline in manufacturing profitability, entered a deep recession at the end of 1979, characterised by high interest rates and inflation, falling manufacturing output, and unemployment rising to a very high level. Sterling remained strong until mid-1981, when it fell dramatically against the US dollar. Capital outflow followed the removal of sterling exchange controls in 1979, and import penetration of the domestic market is high. Economic prospects remain bleak.

In the seventies, there was no shortage of external finance, including equity financing, but although the proportion of the latter increased after 1976, companies relied much more on retained earnings and bank borrowing. In the 1979 recession, the latter increased sharply, and companies' internal funds dropped. Government borrowing through the Stock Exchange is continuous, heavy, and somewhat pre-emptive of equities, however much the Conservative Government wishes to reduce PSBR.

The size of the UK Stock Exchange, in comparison with its EC partners, is outstanding on most definitions. In structure and organisation, the Exchange is characterised by a high degree of self-regulation, a massive gilts market, the 'single-capacity' system of dealing and minimum brokers' commissions. Supervision is largely non-statutory, but within a legal framework. The Exchange has also seen a swift growth of trading by financial institutions in recent years.

The disparity between performance of government bonds and equities in the Stock Exchange is marked. By a number of performance measurements, the equity market has been much less dynamic, with low yields and volatile prices. The corporate bond market has almost disappeared. On the other hand, information and surveillance standards are high. The Exchange stands up well to statistical testing of the 'efficient market hypothesis'.

Among recent reforms must be mentioned legislation on insider dealing and 'warehousing' and company equity repurchasing. In the more important area of non-statutory reforms, with the establishment of the Council for the Securities Industry, a number of guidelines on trading practices has been issued, e.g. on 'dawn raids' and licensed dealers in securities. Some further improvements are suggested, such as greater encouragement to employee equities, more detailed trading information, and more careful management of gilt-edged issues.

In the UK, savings and investment is more than usually well supported by governmental incentives, ranging from fiscal concessions on dividend and capital gains to elaborate regional and direct industrial investment incentives.

Notes and references

1   'Capital Requirements and Industrial Finance', *Midland Bank Review*, February 1976.
2   National Economic Development Organisation, *Finance for Investment*, London 1975.
3   Committee to Review the Functioning of Financial Institutions, *Report*, HMSO, London June 1980.
4   'How Profits are Moving', *Investor's Chronicle*, 16 January 1981.
5   Williams, N.P., *Influences on the profitability of 22 industrial sectors*, Bank of England discussion paper no.15.
6   *A Survey of European Stock Exchanges in 1979* (a supplement to the Stock Exchange Fact Book), UK Stock Exchange, London August 1980.
7   Committee to Review the Functioning of Financial Institutions, *Second Stage Evidence*, vol.4, The Stock Exchange, HMSO, London March 1979.
8   The Stock Exchange, *Evidence to the Committee to Review the Functioning of Financial Institutions — the Role and Functioning of the Stock Exchange*, London 1977.
9   Ferguson, Graham, 'The Advantages of the Jobbing System', *Bankers' Magazine*, April 1980.
10   The Stock Exchange, *Evidence to the Committee to Review the Functioning of Financial Institutions — The Provision of Funds for Industry and Trade*, London 1977.
11   The Stock Exchange, *Fact Book*, December 1980.

12 Greenwell, W. and Co., *The United Kingdom Gilt-Edged Market*, London February 1980.

13 Central Statistical Office, Press and Information Service, *Institutional Investment, Fourth Quarter 1980*, April 1981.

14 Williams, N.P., op.cit. (see note 5).

15 Investors' Chronicle, *Annual Review*, 2 January 1981.

16 Central Statistical Office, *Financial Statistics*, January 1981.

17 Bank of England, *Quarterly Bulletin*, March 1981.

18 Richards, P.H., *U.K. and European Share Price Behaviour: the Evidence*, Kogan Page, London 1979.

19 West, P.R., 'On the Difference between Internal and External Market Efficiency', *Financial Analysts' Journal*, November/December 1975.

20 Samuels, J., 'The Performance of Unit Trusts', *Bankers' Magazine*, 1968.

21 Richards, P.H., 'Sharpe Performance among Pension Funds', *The Investment Analyst*, no.51, 1978.

22 Council for the Securities Industry, *Rules Governing Substantial acquisitions of Shares*, CSI no.2, London December 1980.

23 Council for the Securities Industry, *Code of Conduct for Dealers in Securities*, May 1980; *Guidelines for Personal Dealings by Fund Managers*, March 1981.

24 The Stock Exchange, *The Stock Exchange Unlisted Securities Market*, London October 1980.

25 Bank of England, *Quarterly Bulletin*, June 1979.

26 *Financial Times*, 8 January 1981, report of a letter from the Chairman of the Stock Exchange to the Chancellor of the Exchequer.

27 Aldous, H., 'Government Incentives and Assistance for Industry in the UK', *Accountants' Digest*, no.104, Spring 1981.

About the author

Dr Paul Stonham is Director of the Commonwealth Bureau of Agricultural Economics, and a Member of Common Room, Wolfson College, Oxford. He was a member of the Invisibles Division of UNCTAD, Geneva, and Assistant Director of the Committee on Invisible Exports, London. Author of a number of academic articles on transport, investment, and international trade, he has acted as consultant to the Statistical Office of the European Communities in Luxembourg since 1976, reporting on financial statistics. He has also undertaken project evaluations in recent years in East and North Africa, the Gulf States, and Australia.